WATER RESOURCES AND AGRICULTURE

WATER RESOURCES AND AGRICULTURE

Edited by

Dr. Pawan Kumar 'Bharti'
Centre for Agro-Rural Technologies (CART-India)
20, Jamaalpur Man, Raja Ka Tajpur
Bijnore (UP) - 246 735 (India)
E-mail: gurupawanbharti@rediffmail.com

&

Dr. Ezeaku Peter Ikemefuna
Department of Soil Science
University of Nigeria, Nsukka
Enugu State, Nigeria

DISCOVERY PUBLISHING HOUSE PVT. LTD.
NEW DELHI-110 002

Published by:
Namit Wasan

DISCOVERY PUBLISHING HOUSE PVT. LTD.
4383/4B, Ansari Road, Darya Ganj
New Delhi-110 002 (India)
Phone : +91-11-23279245, 43596065, 23253475
E-mail : discoverybooksindia@gmail.com
discoverypublishinghouse@gmail.com
namitwasan9@gmail.com
web : www.discoverypublishinggroup.com

First Edition: 2018

ISBN: 978-93-5056-481-3

Water Resources and Agriculture

Printed at:
Infinity Imaging Systems
Delhi

Preface

Water resources are sources of water that are useful or potentially useful. Uses of water include agricultural, industrial, household, recreational and environmental activities. Virtually all of these human uses require fresh water.

97 per cent of the water on the Earth is salt water. However, only three per cent is fresh water; slightly over two thirds of this is frozen in glaciers and polar ice caps. The remaining unfrozen freshwater is found mainly as groundwater, with only a small fraction present above ground or in the air.

Fresh water is a renewable resource, yet the world's supply of clean, fresh water is steadily decreasing. Water demand already exceeds supply in many parts of the world and as the world population continues to rise, so too does the water demand.

Water resources are not distributed evenly in space or time around the world. Global circulation patterns create wet and dry climate zones, and in some regions seasonal or multi-annual climate cycles generate distinct wet and dry phases.

Although developed nations generally have more water available than many countries in Africa and the Middle East, some areas with good water endowments still are subject to 'water stress' because they are withdrawing water from available supplies at extremely high rates. High-intensity water uses in industrialized nations include agricultural production and electric power generation, which requires large quantities of water for cooling. In the United States electric power production accounts for 39 per cent of freshwater withdrawals, although almost all of this water is immediately returned to the rivers from which it is withdrawn. Agriculture requires much more water because irrigation increases transpiration to the atmosphere.

This book provides comprehensive coverage of the fundamental principles and current practices and trends in the field of global water resources, aquatic ecosystem, water demand and agriculture ecology.

This book updates the subject matter, illustrations and problems to incorporate new concepts and issues related to global water resources, water demand and agriculture ecology.

Particularly thanks are due to all contributors from Nigeria, India; and publisher also for their contribution and assistance. I hope this book will be of benefit to both present and future colleagues, who teach, study and working in the field of environment, ecology, freshwater ecology, aquatic ecosystem, environmental pollution, fisheries and agriculture.

Dr. Pawan Kumar 'Bharti'

(*gurupawanbharti@rediffmail.com*)

Contents

CHAPTER

Global Water Resources and Water Demand

Pawan Kumar 'Bharti'

World's available freshwater supply is not distributed uniformly around the globe throughout the seasons or from year to year. Nearly three quarters of the worlds annual rainfall comes down in areas inhabited by less than one third of the world's population, while two third of the world's population lived in areas receiving only one quarter of the world's annual rainfall. A water crisis, which has come about because rain - as a source of water has been ignored. The potential of rain to meet water demand is tremendous. Theoretically, the average rainfall of 100 mm of rain falling on one hectare of land in arid regions like Jaisalmer can yield up to one million liters of water.

Despite several initiatives taken by Government & public bodies, in 1995 some 20 per cent of the world's population of 5.7 billion people still lacked safe, fresh and reliable water supply, while more than 50 per cent were without adequate sanitation system. Today, thirty-one countries having nearly 8 per cent of the total population face water shortages, affecting more than 2.8 billion people, which is more than one third of the world's projected population.

Center for Agro-Rural Technologies (CART-India), 20, Jamaalpur Man, Raja Ka Tajpur, Bijnore (UP)-246 735 (India)

WATER ON EARTH

The amount of freshwater available on Earth today is no more than that was available 2,000 years ago when the Earth's population was less than 3 per cent of its current size. Rising demands of water in agriculture, domestic (municipal) consumption and industry are forcing stiff competition over the distribution of scare water resource, both amongst different regions and types of use. Water is likely to play the same role in world economy in the 21st century that oil played in the 20th century and will be source of conflicts world over to pose a major threat to human security if proper preventive measures are not taken globally. Growing water scarcity has become a very real obstacle to sustainable development.

Water is not only essential for life but predominant inorganic constituent of living matter forming in general nearly three quarters of the weight of living cells. It makes some 5 percent of the body weight of an adult human and can forms as 98 per cent of the mass of certain jellyfish. Organisms that contain relatively small amounts of water are generally in dormant state or show very slow development; seeds and certain invertebrates that live in arid environments are examples. On the other hand high rainfall over a landmass in variably means a large biomass per unit area.

India is a rich country in natural resources. One has to realize the need and importance of water conservation. Conservation and management of water resources was advocated even in ancient times when there was not much pressure on this resource. Water is used in everything people do; for irrigation, for industry, for power generation, for navigation, drinking, cooling, waste disposal and recreation.

Water conservation basically aims at matching demand and supply. The strategies for water conservation may be either demand oriented or supply oriented. The strategies may vary depending upon the field of water use domestic, irrigation or industrial. Some of the supply oriented strategies such as creation of storage; long distance transfer and control of water loss through evaporation are generally common to all the fields of water use, whereas the others may be applicable only to specific field.

Storage of water by construction of various water resources projects has been one of the measures of water conservation. To render it stable the walls have to be lined with timber or with stone and the adjoining soil strengthened by stamping and tramping of elephants, horses etc.

For centuries, streams and rivers have provided a convenient place to dump wastes. Today, water pollution comes from many different sources. These include untreated sewage, industrial discharge, leakage from oil storage tanks, mine drainage and mine drainage and pesticides. Water pollution varies in severity in one region to the next depending on the density of urban development, agricultural and industrial practices and the presence or absence of system for collecting and treating the wastewater. The large industrial cities of the world produce huge amount of sewage, both from households and industries, causing problems not only for human health but also for ecosystems.

Industry is also highly water-intensive. For example, making one tonne of steel can consume as much as 300 tonnes of water. Driven by stiffer regulations and the need to cut costs, such water-intensive industries as chemicals, iron and steel, and pulp and paper have made impressive strides in reducing the amount of water in current production processes. Some of these industries have also redesigned production processes, which require less water per unit of production.

Conserving water for personal use in cities (including use by households and municipalities) requires managing both the supply of and demand for water. Much of the municipal water supply is lost before it can reach consumers, leaking out of water mains, pipes, and faucets, or disappearing through illegal tapes. Moreover, when they have convenient access to running water, consumers often use much, more water than they actually need. In India over 40 per cent of the total municipal water supply is lost in transit, before it reaches the consumers. In most cities, nothing more than tightening the joints in the water pipes and fixing leaky community standpipes and household connections could save more than one third of the water that is currently wasted. Many cities could manage the water supply better if they could eliminate illegal water taps. Beside, treated wastewater can be used for purposes where the quality standard requirements are not very high, for example, flushing toilets, washing cars, cleaning floors, gardening, etc.

Since agriculture accounts for nearly 70 per cent of all water withdrawn from rivers, lakes and underground aquifers for human use, large potential for conservation lies with increasing irrigation, efficiencies. Typically, only about 45 per cent of water withdrawn for irrigated agriculture ever reaches the crops. Even when sufficient irrigation water reaches agriculture fields, it can spoil much of the land unless drained properly. Also, poorly drained irrigation water can raise the groundwater table until it reaches the root zone, thereby water logging and drowning crops. Globally some 80 million hectares of farmland have been degraded by a combination of salinization and waterlogging. Efficient irrigation techniques not only save water but also protect the land. Drip irrigation is one such technique. It consists of a network of perforated piping, usually installed on the surface or just below ground, which delivers water directly to the root zone of crops. This technique keeps evaporation losses low, at an efficiency rate of 95 per cent. Drip irrigation systems can cut water use by an estimated 50 per cent compared with gravity systems.

Another promising conservation technique – low-energy precision application (LEPA) – offers substantial improvements over conventional sprinkler systems that spray water in to air. Instead the low-energy precision application method delivers water to the crops from drop tubes that extend from the sprinkler's arm. When applied together with appropriate water-saving farming techniques, this method also can achieve efficiencies as high as 95 per cent. Since this method operates at low pressure, it results in 20 per cent to 50 per cent energy savings as compared to conventional systems.

Apart from leakage and pilferage, another major reason for large-scale wastage of municipal water in cities is the nominal cost or no cost charged for it. Water should be treated as a commodity and sold to consumers at rates that reflect its value in order to encourage conservation. With higher cost recovery, utilities in developing countries could improve the quality and availability of water even in low-income areas. Water supply projects require huge capital investments, yet cities are faced with diminishing funds for urban water supply to provide for the burgeoning urban populations.

According to a recent analysis of a World Bank financed project, in developing countries, consumers play only about 35 per cent of the costs of supplying water. Recovering a greater percentage of these costs could provide city managers with funds to expand coverage to new areas or to maintain and improve existing facilities. Other measures that could reduce municipal demand include: building codes that require installation of low flush toilets, low water use landscaping – known as xeriscaping – in arid and semi arid areas. Such measures could be adopted in both developed and developing countries.

DISTRIBUTION OF WATER

About 30 per cent of the area of the continents (except Antarctica) is underlain by relatively homogeneous aquifers containing important groundwater reserves. About 19 per cent is endowed with groundwater, some of which is extensive, in geologically complex regions. Half of the continental area contains generally minor occurrences of groundwater that are restricted to near-surface unconsolidated gravels, sands, and rock debris; but these groundwater resources are still sufficient to sustain small to medium-sized population centres. Fifteen percent of the world's land area receives less than 200mm average annual precipitation (c. 200 litres per square metre). In these low rainfall regions there is normally very little groundwater recharge, so groundwater used will not generally be replaced for hundreds - perhaps thousands of years. Extraction in these areas must therefore be considered as "mining" a limited resource, rather than tapping a continuous supply. The geological conditions and hydro-geological characteristics of the rocks are critical controls on groundwater quantity, quality and flow regime. According to the UN, Planet Earth's mean annual renewable volume of water is 43,000 cubic kilometres. This is about half of all the fresh water contained in all the Earth's natural lakes and about ten times the volume of all man-made reservoirs. Groundwater recharge accounts for about 10,000 cubic kilometres annually, (c. 0.1% of all groundwater resources). Thus, only a tiny proportion of the total volume of groundwater reserves is recharged each year, compared to the large volume in stock (www.yearofplanetearth.org).

Some groundwater systems are non-renewable under current climatic conditions because they formed under much wetter climates that prevailed perhaps 1000 or 10,000 years ago. These groundwater reservoirs are being increasingly "mined" in the arid zones of the world. For example, in the north-eastern Sahara, the Nubian Sandstone Aquifer System underlies an area of more than two million square kilometres in Chad, Egypt, Libya and Sudan, and contains huge amounts of fresh groundwater. It is thought to contain about a hundred times the present annual global water consumption. Giant groundwater deposits of comparable size and limited recharge are thought to exist on nearly all continents, but the amount of groundwater that can be pumped out is unknown. Information about the age, travel times and flow of the water underground, and other features such as chemical characteristics and processes are needed.

Water covers nearly 70 per cent of the globe, but most of it is salt water that fills the oceans. By volume, less than 3 per cent of all the water on earth is freshwater, most of which lies frozen in Antarctica and Greenland in Polar ice and is unavailable to humanity. Less than 1 per cent of the all water on earth is easily accessible in the form of surface freshwater, found in lakes, rivers and underground in shallow aquifers. This amount of water is regularly renewed by precipitation in the form of rain and snowfall or by melt by glaciers in the mountains and supplemented by dew and fog drip in some locations.

Atmospheric water is about 0.001 per cent of the total estimated distribution of world's water resources taking part in the hydrological cycle. It is also estimated that the freshwater resources is about 3 per cent, 77.2 per cent of this is in cold storage, frozen in the ice caps and glaciers. Most of the remaining supply of freshwater i.e. 22.4 per cent is groundwater and soil moisture. This leaves only a very small amount of fresh surface water i.e. 0.35 per cent contained in lakes and swamps and less than 0.01 per cent in rivers and streams. The freshwater resources with their estimated volumes in km^3 with average residence time in the earth environment are:

Atmospheric water	–	113,000 (8 to 10 days)
Oceans and open seas	–	1,370,000,000 (4000 + years)
Freshwater lakes and reservoirs	–	125,000 (from days to years)
Saline lakes and inland seas	–	104,000

River channels	–	1,700 (2 weeks)
Swamps and marshes	–	3,600 (years)
Biological waters	–	65,000 (1 week- used by plants)
Moisture in soil & unsaturated zone	–	65,000 (2 week to 1 year - zones of aeration)
Groundwater (10 days to thousands of years)	–	4,000,000 to 60,000,000
Frozen water (Glaciers & ice caps)	–	30,000,000 (10 days to thousands of years)

The total quantity of water on our planet is fixed and its distribution is highly uneven. Almost 95 per cent of the total water present on the earth is chemically bound in to rocks and does not cycle. Of the remainder, about 97.3 per cent is in the ocean, about 2.15 exists as ice in the polar caps and permanent glaciers and the rest is freshwater present in the form of atmospheric water vapour, ground water, and inland surface water. Thus, less than one percent of the total freshwater precipitates in the hydrological cycle.

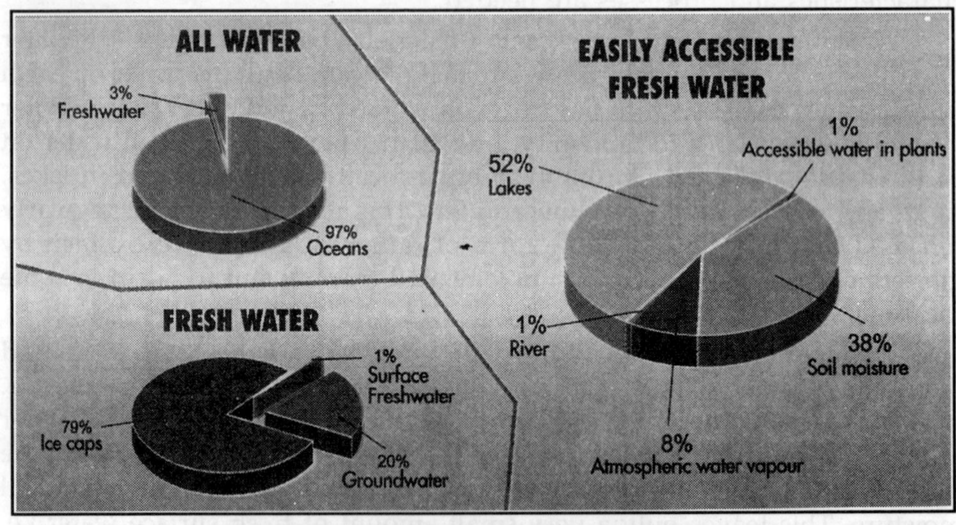

Fig. 1.1: Global Distribution of Water
Source: **Prakash and Prakash, 2001**

WATER DEMAND AND CRISIS

A water crisis that has come about, because rain, as a source of water has been ignored. The potential of rain to meet water demand is tremendous. Theoretically, the average rainfall of 100 mm of rain falling on one hectare of land in arid regions like Jaisalmer can yield up to one million litres of water.

Table 1.1: Total Estimated Water Resources on Earth

Sl. No.	Reserves	Volume Km³	Percentage
1.	Oceans	1,32,20,00,000	92.200
2.	Ice caps & Glaciers	2,92,00,000	2.150
3.	Underground	41,70,000	0.625
4.	Freshwater Lakes	1,25,000	0.009
5.	Saline Lakes & Inland Seas	1,04,000	0.008
6.	Soil Moisture	67,000	0.005
7.	Atmosphere	13,000	0.001
8.	Rivers	1,250	0.001
	Total	**1,35,56,80,250 Km³**	**100%**

The demand for water is continually growing globally at an accelerated pace. The demand for water in various sectors including domestic use, irrigation, energy and industry etc, during year 1990 and projections four years 2000 & 2025 are given in Table 1.2. The total quantum for water available on the average may be enough to meet all our demands put together. But its availability is highly irregular. It is not available in places where we want it, at times when we want it and in which we want it – hence the need for conservation.

Table 1.2: Demands for Various Sectors

Purpose	Demand (km³) - in the Year		
	1900	2000	2025
Domestic use	25	33	52
Irrigation	460	630	770
Energy	19	27	71
Industrial use	15	30	120
Others	33	30	37
Total	552	750	1050
Surface water	362	500	700
Ground water	**190**	**250**	**350**

Conservation is defined as preservation against loss of waste. Technically conservation of water implies the same meaning in a much wider perspective. Briefly stated it means putting the water resources of the country for the best beneficial use with all the technologies at our command. In other words, surface water running down to sea should be stored to the maximum extant, evaporation and other losses minimized and benefits spread with the sole criteria of maximum benefit to maximum number having due regard to the properties like drinking, irrigation, industrial use, navigation etc.

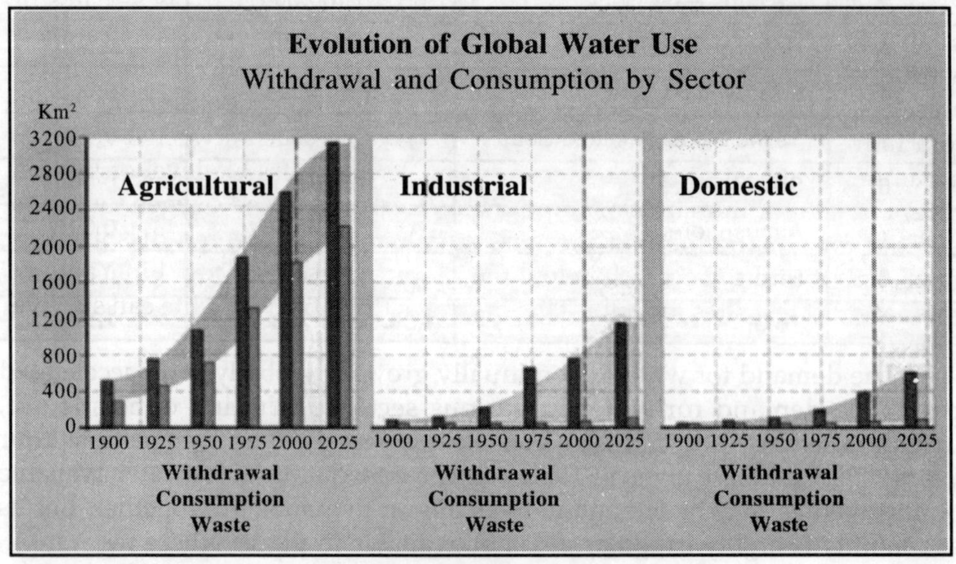

Fig. 1.2: Water Requirement for Various Sectors

Source: **www.yearofplanetearth.org**

World's available freshwater supply is not distributed uniformly around the globe throughout the seasons or from year to year. Nearly three quarters of the worlds annual rainfall comes down in areas inhabited by less than one third of the world's population, while two third of the world's population lived in areas receiving only one quarter of the world's annual rainfall.

Despite several initiatives taken by Government & public bodies, in 1995 some 20 per cent of the world's population of 5.7 billion people still lacked safe and reliable water supply, while more than 50 per cent were without adequate sanitation system. Today, thirty-one countries having nearly 8 per cent of the total population face water shortages, affecting more than 2.8 billion people, which is more than one third of the world's projected population.

Among the country likely to run short of water in the next 25 years are India, Ethiopia, Kenya, Nigeria, Peru, China, Bangladesh. Now more than 25 countries already facing chronic water problems. Groundwater, which now accounts for 80 per cent of rural and 60 per cent of the urban water supply in India, is depleting at an alarming rate. In fact, today 19 major cities of India already face chronic water shortage.

Many rivers are already dead or dying. All the 13 great river systems in India are endangered. They are fought over and dammed in discriminately by states to provide water for irrigation and industrial use. A typical example of dying river is the Yamuna in Delhi. Because of overuse, there is no original water left in the Yamuna at Delhi. Instead it carries only narrow streams of urban and industrial wastewater. The result of tests conducted by a reputed institute of Delhi on Yamuna water is alarming. For example, the biochemical oxygen demand (BOD), which is a measure of the burden of organic waste from industries and sewage, was found to have a value between 4-75 mg/l in Yamuna water at different sites in Delhi. The permissible level of BOD is 3 mg/l or less for human consumption. Similarly dissolved oxygen, which is essential for aquatic life and measures the amount of oxygen dissolved in water, was found to be much below the required level of 5 mg/l in Yamuna water at most test sites in Delhi. This indicates that no aquatic life can survive in the Yamuna along its entire stretch in Delhi. The only exception being the water at the Wazirabad barrage, the point where Yamuna enters Delhi.

The public sector has often failed to deliver sustainable water supply and adequate sewage treatment systems. Although officially 70 per cent of Delhi's sewage is treated, in realty, due to the malfunctioning of ill-maintained sewage treatment plants, half that volume comes out as raw sewage. The polluted water, improper sewage disposal, and poor water management combined together cause serious public health problems. The coliform count, which is an indicator of contamination by bacteria coming mainly through domestic sewage, is found to be between 23,000 and 1,40,000 in most of the Yamuna water in Delhi. The upper level of safe level of coliform count is 500. Once again, Yamuna water only at Wazirabad is found to be safe in terms of coliform count, with a value of only 28.

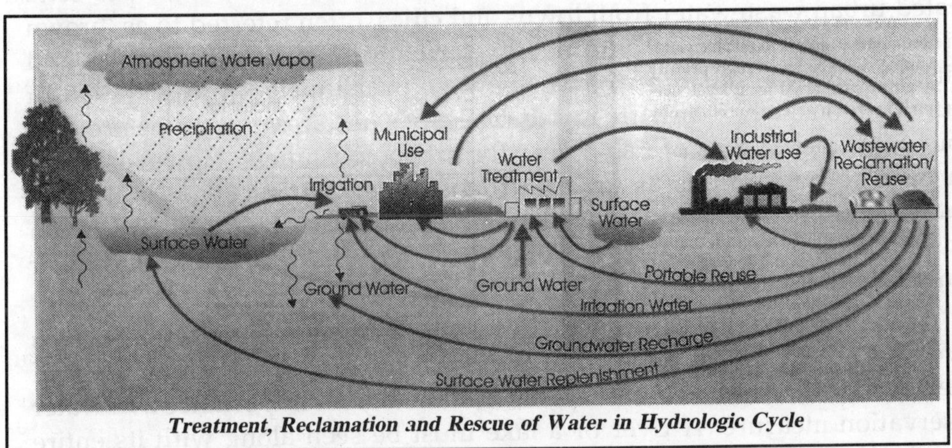

Treatment, Reclamation and Rescue of Water in Hydrologic Cycle

Fig. 1.3: Water Uses and Water Cycle

Source: **Prakash and Prakash, 2001**

The world is now facing water crisis of dimensions that no earlier generation has had to face. It may already be late for some water scare countries with rapid population growth to avoid a water crisis unless they take immediate and drastic steps for sustainable management of urban water resources. But a water crisis in the near future can be avoided if appropriate policies and strategies are formulated and acted upon quickly. In this regard, water conservation and its better management are the effective strategies for consideration. To avoid a catastrophe over the long term, it is also important to act to reduce the demand of freshwater by slowing the population growth. Urgent and decisive action must begin now if regional water crisis are to be avoided during the next century. There is an imperative need to change people's attitudes towards water. Water must be an environmental issue at the top of the agenda of Governments, institutions and individuals alike. Because knowledge of water resources and availability is the key to development, access to reliable water data needs to be given high priority by governments. At local level, everyone must use water more efficiently without wasting it. At the national level, especially in water scare-regions with dense population, adopting a watershed or river basin management perspective or harvesting of rainwater is required as an alternative to uncoordinated water-management policies. At the international level, countries that share river basins can design workable policies to manage water resources more equitably.

Ancient techniques of water harvesting, like digging of deep underground chambers for storing rainwater from the wet season for use during the dry season, or placing of long lines of stones along the contours of gently sloping ground to slow runoff and spread the water across a wider area, are prevalent in some societies. These practices when applied together have been known to increase crop production by as much as 50 per cent. Treated urban wastewater from towns and cities, often referred to as 'brown water', may be channeled onto nearby farms for growing vegetables and fruits. In Calcutta, much of the raw sewage is channeled into a system of natural lagoons, where fish are raised. The city's hectares of lagoons produce about 6,000 metric tons of fish a year for urban consumers. However, there is a need to be cautions as unless urban wastewater receives some pre-treatment, either from natural wetlands or sewage treatment plants, it can transfer disease organisms to vegetables and fruits or fish and endanger human health.

Watershed management, which refers to managing an entire land area served by all the rivers and aquifers that drain into a particular body of water, such as a semi-enclosed bay, has assumed great importance as a water conservation measure. A river or a lake must be seen along with its entire watershed and all its physical, chemical, and biological elements, as part of a complex, integrated system. People living in most of these watersheds have radically altered the natural drainage systems around them. Tempering with watershed has proved ruinous for many developing countries, where hillsides, denuded of vegetation, empty tonnes of soil into watercourses every year, causing floods during the wet seasons and suffocating aquatic life during the dry seasons. Deforestation has ruined land and altered climates, causing less rain in some areas. In others, rainwater runs off so fast that little can be collected for use later. Watershed management is generally complicated and can be contentious because watershed boundaries do not coincide with those of political or administrative jurisdictions. It involves many levels of Government and many different communities, each with its own constituencies and concerns. Balancing the multitude of interests involved which is time consuming and troublesome, is the key to the success of watershed management. But if we carried out properly, watershed or river basin management pays multiple benefits.

Every year India gets an estimated rain and snowfall spread over 400 million hectares of land. Even if rain is captured from just one to two percent of India's land area, it can provide a population of one billion as much as 100 litres of water per person per day. Harvesting rainwater is one of the most effective ways of tackling water crisis. The basic principle is to collect the rainwater where it falls, us it and let it seep into the ground. In fact, India has had a long tradition of water harvesting. Aizawl in Mizoram meets most of its water needs through rooftop harvesting. In 1994 a law was promulgated for the residents of Chennai making it mandatory for new buildings tc harvest rainwater if they wanted municipal water connection. This has also resulted into a few business ventures devoted exclusively to artificial recharge. As a result of rainwater harvesting, the coastal aquifers in Tamilnadu are healthy again after several years.

Check dams can be built to store monsoon flows and recharge aquifers. Rainwater can also be stored in wells by channeling it through pipes from the rooftop terrace. Further, percolation tanks may be built to allow slow percolation and collection of rainwater into the ground. It is efficient both for soft and hard ground. Recharge wells or injection wells are just like tube wells but have the provision for pumping in water from the surface after treatment.

According to some projections, the city of Delhi can actually retrieve around 720 million liters of water every year by artificial recharge. Installing a rooftop harvesting system can cost nearly Rs. 100,000 to Rs. 150,000 for a suitably sized apartment. A rooftop recharge can provide nearly 300 litres a minute at the time of good rain. Delhi's master plan for the year 2001 projects per capita need of 400 litres of water every day and this demand can be met by adopting these new ways of harvesting water. Rainwater can not only provide much needed drinking and irrigation water but can also increase groundwater discharge, reduce urban floods and overloading of sewage treatment plants and sea water ingress in coastal areas.

One solution proposed and already being adopted around the world is to set a price of water to cover its 'real costs'; a price which would take into consideration all of the associated services such as treatment, infrastructure, distribution. Placing a price of water might attract big companies to invest in remote areas where their profit margin – because of a high consumption potential – could be high. It would also 'make it possible to reduce the burden of expenditures which up until now were met by public funds.' But what happens when people simply cannot pay? Or when they live in small, poor communities, which don't interest the big water companies? In such cases, voluntary agencies and NGOs can pay a key role. In Cambodia, for example, NGOs have helped create local drilling teams and encouraged self-management of water projects.

Nowadays, due to water crisis, state/centre dispute occur on water requirement like Kavery river in between Tamilnadu and Karnataka; Yamuna - Satluj in between Haryana, Punjab & Delhi; Sharda river in between Nepal and India; Brahmaputra river in between Bangladesh & India.

GLOBAL WATER SUPPLY AND DEMAND

Total Water Supply

Water supply depends on several factors in the water cycle, including the rates of rainfall, evaporation, the use of water by plants (transpiration), and river and groundwater flows. It is estimated3 that less than 1 per cent of all fresh water is available for people to use (the remainder is locked up in ice sheets and glaciers). Globally, around 12,500 cubic kilometres (km3) of water are considered available for human use on an annual basis. This amounts to about 6,600 m^3 per person/year 4.

Total Water Demand

Today, the quantity of water used for all purposes exceeds 3,700 km^3 per year. Agriculture is the largest user, consuming almost two-thirds of all water drawn from rivers, lakes and groundwater. While irrigation has undoubtedly contributed significantly to world agricultural production, it is extremely water intensive. Since 1960, water use for crop irrigation has risen by 60-70 per cent. Industry uses about 20 per cent of available water, and the municipal sector uses about 10 per cent. Population growth, urbanization and industrialization have increased the use of water in these sectors.

Access to Water

The previous section examined the gross supply of and demand for water on a global basis. However, the world's available freshwater supply is not distributed evenly around the globe, throughout the seasons, or from year to year. About three-quarters of annual rainfall occurs in areas containing less than one-third of the world's population, whereas two-thirds of the world's population live in the areas receiving only one-quarter of the world's annual rainfall. For instance, about 20 per cent of the global average runoff each year is accounted for by the Amazon Basin, a vast region with fewer than 10 million people. Similarly, the Congo River and its tributaries account for about 30 per cent of the entire African continent's annual runoff, but the basin contains only 10 per cent of Africa's population. Throughout much of the developing world freshwater supply comes in the form of seasonal rains, such as the monsoons in Asia. Such rains often run off too quickly for efficient use. India, for instance, gets 90 per cent of its rainfall during the summer monsoon season – at other times rainfall over much of the country is very low. Because of the seasonal nature of the water supply (without storage), many developing countries can use no more than 20 per cent of their potentially available freshwater resources.

Water supplies can also vary from year to year, depending on variations in the weather. For example, monsoons may fail in some years. Also natural phenomena such as the El Nino Southern Oscillation can lead to significant differences in rainfall in the southern Pacific Ocean, affecting south-east Asia and south and Central America. (www.parliament.uk/).

SOLUTIONS

It is estimate that more than more than one billion people drink unsafe water and 2.4 billion, that is, 40 per cent of the human race does not have access to adequate sanitation, and 3.4 million people, mostly children, die every year of water-related diseases (more than one million from malaria alone), the majority of them unnecessarily (Prakash and Prakash, 2001).

But the picture is neither gloomy nor hopeless, says the World Health Organisation (WHO) in a report on water and sanitation. "Clearly, a problem of this magnitude cannot be solved overnight, but simple, inexpensive measures, both individual and collective, are available that will provide clean water for millions and millions of people in developing countries – now, not in 10 or 20 years," said Dr. Gro Harlem Brundtland, Director-General of WHO. "We do not have the luxury of waiting around for large infrastructure investments to provide water supplies and basic sanitation services for all who need them. It makes no sense, and it is not acceptable, to ignore the immediate priorities of the most needy".

Optimistic but realistic, the WHO report, entitled *Water for Health – Taking Charge,* strongly urges several basic measures, including purifying water and improving hygiene, as immediate means of improving people's water supply in developing countries. Chlorination, for example, is, "a proven means of ridding water of disease causing microorganisms in piped water," according to the report. Moreover, research carried out at the Centers for Disease Control and Prevention in Atlanta, Georgia, and by the Pan American Health Organisation, supports chlorination in households without piped water, even through the prevailing wisdom is that chlorination should follow and not precede the creation of water and sanitation services. Even in conditions of very poor sanitation and hygiene, where people collect whatever water is available to use for their household water supply, if the water is chlorinated, the water quality is improved microbiologically, and there are statistically significant decreases in diarrhoel diseases.

A good example of successful chlorination can be found in the Maltheves where a national control programme used it in wells. Rainwater was also collected for drinking. Twenty years after the programme started, the entire populations of the Maltheves islands have their own community rainwater collection tanks, and deaths from diarrhea are virtually unknown.

Another easy, small-scale, and cost-effective technique for providing safe water, individually or collectively, is still little known but highly effective solar thermal technique. It is called SODIS and was promoted by the Swiss Federal Institute for Environmental Science and Technology near Zurich. SODIS, an acronym for SOlar water DISinfection, is a nearly cost free system because sunlight costs nothing, and the only other elements are throw-away transparent plastic soft-drink bottles or used mineral water bottles and a black surface. The transparent bottles are filled with water and placed horizontally on a flat surface for about five hours. The disease-causing microorganisms (pathogens) in the polluted water succumb to the killing effect of the ultraviolet light in solar radiation. The process is enhanced when the solar water disinfection is combined with a 'solar thermal water treatment' which makes use of the fact that black colour absorbs light and heat more efficiently. This is accomplished by painting the bottom half of the bottle black or placing it on black-painted corrugated iron or plastic sheets. Field studies in Bolivia, Burkina Fasco, China, Colombia, Indonesia, Thailand and Togo show that the process works.

A third recommendation of the report calls for 'changing behaviour'. Studies of diarrhea show that the simple act of washing hands with soap and water reduces incidence of the disease by 35 per cent. Elsewhere, good water management has almost eradicated guinea worm, a disfiguring, disabling disease which afflicted 50 million people in Africa and Asia in the mid-1900s. By 1999 that number had fallen to below 10,000. But poor irrigation water management, in sharp contrast, had let to a huge spread of schistosomiasis (snail fever) to areas of the world where it never existed before. An estimated 200 million people are infected today with schistosomiasis, according to WHO.

What should be done differently to prevent water-related diseases and to ensure that everyone access to at least some safe water and sanitation? For one thing, says the WHO report, the health sector must get fully involved in water management. It can no longer be left to water management authorities or to environment ministries. Just as major development projects always have environment impact assessment, they should also require health impact assessments. Those involved in water management should be made responsible for its effects on people's health.

During the past 50 years there has been a strong emphasis on medical interventions including, for example, drug therapy, to tackle water-borne and sanitation related diseases and this has tended to reduce the attention and priority given to safe water supply and adequate sanitation. With the increasing resistance to antibiotics, insecticides and standard drugs, health authorities now understand the limitations of a strictly medical approach. That makes safe water and sanitation more important than ever before.

INTERLINKING OF RIVERS

A familiar phenomenon in human history is the fight to secure natural resources. This essay shall examine how one country, India, is seeking to solve its water problems via the interlinking of all its rivers. River interlinking is a project that is both visionary and controversial in claiming to cure all of the country's water problems. The goal of the project is to interlink all the country's rivers together. This, allegedly, will provide water to all by diverting water from areas that have a 'surplus' to those that don't and "by preventing the unnecessary spillage of water into the sea." Furthermore, such water transfers would also be aimed at flood control during the erratic monsoon season, where floodwaters could simply be diverted away. However, Interlinking at the same time has the potential to become another grand, large-scale project of the sort that creates more problems than it proposes to solve. To assess the risk of this fate, the author provides comparisons with other countries that have undertaken similar projects. These comparisons will show that such large-scale projects typically tend to run into difficulty and usually fail. The goal of this essay is to evaluate why, in spite of these historical precedents against large projects, governments nonetheless tend to follow through with them. Two possible answers come to mind. The first is that governments believe that these are genuinely beneficial projects based on some explicit or implicit calculation of costs and benefits. The second is that government officials are acting self-interestedly, prompted by the influence of special interest groups. The author believes that the answer lies in examining the nature of the benefits and costs involved, and the distribution of these benefits in relation to political power and government self interest. Therefore, in this essay begins with an examination of the cost-benefit procedure, and then examines Interlinking using a qualitative cost-benefit analysis. It follows with possible reasons behind the motivation of Interlinking based on the distribution of costs and benefits and the interests of government leaders, and ends with questioning whether such a project would pass through the legislature regardless (Dev Goel, 2005).

India is on the brink of executing a stupendous hydrological phenomenon of inter basin transfer of water, not of one or two river basins as has been done hither to over different parts of the world, but interlinking of all the major rivers viz. Ganges and Brahmaputra and connecting them with the southern rivers of Mahanadi, Godavari, Krishna and Kaveri. The scheme, after completion will perhaps be a hydrological marvel of the world. The project, at an estimated cost of 100 billion US dollars, on completion is expected to contribute significantly to food production, water, energy and transport needs and to mitigate drought and floods in the country. Many arguments supporting and otherwise of the concept were discussed with scientific basis.

DRINKING WATER PROBLEMS IN SAARC COUNTRIES

The drinking water problems of SAARC countries were discussed at a special colloquium. The presentations indicate that South Asia remains a region divided- divided between the hopes of the rich and despair of the poor. The rural people in almost all the SAARC countries has still to walk at least 3-4 km every day to fetch a pot of drinking water. Contamination from arsenic, fluoride and anthropogenic sources add fuel to fire.

Most of the presentations are focused around a pragmatic approach with peoples' participation on a local scale complemented by proactive government response.

NEGATIVE IMPACTS OF RIVER LINKING

The Rs. 4000 crore Ken-Betwa river linking project which includes a dam on the river Ken and a 231 km. canal linking it to the Betwa will submerge significant forest areas including parts of the Panna Tiger Reserve. The feasibility report of the project says that the project will submerge some 100 sq. km. in Panna, Chatarpur and Damoh districts – including 19 villages and about 37.5 sq. km. of forestland as well as 30 km. stretch of the Gangau-Shahpura road in Madhya Pradesh. The agreement for the project was recently signed by the Madhya Pradesh and Uttar Pradesh Chief Ministers, Babulal Gaur and Mulayam Singh Yadav, and Union water resources Minister Priya Ranjan Das Munshi in New Delhi in the presence of Prime Minister Manmohan Singh (PAU, 2005).

Leading scientists of India have a doubt that the interlinking of rivers may affect the local weather, monsoon cycle and contribute to Climate change.

REFERENCES

Bharti, Pawan K. (2012): Ground Water Pollution, Biotech Books, Delhi, pp: 246.

Dev Goel, (2005): "A Political-economic Analysis of India's River Interlinking Project" (August 30, 2005) *Florida State University D-Scholarship Repository*, Article #132. (http://dscholarship.lib.fsu.edu/undergrad/132)

http://www.appliedhydrology.org

http://www.yearofplanetearth.org

http://www.parliament.uk/

PAU (2005): Ken Betwa River Link to Submerge Parts of Panna TR. In: Protected Area Update, October, 2005, (No. 57) Vol. XI, No. 5, pp: 10.

Prakash, G. and Prakash, J. (2001): Water-present, Past and Future, *Science Reporter*- Cover Story, July, pp: 10-14 & 62-63.

CHAPTER

Water Quality of River Kunda, District Khargone Madhya Pradesh with Special Reference to Physico-Chemical Parameters

Shailendra Sharma*; Sudha Dubey**
Rajendra Chaurasia;Vibha Dave*****

ABSTRACT

The study on some physico-chemical characteristics of River Kunda at its source has been calculated for the period of one year (August 2010 to July 2011). The sampling points were selected on the basis of their importance. For surface water determination of water quality index becomes essential and pre-requisite. Analysis of some physico-chemical characteristics like water temperature, pH, transparency, dissolved oxygen, BOD, total hardness, alkalinity, Chloride, Nitrate and Phosphate has been done during the investigation period. Increase in temperature, pH, Transparency, Chlorides and Phosphates values were higher in Siptan Station, whereas the increase in Total Hardness and Nitrates values were higher in Khargone station to the intensity of expulsion of contamination. The Total Alkalinity, Dissolved oxygen and BOD values higher in

* Department of Biotechnology, Adarsh Institute of Management & Science, Dhamnod (M.P.), India.

** Department of Zoology, Govt. Holkar Science College Indore - 452 017, India.

*** Department of Zoology, P.M.B.Gjarati Science College Indore - 452 001, India.

Confluence with Undri River station owing to unpolluted water. The Kunda River has been facing severe anthropogenic activities, mostly due to municipal sewage and industrial waste and dense population etc.

Key words: Water quality, DO, BOD, Kunda River, Anthropogenic activity

INTRODUCTION

The health a water body or his quality is assessed using physical, chemical and biological parameters (APHA, 2002). Blockeel *et al.*, (1999) Suggested that physical and chemical properties give a specific picture of water quality in fresh water at a particular point in time, while the biota (biological property) act as a continuous monitor and give more general pictures of water quality over a period of time. Measurement of physical attributes serves as indicators of some forms of pollution, changes in temperature may, indicate the presence of certain effluents while changes in stream width, depth and velocity, turbidity and rock size may indicate dredging in the area (Chris Kreger, 2002).

Chemical characteristics of a healthy water body affect its toxicity and also aesthetic qualities such as how water looks, smell and tastes. Assessment of water quality by its chemistry includes measures of many elements and molecules dissolved or suspended in the water and can be used to detect imbalances within the ecosystem. Such imbalances may indicate the presence of certain pollutants as suggested Dzeroski *et al.*, (2002). The commonly measure chemical parameters includes pH, alkalinity, hardness, nitrates, nitrites and ammonia, ortho and total phosphate and dissolved oxygen for Biochemical Oxygen Demand (BOD). Measurements such as conductivity and density in chemical measurement actually indicate the physical presence of pollutants in water (Chris Kreger, 2002).

Water is one of the most important natural resources in the United States and around the world (EPA 2001). It is necessary for life and provides a variety of uses from drinking water in cities to the irrigation of crops in agricultural areas. Water also provides recreational uses as well as habitat for wildlife. According to the Environmental Protection Agency (2001) "rivers, lakes, estuaries and wetlands are among the Nation's most precious resources". In the Khargone present is six river, its name is Kunda, Veda, Bakund, Indravati, Morani and Undri river. Population of Khargone district water supply main source is Kunda river, its river situated it Bhagwanpura block of Khargone district. In the Khargone district present is 4 Tanki and its water capacity 8 Lac Gallon. On the Nagar Panchayat drinking water arrangement 75 Thousands Population is depend. Its tributary river of Undri river. Khargone district in present is small and large dam. Their districts on the view of water structure are divide two parts. Area of Department of water resources Khargone one medium and 27 short irrigation scheme. The area of Khargone are made small and large dam, some dams name is following- Dejla-Devada, Adampura, Garhigaltar, Nand Gaugaon, Momdia, Bhikarkhedi, Silatia, Baghai Mata, Ban Ganga, Chand Gaghd, Oon, Sagaon and is Sangaon-2. Main dams of Khargone district in Dejla Devada dam canal length is about 26 Kms. Dejla Devada dam water capacities is 13m. Besides it main canal together also present is small Accessory canal. These canal area of Devada, Bhagwanpura, Taradpura, Badda, Umar Khali, Tanda, Barud, Sinkheda etc. these region supply irrigation water.

Khargone has a transitional climate between a tropical wet and dry climate and a humid subtropical climate. Three distinct seasons are observed: summer, monsoon and winter. Summers are extremely hot and dry in this region, lasting from mid-march to mid-june followed by the monsoon season. The temperatures in summer are usually above 40° C during April-May. During these months when temperatures become very high the dry and hot wind (Locally known as loo) blows in this area widely affecting the local ecology. The temperature also remains quite high during the night. The monsoon arrives in late June, with temperatures around 29° C and about 36 in. rainfall. The rainy season is humid and has substantial rainfall. Local people are commonly affected by the flooding of river Kunda which flows from outskirts of the city. Winters start in mid-November and are dry, mild and sunny. Temperatures average about 4-15° C (39-59° F), but can fall close to freezing on some nights.

Khargone District climate is changed. Water of river is absorbed and water pollution amount is increased day by day. Its district Noise pollution, Soil pollution and Water pollution and many more pollution also increases. On the Kunda river reach daily 4 gutters and do polluted water, Every month 1 ton or its more waste material reach in Kunda river. Khargone district and its attached in Panchayat of water also increase in quantity of chlorides and yet increase is disease of Allergy, And through chemical manure reach sulpher in water sources, and soil also polluted. Currently it district of average $_{p}$H value is 7.5 and $_{p}$H value more 8 yet soil is unfertile. Many years ago $_{p}$H of soil was 7 and more quantity use of chemical manure soil and water polluted.

Many dirty gutters are joining Kunda river form new bridge to old bridge in urban areas. These dirty gutters are polluting to this River. Due to increasing population of urban up to today, there are many gutters. In these gutters dirtiness is also increase these gutters are seen near the old bridge on the way of Kaladeval, near Ganesh temple, near Pathanwadi, near the church of Saint Thomas, near the temple of Kalika Mata and near the Islampura. These all the gutters carry dirty water to the river kunda. It is going up to today. Yet Khargone district day by day population, pollution and many gutters increase and in these gutters also increased waste material, And it gutters mixed in kunda river and it process continued modern time.

Kunda river in urban areas on duration of one year any year 9 month or any year 7 month fulfill in waste material, yet year in the region of Bhagwanpura is raining heavy and some some days duration this river small or large flooded yet Freshness of river only 3 month only July to September and after 9 month it river fulfill of waste material, on this river last 2 years duration of 3 to 4 Km. distance it river are constructed 7 stopdams while rainy season relief one or two month it river changed in gutter and fill for water but it not possible stop dam from on near of new bridge next year after rainy season stopped water it reason of gutter stopwater fulfill for dirty, fresh and clear water fulfill plastic bags, dirty clothes, old flowers and dirty materials.

The basic economy of the city constitutes the agricultural and the cotton industries. While there is a good market for clothing, jewellery and sarees, most of the general purpose requirements of the public are easily fulfilled by local markets. Both the auto and the electronic businesses are also growing. All of them use Kunda river water for their water requirements. Either directly or indirectly all their effluents reach Kunda river causing severe pollution, affecting agriculture and causing severe environmental damage. The present study has been carried out to evaluate the physico-chemical parameter of river Kunda by using standard method, which enables the common man to understand the quality of water.

MATERIALS AND METHODS

Study Area

The Kunda River is a Main river of Khargone district. It is a tributary river of Narmada river. It's originated from forest, Amba and Sirvel village. River Kunda has a length of approximately 169Kms. and its catchment area of 3825 sq.km. Its river situated in the west directions of M.P. and its flows from South to North through four block of Khargone district Bhagwanpura, Goganwa, Khargone, and Kasrawad. Its Latitude 21°49′16″ N and Longitude 75°36′4″E. On the Kunda River there are two Dams constructed Dejla-Devada dam & Vanihar dam. It's Provides of drinking water for the Khargone city. There is on a Shiv temple and Ahilyaghat before Siddhi vinayak ganesh temple at the bank of Kunda River in Khargone. There are 7 stop dams is being constructed in last two years. These Stop dams provide drinking water & irrigation facility to Khargone District. Its water works water capacity 20 crore litre. Its 7 stop dams are water holding capacity 0.646 million cubic meters. Its capacities in stop water 1.5 million cubic meter and these stopdams made in front of Kalika mata temple.

Sampling Stations

The sampling would be collected from various shoreline area of following selected station.

1. DEJLA-DEVADA DAM

Dejla-Devada Dam is situated on Kunda River. It is 5km. away from Bhagwanpura Tehsil in Khargone district of western Madhya Pradesh. Its total length is 6010m. And Its 357.20m. high from the deepest foundation level. Its Irrigation area is about 8000 hectare. Its water holding area is 335.40 sq. km. and its complete storage capacity is 56.35million cubic meter, its total dam surface 383.20m. And its maximum dam surface 38920m.

Its latitude 21°36′45″ (DMS) N & longitude 75°37′30″ (DMS) E

2. CONFLUENCE WITH UNDRI RIVER

Undri River is a tributary river of Kunda river. This place is situated 12 km. away From the Dejla-Devada dam. At this village Undri river confluence in Kunda River this village is called Bagdhari. At this place Garhi-Galtar project has made, which provided Irrigation facility to near about 1157 km. hectare Land.

Its latitude 20°41′30″ (DMS) N & longitude 75°52′15″ (DMS) E

3. KHARGONE

Khargone district formerly known as West Nimar district. It is a district of Madhya Pradesh state in central India. The district lies in Nimar region, and is part of Indore Division. Khargone town is the headquarters of this district. It is situated on the bank of Kunda River. Khargone is located at South-West border of Madhya Pradesh, 283 meters above sea level. Area of the district is 8030 square km. The district is surrounded by Dhar, Indore and Dewas in the north, Maharashtra state in the south, Khandwa, Burhanpur in the east and Barwani in the west. The district forms almost the central section of Narmada valley which is bordered by Vindhachal ranges in the north and Satpura ranges in the south. Narmada is the main river flowing through the district. Its river flows in a path of 50 Km. inside the district. Kunda and Veda are other main rivers in the district. Khargone is fastly growing as a city. Khargone district Total population is above 1872413. It district water use 141 Lac liter per day and its situated Intecvel its water capacity 1.062 Crore liter. It's situated in small and large 146 dam. Dejla-Devada, Garhi-Galtar & Ambaknala are main irrigation projects. Khargone generally has hot climate with little rain. The average rain fall 831mm. The summers are long ranging from March to July. Monsoon is brief and arrives in mid August.

Its latitude 20°22′ and 22°35′ N & longitude 74°25′ and 76°14′ E

4. SIPTAN

Siptan is a small town. It is a terminal point of Kunda river, At this point Kunda river confluence with the Veda River. After this place Kunda river is called Veda River. Siptan is situated 35 km. away from administrative headquarters of Khargone district.. Siptan is near the village named Bhulgori. Siptan catchments area is about 798.10 sq.m.

Its latitude 21°41′30″ (DMS) N & longitude 75°41′30″ (DMS) E

Water Analysis

The water samples were collected from the four selected sampling stations viz., Dejla-Devada dam = Station 1, Confluence with Undri river = Station 2, Khargone = Station 3 and Siptan = Station 4 in the Kunda River for the period of one year from August 2010 to July 2011. In the analysis of the physico- chemical properties of water, standard method prescribed in limnological literature were used. Temperature, pH, Transparency, Dissolved Oxygen were determined at the site while Biochemical oxygen demand, Total Hardness, Alkanity, Chloride, Nitrate, Phosphate were determined in the laboratory. The Physico- Chemical parameters were determined by standard methods of APHA (2002), Welch (1998), Golterman (1991). All the chemicals used were of AR grade.

RESULTS AND DISCUSSION

The physico-chemical characteristics of the four samples points were given in Tables 2.1, 2.2, 2.3 and 2.4 along with the respective values and the mean values with range values were given in the Table 2.5 and Monthly Fluctuation of physicochemical parameters are presented in figures 2.1-2.10.

Temperature is an important biologically significant factor, which plays an important role in the metabolic of the organism. Temperature value was found to be ranging from 20° C to 43° C. An increase in the Temperature was observed at Siptan (20° C to 43° C) further increased values could be noticed at Dejla- Devada dam (25° C to 42° C) and Confluence with Undri river (25° C to 40° C) and Khargone (22° C to 41° C). The mean value of Temperature in Dejla- Devada dam 32.33°C and Confluence with Undri river 31.70°C and Khargone 31.25°C and Siptan 31.41°C.

Lowest water temperature was observed in the Siptan 20° C. A study increase in water temperature in the course of River Kunda was noticed. There was an increase in water temperature after the discharge of the effluents into the river. An increase in temperature was observed from upstream station to lower (Dejla- Devada dam to Confluence with Undri river to Siptan to Khargone). This might be due to mixing of the effluents. Our property of water is that with change in temperature, its density varies and it becomes less with warming up and more with cooling Bhagavathi *et al.*, (2001). The pH value was found to be ranging from 7.2 and 9.4. An increase in the pH was observed at Siptan (7.2 and 9.4.) further increased values could be noticed at Dejla- Devada dam (7.61 and 9.22) and Confluence with Undri river 7.9 and 8.8 and Khargone (7.5 and 9.3). The mean value of pH in Dejla - Devada dam 8.465 and Confluence with Undri river 8.36 and Khargone 8.325 and Siptan 8.29.

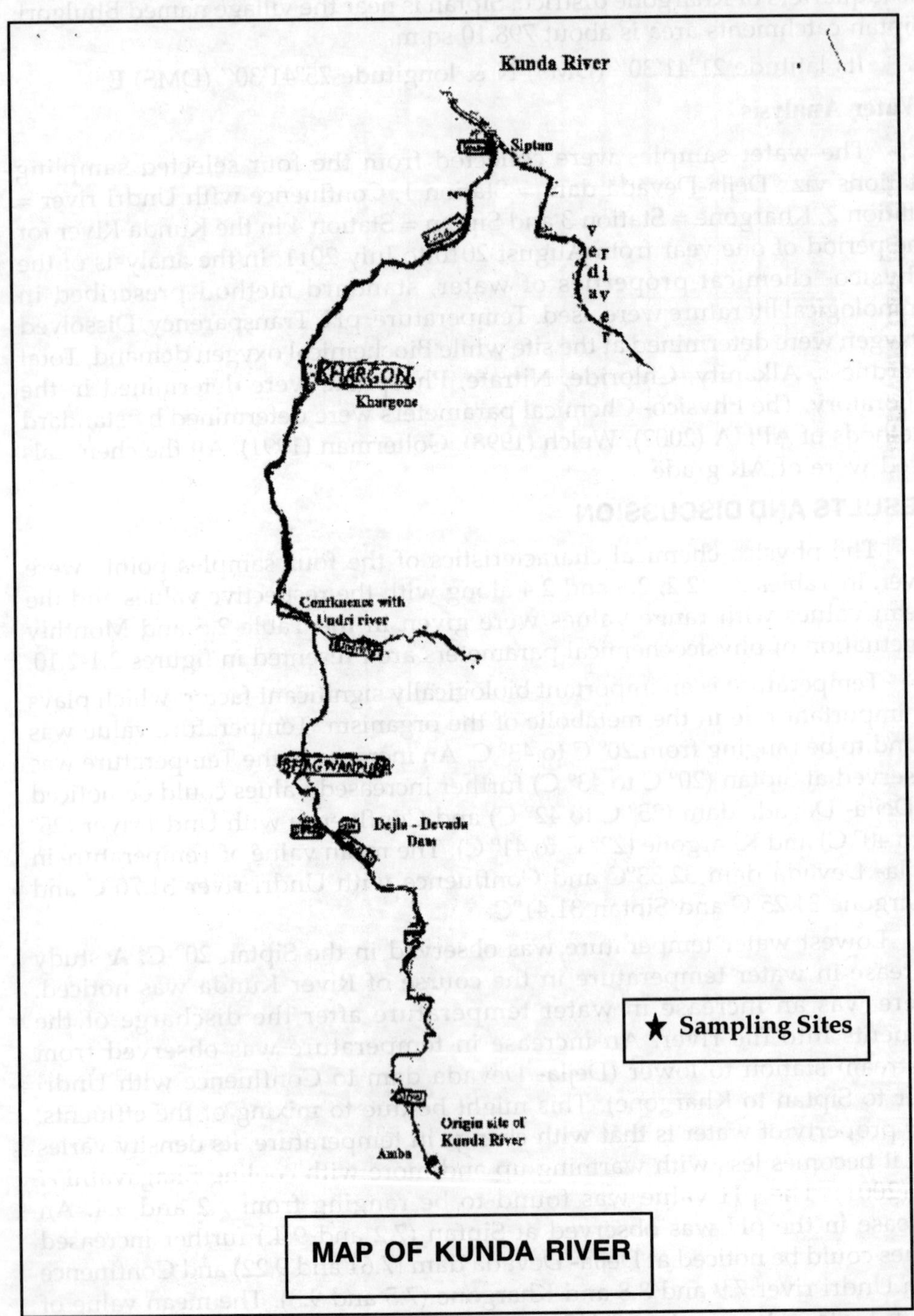

Map 2.1: Location Map Showing the Kunda River and Four Sampling Points, Khargone, M.P. India.

Table 2.1: [Station I] Physico-chemical Characteristics of River Kunda at Dejla-Devada Dam for One Year (August 2010 to July 2011)

Month	August	September	October	November	December	January	February	March	April	May	June	July
Temp. (°C)	28	30	35	31	29	25	27	33	35	42	41	32
pH	9.1	8.7	8.2	8.5	7.61	7.84	7.8	8.2	8.1	9.2	9.22	9.11
Transperancy (N.T.U.)	16	25	38	50.5	51.2	53	45	39	28	24	22	9.11
D.O. (Mg/l)	8.2	6.23	6.50	6.35	6.39	6.21	6.9	7.2	7.5	8.7	9.1	9.12
B.O.D. (Mg/l)	5.63	5.5	4.8	3.1	3.2	3.31	3.9	4.0	4.5	4.81	5	5.45
Total Hardness (Mg/l)	80	78	73	71	89	107	121	157	145	147	190	85
Alkalinity	245	255	230	250	235	250	245	264	258	298	300	278
Chloride (Mg/l)	49	38	0.3	25.4	21	26	36.5	39.1	46.7	49.1	53.4	53.1
Nitrate (Mg/l)	0.125	0.3	0.131	0.121	0.11	0.89	0.76	0.78	0.89	0.102	0.109	0.112
Phosphate (Mg/l)	0.46	0.49	0.5	0.16	0.17	0.21	0.23	0.27	0.31	0.35	0.42	0.45

Table 2.2: [Station II] Physico-chemical Characteristics of River Kunda at Confluence with Undri River for One Year (August 2010 to July 2011)

Month	August	September	October	November	December	January	February	March	April	May	June	July
Temp. (°C)	27.1	30.1	35	31.3	29.2	25.2	29	33.3	34	40	35.1	31.2
pH	8.5	8.7	8.2	8.5	7.61	7.84	7.8	8.2	8.1	9.2	9.22	9.11
Transperancy (N.T.U.)	20	30	42	55	48	58	45	36	28	22	20	12
D.O. (Mg/l)	6.2	9.2	9.8	6.5	7.2	7.5	8.1	7.3	6.4	5.7	4.9	5.4
B.O.D. (Mg/l)	6.3	5.7	5.08	3.0	2.8	3.1	3.8	4.3	4.7	5.1	5.5	5.7
Total Hardness (Mg/l)	128	136	170	165	155	180	188	200	170	210	205	166
Alkalinity	365	415	390	415	385	255	245	256	375	230	160	335
Chloride (Mg/l)	30	18	20	23	38	32	37	24	18	40	47	27
Nitrate (Mg/l)	0.120	0.135	0.139	0.120	0.110	0.890	0.765	0.780	0.850	0.115	0.190	0.122
Phosphate (Mg/l)	0.66	0.40	0.55	0.16	0.20	0.31	0.20	0.37	0.29	0.31	0.49	0.40

Table 2.3: [Station III] Physico-chemical Characteristics of River Kunda at Khargone for One Year (August 2010 to July 2011)

Month	August	September	October	November	December	January	February	March	April	May	June	July
Temp. (°C)	25	31	33	32	28	22	26	33	35	41	39	30
pH	9.3	8.8	8.4	8.0	7.5	7.9	8.0	8.6	7.8	8.8	9.0	7.8
Transperency (N.T.U.)	19	28	40	55	52	58	42	37	22	20	24	15
D.O. (Mg/l)	7.8	6.50	6.25	6.65	6.89	6.10	6.90	7.50	7.10	8.90	9.30	8.80
B.O.D. (Mg/l)	5.63	5.5	4.8	3.1	3.2	3.31	3.9	4.0	4.5	4.81	5	5.45
Total Hardness (Mg/l)	115	125	165	188	165	190	205	235	210	245	215	170
Alkalinity	250	258	239	260	230	252	240	275	252	285	305	267
Chloride (Mg/l)	41	35	28	24	20	27	35	40	42	50	55	58
Nitrate (Mg/l)	0.140	0.125	0.135	0.115	0.105	0.095	0.076	0.070	0.890	0.125	0.119	0.122
Phosphate (Mg/l)	0.39	0.55	0.50	0.36	0.25	0.17	0.28	0.33	0.30	0.45	0.66	0.29

Table 2.4: [Station IV] Physico-chemical Characteristics of River Kunda at Siptan for One Year (August 2010 to July 2011)

Month	August	September	October	November	December	January	February	March	April	May	June	July
Temp. (°C)	22	30	32	30	26	20	24	35	37	43	38	28
pH	9.0	8.2	8.8	8.4	7.9	7.5	8.5	8.9	7.2	8.0	9.4	7.7
Transperancy (N.T.U.)	21	25	35	50	59	60	46	35	30	18	22	18
D.O. (Mg/l)	6.9	6.5	6.0	6.5	6.2	6.0	7.0	7.9	7.7	8.4	9.5	9.0
B.O.D. (Mg/l)	5.0	5.7	4.5	3.6	3.8	3.0	3.8	4.4	4.9	5.1	5.5	5.9
Total Hardness (Mg/l)	135	145	185	195	165	180	198	210	180	220	235	176
Alkalinity	220	245	220	230	210	245	260	287	260	299	315	255
Chloride (Mg/l)	50	45	39	32	28	36	48	55	60	69	56	43
Nitrate (Mg/l)	0.130	0.115	0.145	0.125	0.115	0.090	0.080	0.095	0.780	0.145	0.120	0.125
Phosphate (Mg/l)	0.55	0.75	0.69	0.45	0.39	0.25	0.30	0.39	0.44	0.57	0.86	0.49

Table 2.5: Physico-chemical Characteristics of River Kunda (Dejla-Devada Dam, Confluence with Undri River, Khargone, Siptan) at Four Stations (Mean Values for One Year (August 2010 to July 2011)

Physical Characters	Dejla-Devada Dam	Confluence with Undri River	Khargone	Siptan
Temperature (ºC)	32.33 (25-42)	31.70 (25.2-40)	31.25 (22-41)	30.41 (20-43)
pH	8.465 (7.61-9.22)	8.36 (7.9-8.8)	8.325 (7.5-9.3)	8.29 (7.2-9.4)
Traneperancy (N.T.U.)	33.89 (15-53)	34.66 (12-58)	34.33 (15-58)	34.91 (18-60)
D.O. (Mg/l)	7.36 (6.21-9.12)	7.01 (4.9-9.8)	7.39 (6.10-9.30)	7.3 (6.0-9.5)
B.O.D. (Mg/l)	4.43 (3.1-5.63)	4.59 (2.8-6.3)	4.43 (3.1-5.63)	4.6 (3.0-5.9)
Total Hardness (Mg/l)	111.9 (71-190)	172.75 (128-210)	185.66 (115-245)	185.33 (135-235)
Alkalinity	259 (230-300)	318.83 (160-415)	259.41 (230-305)	253.83 (210-315)
Chloride (Mg/l)	36.46 (0.3-53.4)	29.5 (18-47)	37.91 (20-58)	46.75 (28-69)
Nitrate (Mg/l)	0.355 (0.11-0.131)	0.361 (0.110-0.890)	0.176 (0.070-0.890)	0.172 (0.080-0.780)
Phosphate (Mg/l)	0.335 (0.5-0.49)	0.361 (0.16-0.66)	0.03 (0.17-0.66)	0.510 (0.25-0.86)

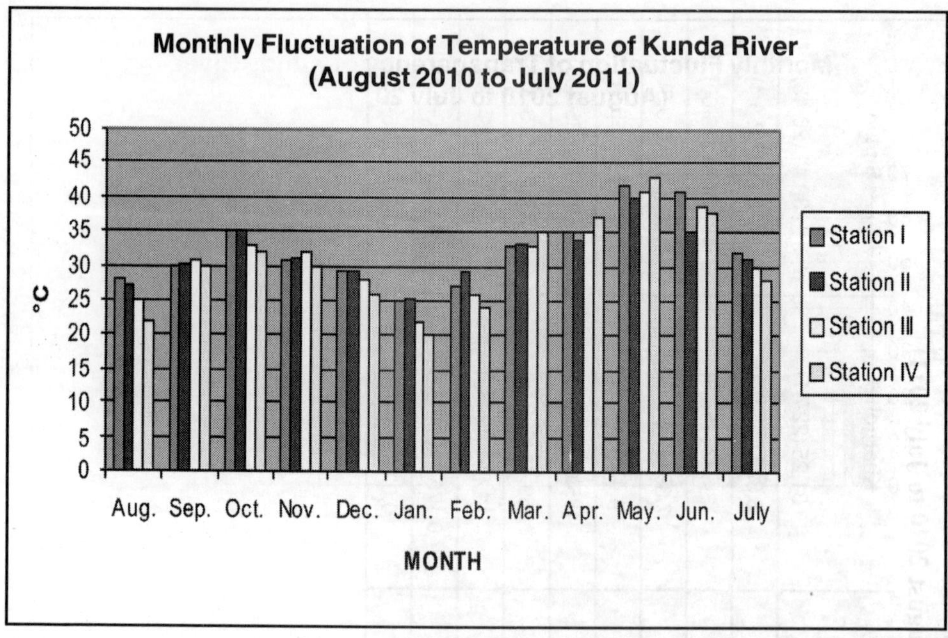

Fig. 2.1: Bar Diagram Showing Monthly Fluctuation of Temperature of Kunda River (August 2010 to July 2011)

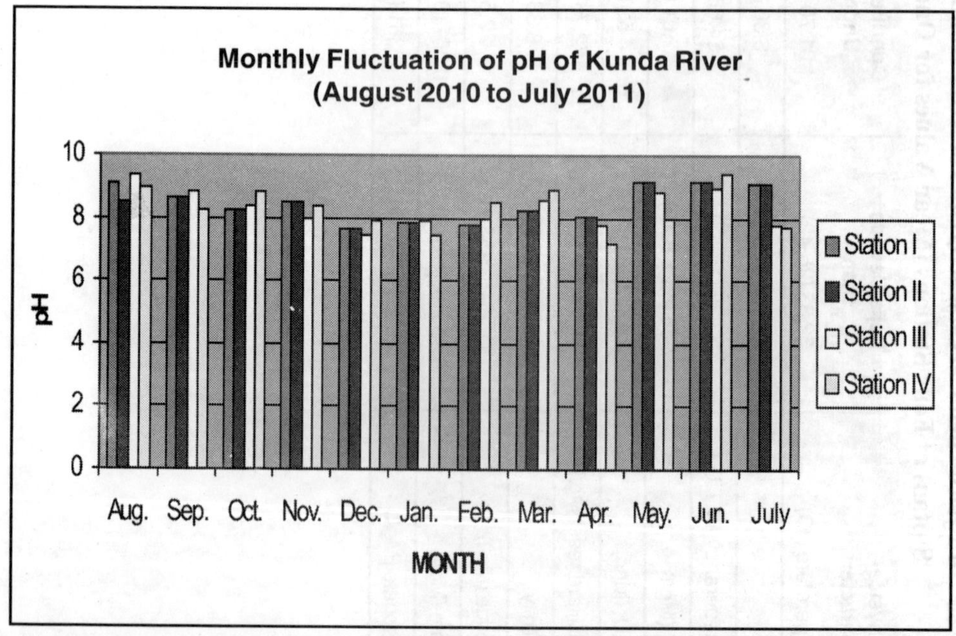

Fig. 2.2: Bar Diagram Showing Monthly Fluctuation of pH of Kunda River (August 2010 to July 2011)

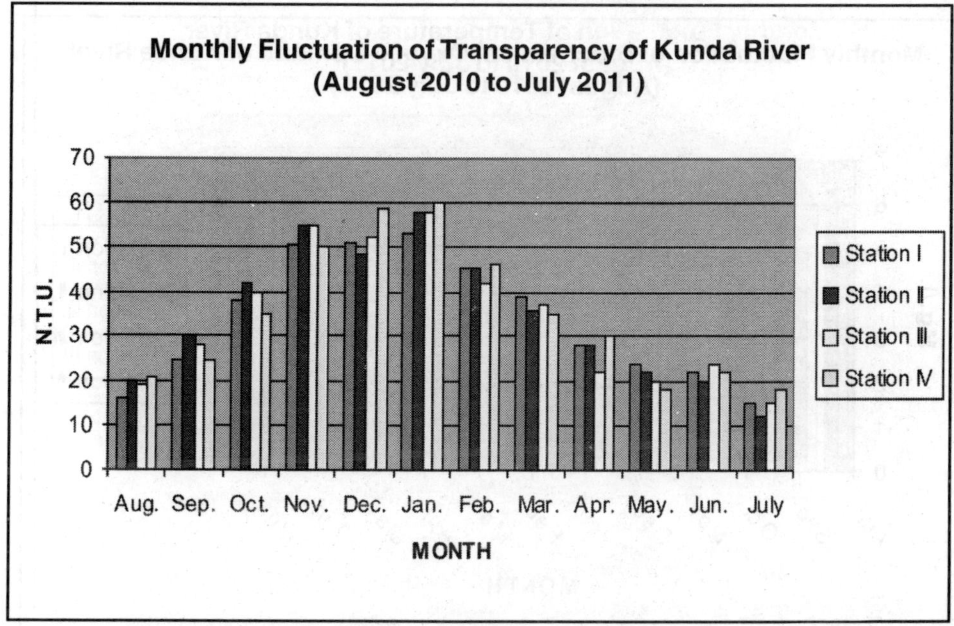

Fig. 2.3: Bar Diagram Showing Monthly Fluctuation of Transparency of Kunda River (August 2010 to July 2011)

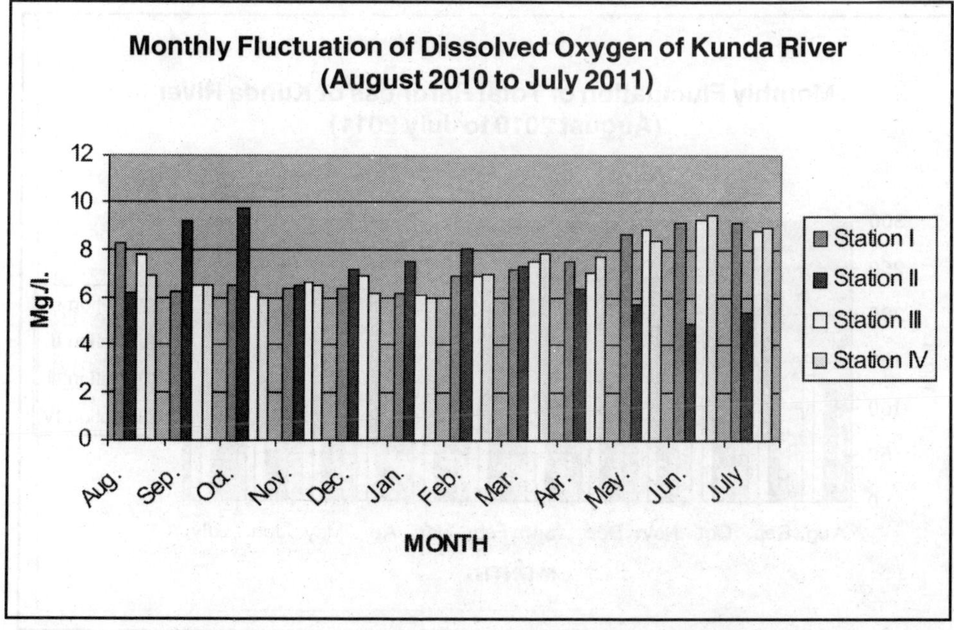

Fig. 2.4: Bar Diagram Showing Monthly Fluctuation of Dissolved Oxygen of Kunda River (August 2010 to July 2011)

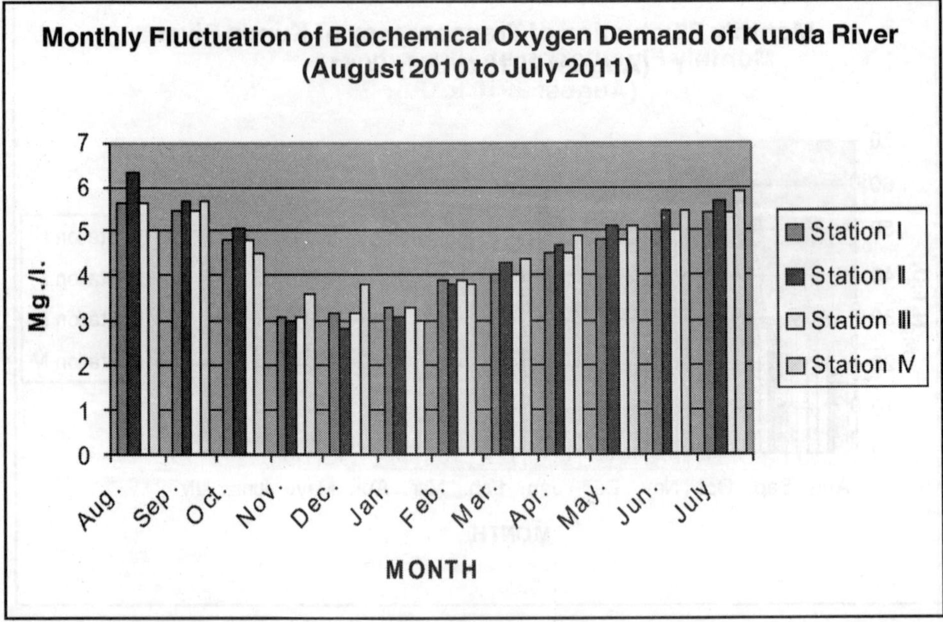

Fig. 2.5: Bar Diagram Showing Monthly Fluctuation of Biochemical Oxygen Demand of Kunda River (August 2010 to July 2011)

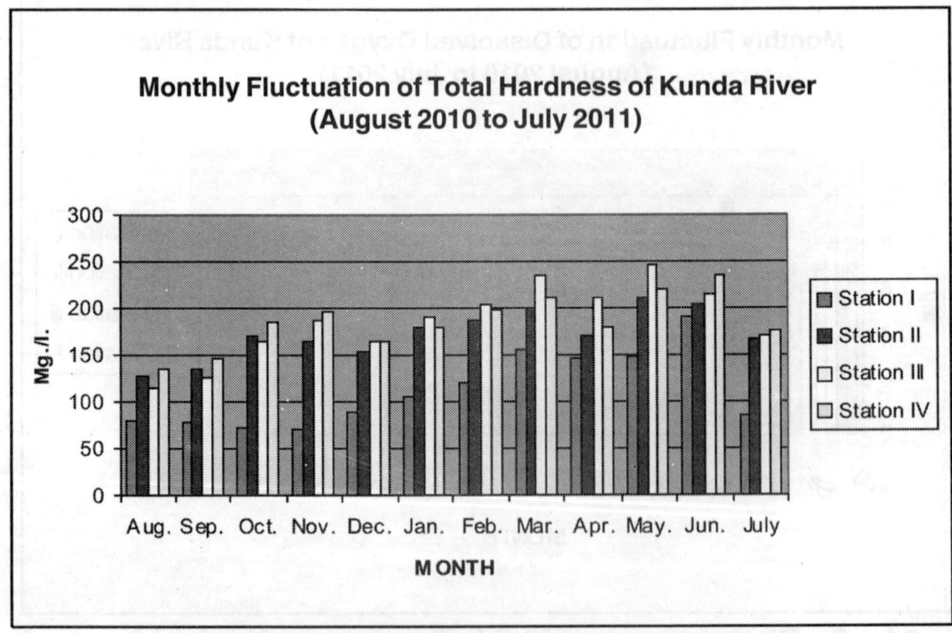

Fig. 2.6: Bar Diagram Showing Monthly Fluctuation of Total Hardness of Kunda River (August 2010 to July 2011)

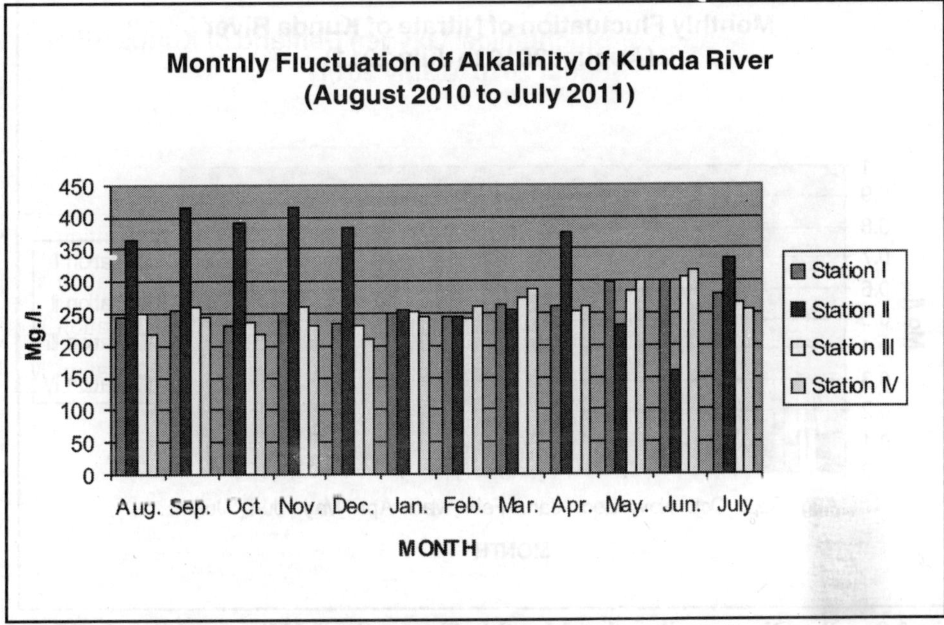

Fig. 2.7: **Bar Diagram Showing Monthly Fluctuation of Alkalinity of Kunda River (August 2010 to July 2011)**

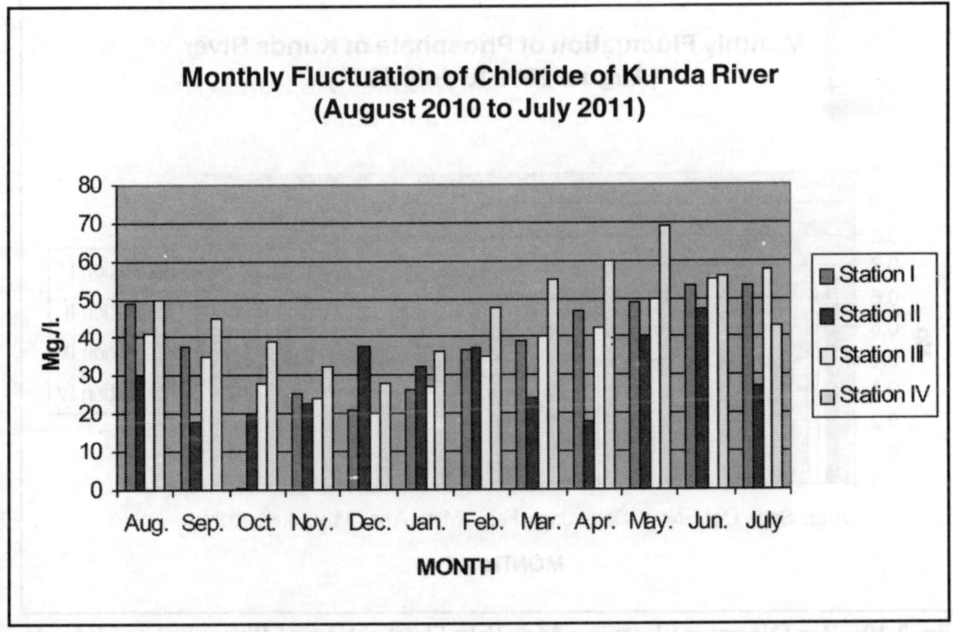

Fig. 2.8: **Bar Diagram Showing Monthly Fluctuation of Chloride of Kunda River (August 2010 to July 2011)**

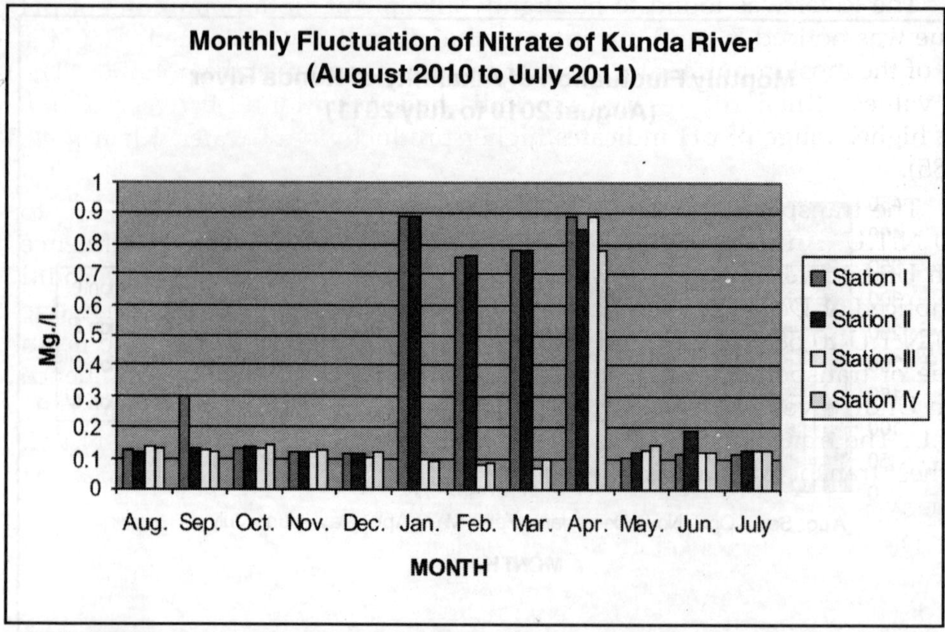

Fig. 2.9: Bar Diagram Showing Monthly Fluctuation of Nitrate of Kunda River (August 2010 to July 2011)

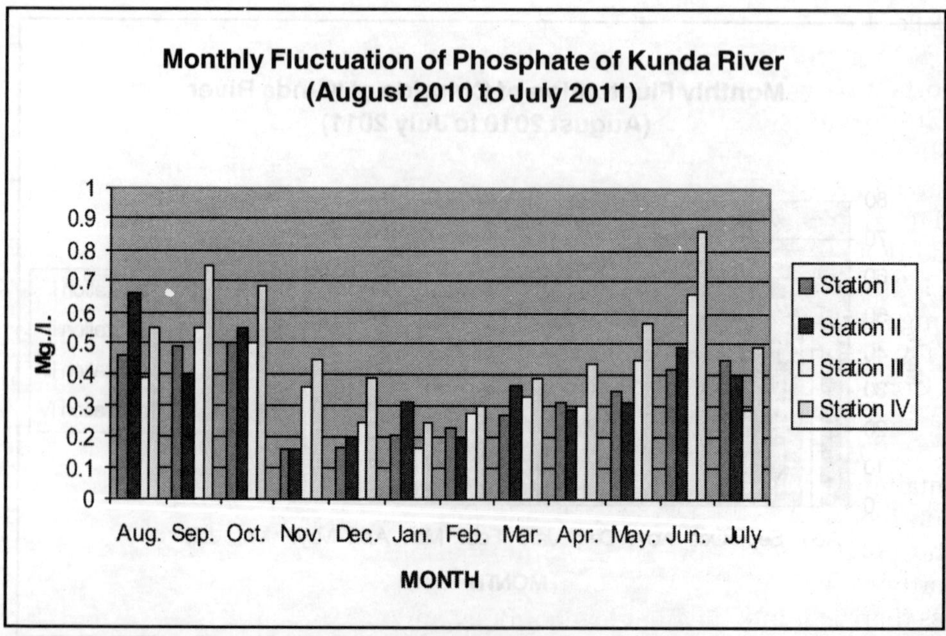

Fig. 2.10: Bar Diagram Showing Monthly Fluctuation of Phosphate of Kunda River (August 2010 to July 2011)

The River was found to be slightly alkaline at Siptan minimum of pH value was noticed 7.2 and maximum value pH value was noticed 9.4. pH is one of the most important factors that serve as an index of the pollution. The pH values of majority reservoir in India have been found between 6 to 9. The higher range of pH indicates higher productivity of water. Khan *et al.*, (1985).

The transperancy value was found to be ranging from 12.0 N.T.U to 60.0 N.T.U. An increase in the transperancy was observed at Confluence with Undri river (12.0 N.T.U to 60.0 N.T.U.) further increased values could be noticed at Dejla- Devada dam (15.0 N.T.U to 53.0 N.T.U.) and Khargone 15.0 N.T.U to 58.0 N.T.U. and Siptan (18.0 N.T.U to 60.0 N.T.U. The mean value of transperancy in Dejla - Devada dam 33.89 N.T.U and Confluence with Undri river 34.66 N.T.U. and Khargone 34.33 N.T.U. and Siptan 34.91 N.T.U. The transperancy value was ranging from 12.0 N.T.U to 60.0 N.T.U. Highest transperancy value was noticed at Siptan 60.0 N.T.U and the lowest value was noticed in Conflucnce of Undri river 12.0 N.T.U.

Dissolved Oxygen an important limnological parameter indicating level of water quality and organic pollution in the water body Wetzel *et al.*, (2006) The dissolved oxygen value was found to be ranging from 4.9 mg/l to 9.8mg/l. An increase in the dissolved oxygen was observed at Confluence with Undri river (4.9 mg/l to 9.8 mg/l) further increased values could be noticed at Dejla- Devada dam (6.21 mg/l to 9.12 mg/l) and Khargone (6.10 mg/l to 9.30 mg/l) and Siptan (6.0 mg/l to 9.5 mg/l). The mean value of dissolved oxygen in Dejla- Devada dam 7.36 mg/l and Confluence with Undri river 7.01 mg/l and Khargone 7.39 mg/l and Siptan 7.3 mg/l. Dissolved oxygen is an important parameter of the river, which is essential to the metabolism of all aquatic organisms Wetzel, R.G. (1975) The Dissolved oxygen percent saturation was low at Confluence with Undri river. These tallies with the research finding of Turkish Standards (1988). The biochemical oxygen demand (BOD) value was found to be ranging from 2.8mg/l to 6.3mg/l.An increase in the BOD was observed at Confluence with Undri river (2.8 mg/l to 6.3 mg/l) further increased values could be noticed at Dejla- Devada dam (3.1 mg/l to 5.63 mg/l) and Khargone (3.1 mg/l to 5.63 mg/l) and Siptan (3.0 mg/l to 5.9 mg/l). The mean value of BOD in Dejla- Devada dam 4.43 mg/l and Confluence with Undri river 4.59 mg/l and Khargone 4.43 mg/l and Siptan 4.6 mg/l. BOD were decreased with low in the pollution level Borse *et al.*, (2001). Pointed out that the minimum oxygen content in water for maintaining fish life healthy condition. An increase in the BOD was observed at Confluence with Undri river (2.8 mg/l to 6.3 mg/l). This range is contrary to the BOD range value of EPA international standard of fresh water. According to EPA, the BOD standard for fresh waters of unpolluted rivers is less than 5.0mg/l. the high level of BOD might have been attributed to the discharge of pollutants into the river through washing, sewage contamination, industrial affluent and a like.

The Total Hardness in water depends on the presence of principle cations Ca++ and Mg++. The Total Hardness value was found to be ranging from 71mg/l to 245mg/l.An increase in the Total Hardness was observed at Dejla - Devada dam (71mg/l to 245mg/l) further increased values could be noticed at Confluence with Undri river (128 mg/l to 210 mg/l) and Khargone (115 mg/l to 245 mg/l) and Siptan (135 mg/l to 235 mg/l). The mean value of Total Hardness in Dejla- Devada dam 111.9 mg/l and Confluence with Undri river 172.75 mg/l and Khargone 185.66 mg/l and Siptan 185.33 mg/l.

Alkalinity is not a pollutant. It is a total measure of the substances in water that have "acid-neutralizing" ability. Alalinity value was found to be ranging from 160mg/l to 415mg/l. An increase in the Alalinity was observed at Confluence with Undri river (160 mg/l to 415 mg/l) further increased values could be noticed at Dejla - Devada dam (230 mg/l to 300 mg/l) and Khargone (230 mg/l to 305 mg/l) and Siptan (210 mg/l to 315 mg/l). The mean value of Alalinity in Dejla - Devada dam 259 mg/l and Confluence with Undri river 318.83 mg/l and Khargone 259.41 mg/l and Siptan 253.83 mg/l. Alkalinity is important for fish and aquatic life because it protects or buffers against pH changes and makes water less vulnerable to acid rain.

Chloride is a material that is both a natural component of water in northeast Ohio and also a very common industrial material. It enters rivers from industrial processes, domestic sewage, and surface runoff. Chloride value was found to be ranging from 0.3mg/l to 69mg/l. An increase in the Chloride was observed at Dejla - Devada dam (0.3 mg/l to 69 mg/l) further increased values could be noticed at Confluence with Undri river (18 mg/l to 43mg/l) and Khargone (20 mg/l to 58 mg/l) and Siptan (28mg/l to 69 mg/l). The mean value of Alalinity in Dejla- Devada dam 36.46 mg/l and Confluence with Undri river 29.5 mg/l and Khargone 37.91 mg/l and Siptan 46.75 mg/l. Chloride is often termed a conservative pollutant. That is, it does not react as readily as many other materials in the water; nor does it settle out as readily. As a result, it is often a very good indicator of the aggregate amount of anthropogenic materials dumped into the river from all sources Jammal, A. (1998) similar results has been observed by Ahmed, A.M. (2004).

Nitrate is the number one limiting factor that prevents the completion of this cycle. Nitrate value was found to be ranging from 0.070mg/l to 0.890mg/l. An increase in the Chloride was observed at Khargone (0.070 mg/l to 0.890 mg/l) further increased values could be noticed at Dejla- Devada dam (0.11 mg/l to 0.131mg/l) and Confluence with Undri river (0.110 mg/l to 0.890 mg/l) and Siptan (0.080mg/l to 0.780 mg/l). The mean value of Nitrate in Dejla- Devada dam 0.355 mg/l and Confluence with Undri river 0.316 mg/l and Khargone 0.176 mg/l and Siptan 0.172 mg/l. Nitrate is attributed mainly due to anthropogenic activities such of run of water from agricultural lands, industrial wastes, discharge of house hold and municipal sewage from the market place and other effluents containing nitrogen.

Phosphate is the most important factor in the cultural eutrophication of rivers and streams throughout the world. Phosphate value was found to be ranging from 0.16mg/l to 0.86 mg/l. An increase in the Phosphate was observed at Siptan (0.25 mg/l to 0.86 mg/l) further increased values could be noticed at Dejla - Devada dam (0.5 mg/l to 0.49 mg/l) and Confluence with Undri river (0.16 mg/l to 0.66 mg/l) and Khargone (0.17 mg/l to 0.66 mg/l). The mean value of Phosphate in Dejla - Devada dam 0.355 mg/l and Confluence with Undri river 0.361 mg/l and Khargone 0.03 mg/l and Siptan 0.510 mg/l. Phosphates stimulate the growth of plankton and water plants that provide food for fish. Phosphates come from fertilizers, Pesticides, industry and cleaning compounds. Natural sources include phosphate-containing rocks and solid or liquid wastes. This may increase the fish population and improve the waterway's quality of life. If too much phosphate is present algae and water weeds grow wildly, choke the waterway, and use up large amounts of oxygen. Many fish and aquatic organisms may die.

The results of the physico-chemical analyses have classified for water quality in by the Dzerosi *et al.,* (2002). All physicochemical parameters determined in the Narmada river, Bhavani river, Challawa river and Abeokuta, Nigeria Sharma *et al.,* (2012); Varunprasath *et al.,* (2010);. Indabawa I.I. (2010); Shittu et al., (2008). Cekerek stream are similar to those reported in the River Yesilirmak, Tuzen *et al.,* (2001). The physico-chemical parameters of lakes, ponds and rivers have considerable effect on the aquatic life. These parameters Provide information on the characteristics and quality of a water body Haruna *et al.,* (2006).

CONCLUSION

The assessment of water quality at Kunda river for a period of One Year via physicochemical analysis indicated that the temperature, pH and Transparency lies within the standard limit of good water quality set for freshwater according to EPA and WHO, while dissolved oxygen concentration and Biochemical oxygen demand recorded have exceeded the minimum standard values limit set by EPA and WHO. There is therefore a need of for a regular monitoring of the water to reduce the pollution level.

REFERENCES

1. Ahmed, A.M. (2004); Ecological Studies of the River Padma at Mawa Ghat, Munshiganj Physico-chemical Properties. Pakistan Journal of Biological Sciences. 7(11): 1865-1869.
2. APHA (2002); Standard Method for Examination of Water and Waste Water, American Public Health Association Inc. New York, 22nd Ed.
3. Bhagavathi, S.K., S. Ghan and A. Bhagavathi, (2001). A Comparative Study of Drinking Water Sources of Two Villages having Different Environmental Settings. J. Ecobiol., 13(3): 175-181.

4. Blockeel H; Dzeroski S, and Grbovic (1999); Simultaneous Prediction of Chemical Parameters of Rivers Quality with TILDE, 2nd Edition European Conference on Principle of Data Minimum and Knowledge pp. 15-18, Springler, Berlin.
5. Borse, S.K. and P.V. Bhave, (2001); Seasonal Variations in Temperature, Dissolved Oxygen Ph and Salinity and Their Influence on Planktons in River Water, Jalagon, Maharastra. Poll. Res., 20(1): 79-82.
6. Chris Kreger (2002); Water Quality Control and Assessment, Centre for Education Technologies Wheeling Jesuit University USA; Website Report Published, May 5, 2002.
7. Dzeroski S. Grbovic T. and Demsor D. (2002); Predicting Chemical Parameters of River Quality from Bioindicator Data. Applied Intelligence.
8. Environmental Protection Agency, EPA (1987); Surface Water Monitoring, a Framework for Usage. Office of Water Policy Planning and Evaluation, Washington DC.
9. Environmental Protection Agency (2001): Protecting and Restoring America's Watersheds: Status Trends and Initiatives in Watershed Management. EPA-840-R-00-001.5-7.
10. Golterman, H.L. (1991) Physiological Limnology: An Approach to the Physiology of Lake Ecosystem. Elsvier Scientific Publication Comp. Amsterdam. Oxford, New York, 249- 277.
11. Haruna, A.B., Abubakar, K.A., and Ladu, B.M.B. (2006). An Assessment of Physico-chemical Parameters and Productivity Status of Lake Geriyo, Yola, Adamawa State, Nigeria. Biological and Environmental Sciences Journal for the Tropics 3(1): 18-23.
12. Indabawa I.I. (2010); The Assessment of Water Quality at Challawa River via Physico-chemical and Macro Invertebrate Analysis, Bioscience Research Communications Vol. 22, 227-233 pp.
13. Jammal, A., (1998); Physico-chemical Studies in Uyyakondan Channel Water of Cauvery. Poll. Res., 17(2): 111-114.
14. Khan, I.A. and A.A. Khan, 1985. Physical and Chemical Condition in Seika Jheelat, Aligarh, Ecol.,3: 269-274.
15. Sharma S., Tali I., Pir Z., Siddique A., Mudgal L.K. (2012); Evaluation of Physico-chemical Parameters of Narmada River, MP, India Researcher 4(5): 13-19 pp. (ISSN: 1553-9865) http://www.science pub.net/researcher.
16. Shittu, O.B., Olaitan, J.O., Amusa, T.S. (2008); Physico-Chemical and Bacteriological Analyses of Water Used for Drinking and Swimming Purposes in Abeokuta, Nigeria, African Journal of Biomedical Research, Vol. 11, 285-290 pp. ISSN 1119-5096.
17. Turkish Standards Su Kirliligi Kontro Yonetmelioi (1988); Regulations of Water Pollution Control, 19919 Sayili Resmi Gazete (The Official Gazette).
18. Tuzen, M.E. Aydemir and H. Sari: (2001). Investigation of Some Physical and Chemical Parameters in the River Yesilirmak in Tokat Region, Turkey. Fresenius Environ. Bull., 11(4), 161-170 pp.
19. Varunprasath K., Nicholas A. Daniel. (2010); Physico-Chemical Parameters of River Bhavani in Three Stations, Tamil Nadu, India Iranica Journal of Energy and Environment 1(4): 321-325pp. ISSN 2079-2115.
20. Welch P.S. (1998) Liminological Methods Mcgran Hill Book Co. New York.

21. Wetzel, R.G., (1975); W.B. Limnology, Sundersa Co., Philadelphia.

22. Wetzel R.G., Likens G.E. (2006) Limnological Analysis.3rd ed. Springer-Verlag, New York, 391.

23. World Health Organisation (WHO). (2002), World Health Report: Reducing Risks, Promoting Healthy Life. Life. France. Retrieved 14 July 2009, from http://www.who.int/whr/2002/en/whr02-en.pdf.

CHAPTER

Effects of Oil Spill on Water Quality and Fish Production in Otu- Jeremi and Environs Delta State, Nigeria

V.N. Ojeh[1]; I.P Udo-James[2]; E.D Oruonye[3]

ABSTRACT

The effects of oil spill on water quality and fish production in Otu-Jeremi and its environs were examined. Water samples were collected from rivers where oil spillages were recorded over time (Otu-Jeremi and Eyara Rivers). Each river was stratified into five sampling points and a total of ten samples were collected from the two rivers in the study area. Water sample were obtained with the aid of ten sterilized 2 - litre plastic containers. Additional data were collected via the questionnaires and oral interviews. Physico-chemical properties and heavy metal contents of water samples were obtained from the laboratory analyses. The water sample parameters analysed include pH, Electrical conductivity (EC), total dissolved solids (TDS), total suspended solids (TSS), turbidity, biological oxygen demand (BOD), chemical oxygen demand (COD), Salinity, total hydrocarbon content (THC) and heavy metals (Cu, Ze, Cr, Fe and Pb). Results were compared with DPR standard for quality water.

1, 2. Department of Geography and Regional Planning, Delta State University, PMB 1, Abraka, Nigeria.

3. Department of Geography, Taraba State University, PMB 1167, Jalingo, Nigeria

These indicated that the rivers were polluted and pose great danger to fish production and as such food security for sustainable development is not guaranteed. The study also revealed a significant variation in the total number of fishes harvested before and after oil spillage in the communities. This was ascertained with paired 't' test statistics which showed that there was significant difference in the number of fishes harvested before and after pollution at P d" 0.05. This study recommends that oil companies operating in the area should strictly follow safety measures of operations in-order to minimize oil spill occurrence which adversely affects fish production.

Keywords: Delta State, Fish Production, Oil Spill, Otu-Jeremi and Water Quality.

INTRODUCTION

In the last fifty-five years, Nigeria has experienced increased activities in the areas of oil exploration and exploitation, refining and products marketing operations. While these activities have generated immense financial benefits for the country, they have also created serious health and environmental problems to host communities. Oil industry operations have introduced pollutants as liquid discharges and oil spills into the environment. Literature is replete with incidence of oil spillage in the Niger Delta region of Nigeria. The effects of oil spill on the environment have been very glaring in terms of its negative impacts on the region. Eteng (2007), stated that oil exploration and exploitation, have over the years impacted on the social-physical environment of the Niger Delta region. Oil producing communities have been threatened by massive oil spill thus affecting the peasant economy and the entire livelihood system of the people.

There is no doubt that the Nigeria oil industries have affected the country in a variety of ways and at the same time it has fashioned a remarkable economic landscape for the country. However on the negative side, oil spill resulting from petroleum exploration and exploitation has led to environmental pollution with adverse effects on fish production, especially in the study area. This according to Ikporukpo, (1998) has a far reaching effect on the environment. The toxicity of the oil adversely affects the soil, plants and water resources. According to Ekekwe (2010), oil spill in rural communities in the Niger Delta area has led to the destruction of farmlands, vegetation and pollution of streams. As a result of oil spillage, these rivers carry large quantities of hydrocarbons including heavy metals.

In June 2005, an oil spill occurred in the Otu-Jeremi community in Ughelli Local Government Area of Delta State, Nigeria. An estimated spill of 30,000 barrels of crude oil was released into the environment as a result of valve failure. The area affected by the oil spillage use to be flooded seasonally, and contained numerous fish traps, creeks and lakes which serve as a source of drinking and domestic water for the community. The oil spillage contaminated the water, and destroyed fishes, crabs, molluses, periwinkles and other aquatic lives in the river (The Nigeria Tribune, 2005).

Also in March 2008, another oil spill was reported in Eyara, Ughelli North Local Government Area of Delta State, Nigeria where an estimated crude oil of 26, 600 barrels spilled into the environment covering over eight hectares of arable farmlands and water bodies. The oil spillage destroyed farmlands, vegetations and contaminated surface water which resulted in the death of fishes and other marine lives (Staigen, 2008). According to Badejo and Nwilo (2005), oil spillage is a major environmental problem in the Niger Delta area of Nigeria. Their study adduced that as a result of oil spillages the resultant degradation of the surrounding environment causes significant tension between the people living in the region and multinational oil companies operating in the area. Gbadagesin (1997) indicated that apart from loss of fishing ponds and farmlands, oil spillage have led to extensive deforestations which in effect has shortened fallow periods, compounded land use degradation and led to loss of soil fertility and consequently erosion of the top soil. Oil spill has led to the destruction of fauna and resort centres, pollution of domestic and industrial water sources, destruction of properties and lives as well as regional crisis in the Niger Delta region, where the bulk of oil production and exploration takes place. Oil spilled on water surface could prevent natural aeration and leads to the death of fishes and other marine organisms trapped below and in some cases fish ingest the spilled oil or other foods impregnated with oil thus leading to their death. They are also passed on to humans along the food chain.

According to Choker (2004), fishing is the major source of income and means of livelihood for the rural populace of the Niger Delta region and one determinant of socio-economic wellbeing of the people within the study area. Pollution of surface water, a major economic asset where fishing takes place as a source of livelihood of the people of Ughelli is a serious threat to the communities. Egboh (2010), observed that oil spillage affects the socio-economic lives of man in a number of ways, such as loss of farmlands, cash crops, economic trees, fishing ground, destruction of main source of livelihood such as fishing in Niger Delta region. Therefore this study examines the effects of oil spillage on water quality and fish activities in Otu–Jeremi and its environs in the Niger Delta area of Nigeria and how future occurrence could be minimized or prevented.

STUDY AREA

Otu-Jeremi, the study area is located in Delta State of Nigeria and its Latitude is approximately 4° 45′ and 5° 15′ North of the Equator, and between Longitude of 5° 31′ and 5° 59′ East of the Greenwich Meridian. Otu-Jeremi which is the headquarters of Ughelli South Local Government Area of Delta State, is bounded in the North by Uvwie Local Government Area, to the South by Udu Local Government Area, to the East by Burutu and Patani Local Government Areas and on the West by Ughelli North Local Government Area (Map 3.1). The area is situated on lowland bordering the Forcados River and Okpara Creek hence the people of these communities are engaged in fishing activities as their main source and means of livelihood.

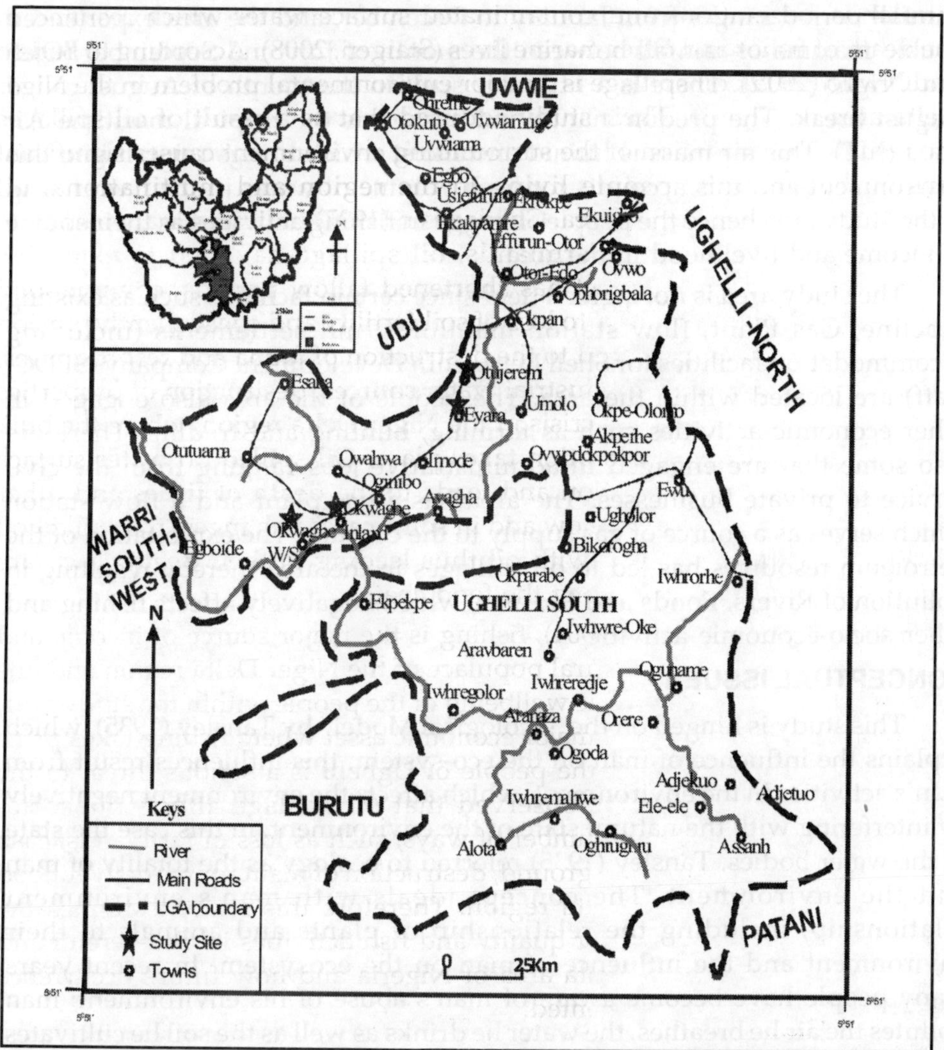

Map 3.1: Map of Ughelli-South Showing OTU-Jeremi and Environs.

Source: Modified After Ministry of Lands, Survey and Urban Development Asaba, 2008

Otu-Jeremi lies on a coastal plain, which is generally low with lowland rising to 15 metres above sea level. The area has a high water table especially during the wet season. The study area is drained by Rivers Otu–Jeremi and Eyara which flows in a southerly direction into the Forcados River and Okpara Creek. Also the area is riddled with an intricate system of natural water channels and valleys culminating in the dominance of fishing as the major economic activities. Otu-Jeremi and its environs experience an average monthly temperature of about 28°C and an annual average rainfall of 3000mm. Rainfall period ranges from January to December, and the area experienced double maxima of rainfall between the month of July and September (Ojeh and Origho, 2012). There is a little dry spell in the month of August called August break. The predominant wind system is the tropical maritime Air Mass (MT). This air mass is humid and moist which brings rainfall into this environment and this accounts for high volume of water in the river found in the study area hence the people engaged in fishing activities as their source of income and livelihood in the area.

The study area is not a green field since certain facilities such as existing pipeline, Gas Plant, flow station manifolds and settlements (including accommodation facilities for Shell Petroleum Development Company (SPDC) staff) are located within the area. The people of the area also engaged in other economic activities such as farming, hunting and trading. There are also some that are engaged in administrative jobs ranging from the civil service to private businesses. The area has a gas plant and a flow station which serves as a source of gas supply to the country. The exploitation of the petroleum resources has led to oil spillages in the area thereby resulting in pollution of Rivers, Ponds and Streams, which negatively affects fishing and other socio-economic activities.

CONCEPTUAL ISSUES

This study is hinged on the "Ecological Model" by Tansley (1935), which explains the influence of man on the eco-system, this influences result from man's activities in the environment, which affects the environment negatively by interfering with the natural state of the environment, in this case the state of the water bodies. Tansley (1935) referred to ecology as the totality of man and the environment. The concept ideals with man's environment relationship, including the relationship of plants and animals to their environment and the influence of man on the ecosystem. In recent years many people have become aware of man's abuse of his environment; man pollutes the air he breathes, the water he drinks as well as the soil he cultivates for food which invariably affects or contaminates plants and animals.

Similarly, man interferes with the environment through exploration and exploitation of the resources found therein, the effect of oil spill on rivers during exploration and exploitation is a major reason for the contamination of water sources. Many ecologists according to Odu (1987) have expressed dismay at the increasing rate of indiscriminate act of oil spills in rivers without any consideration on its effect on the ecosystem, especially surface water and marine lives. Agboola (1985) looked at the environment as the sum of all elements that influence man on a regular basis, the continuous interaction of man with the natural environment has resulted into environmental problems. Further support for this view comes from Isichei and Sanford (1976), which state that "people live and run various kinds of business, extracting resources from the surrounding environment and discharging domestic wastes into the same environment, therefore as long as people's impacts stay within this ability, the ecosystem remains imbalance". This concept is relevant to this study because as man discharge oil into water bodies, they alter and pollute the water, making it unfit and unhealthy for fish to survive and reproduce.

MATERIALS AND METHODS

The researcher adopted the experimental and ex post factor survey designs. This involved the administration of 244 copies of questionnaires aided with oral interview and the collection of water samples from polluted sites (Otu-Jeremi and Eyara Rivers) for laboratory analysis. 2 - litre plastic containers were used for collecting samples. The plastic containers were rinsed first with distilled water before filling, rinsed a further two or three times with the water being sampled, and then the water sample was taken.

Standard methods for the examination of water and waste water from the US Environmental Protection Agency (USEPA) (1986) were used for the determination of trace elements/compounds such as lead, cadmium, zinc, copper and iron. All these elements were analyzed using atomic absorption spectrophotometer. Other parameters include BOD, COD, the pH, temperature, electrical conductivity (EC) and total dissolved solids (TDS) of the water samples were done in the field and results recorded in the field logbook to determine the quality of water from the rivers. The water quality parameters analysed, were compared with DPR guidelines for oil operating companies in Nigeria. In the process of the analysis, two sets of internal standard were run, one at the beginning and the other in between the analyses to have a check on the accuracy and precision of the results following Balaram (1992) method. The Directorate of Petroleum Resources (DPR) standards were used for comparison. The parameters were determined three times and the mean was taken.

Population of the Study

The study area is part of Ughievwen community within Ughelli South Local Area of Delta State. Ughievwen clan is made up of 32 villages. Three communities were chosen for this study due to their peculiarity in their occupation as fishing and oil producing communities in the clan. These communities had a total population of 24,386 (National Population

Commission [NPC], 2006). In line with research standard 10 per cent of the population was selected to represent the entire population used in this study.

Table 3.1: Selected Area for the Study

Zones	Area	Villages	Population	No. of Questionnaires
A	High density	Okwagbe	11,435	114
B	Low density	Eyara	4,880	49
C	Industrial zone	Otu-Jeremi	8,071	81
Total				**244**

Source: Fieldwork (2011).

In all, a total number of 212 questionnaires which represent ten percent of the population were distributed within the communities. The responses to these questionnaire was used to determine the quantity of fish harvested before and after oil spillages, in addition a total number of fifteen water samples were collected in three rivers in the study area, at equal distance of 30cm beneath the water level. Five sampling points from each river were collected randomly into clean plastic containers, and analyzed to determine the water quality in the rivers.

Sampling Technique

The simple random sampling technique was adopted in this study. Based on the peculiarities of the two identified zones, in the study area (high density, low density and industrial zones), the researcher with the aid of an interpreter distributed the questionnaires to each household and conducted the oral interview. Water samples were collected randomly from two locations to determine water quality of the rivers. For a representative sampling of the population to be selected, the study area was structured into three zones, namely high density zone, low density zone and industrial zone.

The questionnaires were administered to the male head to filled but in case he was not present, the female head or a representative filled it. The researcher, with the aid of a research assistant delivered and administered the questionnaire by hand, the respondents were given time to fill and return same on the same day. This method was adopted to guard against the lost of questionnaire (see Table 3.2). For the collection of the oral interview data, the researcher directed pre-prepared questions to the interviewees at different occasions and recorded the obtained responses on a face-to-face interaction.

To obtain the water quality data from the rivers in the study area, the researcher used fifteen sterilized 2 - litre plastic cans to collect five water samples each from the two rivers in the area, a total number of ten water sampling points, at equi- distance of 30 cm beneath the water, long the river course. The locations of the various sampling points were Eyara river and Otu-Jeremi River. Running water from the rivers were carefully collected with the 2 - litre plastic can, as soon as the cans were filled to the brim, the cap was used to seal it firmly to avoid air bubbles, it was labelled appropriately with the name of each river which ranges between 1-5 in each of the rivers in the field. Analysis of unstable parameters such as pH, temperature, electrical conductivity (EC) and total dissolved solids (TDS), were analyzed in the field. Results of such analysis were recorded in the field logbook, while the water samples for the analysis of stable parameters such as BOD, COD and heavy metals were kept in a cooler box and sent immediately to the Nigeria National Petroleum Company laboratory for analysis. The water quality parameters analyzed, were compared with DPR guidelines for oil operating companies in Nigeria.

Table 3.2: Numbers of Questionnaire Administered and Returned

Sl. No.	Name of Community	No. of Questionnaire Administered	No. of Questionnaire Returned	Percentage of Questionnaire Returned
1.	Otu-Jeremi	145	128	60.4%
2.	Eyara	99	84	39.6%
Total		**244**	**212**	**100%**

Source: Fieldwork, 2011.

RESULT OF THE FINDINGS

A total of fifteen (15) parameters were investigated from the two rivers. The results obtained for the physico-chemical properties of Rivers Otu-Jeremi and Eyara was presented in Table 3.3.

Table 3.3: Mean Values of Physico-chemical Parameters of the Two Rivers

Parameters	Otu-Jeremi River	Eyara River	DPR Limit
P^H	13.08 ± 0.037	12.3 ± 0.063	6.5-8.5
Temp. (°C)	32.32 ± 0.115	35.16 ± 0.040	30.0
EC (US/MC)	312.72 ± 3.565	249.3 ± 0.305	200.0
TDS (mg/L)	654.74 ± 1.529	552.72 ± 1.915	500.0
Turbidity (NTU)	15.82 ± 0.086	12.7 ± 0.031	10.0
TSS (mg/L)	48.24 ± 0.081	36.22 ± 0.086	30.0
Salinity (mg/L)	748.26 ± 0.067	650.16 ± 10.483	600.0
THC (mg/L)	13.26 ± 0.112	12.36 ± 0.051	10.0
BOD (mg/L)	16.16 ± 0.050	12.18 ± 0.020	10.0
COD (mg/L)	17.74 ± 0.229	14.82 ± 0.269	10.0
Fe (mg/L)	1.14 ± 0.024	1.236 ± 0.008	1.0
Cr (mg/L)	0.068 ± 0.002	0.062 ± 0.002	0.03
Cu (mg/L)	1.776 ± 0.002	1.634 ± 0.006	1.5
Zn (mg/L)	1.07 ± 0.0045	1.026 ± 0.002	1.0
Pb (mg/L)	0.072 ± 0.002	0.066 ± 0.002	0.05

Source: Fieldwork, 2011. Values are mean ± standard error.

Turbidity: the turbidity obtained for River Otu-Jeremi was 15.82 ± 0.08602 NTU, while that of River Eyara was 12.7 ± 0.03162 NTU. The values of the two rivers were higher than the DPR value of 10.0 (NTU) for domestic and fishing purposes. The highest value was recorded for River Otu-Jeremi which may be as a result of frequency of oil spillage in the area.

Temperature: The surface water temperature of River Otu-Jeremi was 32.32 ± 0.1157°C, while that of River Eyara 35.16 ± 0.040°C. The values of the two rivers were higher than the DPR value of 30.0(°C). The highest value was recorded in River Eyara.

pH: The pH value of River Otu-Jeremi was 13.08 ± 0.03742, while that of River Eyara was 12.3 ± 0.06325. The values of the two rivers were higher than the DPR standard of 6.5-8.5 for water quality in Nigeria for drinking water and aquatic life. Azua (2008) reported the mean stational pH of 7.20 ± 0.02 for River Benue. Adakole and Annune (2003) reported pH range of 6.4-8.80 in River Kubani. Manilla and Njoku (2009) recorded low pH value of 6.5 ± 0.16 for the Nworie River in Owerri, Imo state. pH and temperature are very significant as they determine physiological activities in aquatic environment. Thus, the pH values of the study area is higher than these other rivers and have negative implication on fish production in the rivers.

TDS: The TDS value of River Otu-Jeremi was 654.74 ± 1.52958 mg/L, while that of River Eyara was 552.72 ± 1.91505mg/L. The values of the two rivers are higher than the DPR value of 500.0 (mg/L) for water quality in Nigeria for drinking water and aquatic life. The highest value was recorded in River Otu-Jeremi. An earlier study conducted on River Benue reported (Azua 2008) a higher mean stational TDS value of 75.6 ± 2.8 mg/L. Manilla and Frank (2009) reported low mean TDS value (22.9 to 40.0 mg/L) for the floodplain Lakes of the Niger Delta which was not consistent with the present work.

TSS: The TSS value of River Otu-Jeremi was 48.24 ± 0.08124 mg/L, while that of River Eyara was 36.22 ± 0.08602 mg/L. The values of the two rivers are higher than the DPR value of 30.0(mg/L) for water quality in Nigeria for drinking water and aquatic life. The highest value was recorded in River Otu-Jeremi.

BOD: BOD levels are used as indicators of organic pollution in water quality monitoring (Law 1980). The BOD value of River Otu-Jeremi was 16.16 ± 0.05099 mg/L, while that of River Eyara was 12.18 ± 0.08602 mg/L. The BOD values of the two rivers were higher than the DPR value of 10.0 mg/L for water quality in Nigeria for drinking water and aquatic life. The highest value was recorded in River Otu-Jeremi.

Cr: The Cr concentration of River Otu-Jeremi was 0.068 ± 0.002 mg/L, while that of River Eyara was 0.068 ± 0.002 mg/L. The values of the two rivers were found higher than the permissible limit of DPR value of

0.03 mg/L for water quality for various uses in Nigeria. The highest value was recorded in River Otu-Jeremi. Eneji (2010) reported mean stational concentration of Cr value of 0.381mg/L for the River Benue. Emoyan *et al* (2006) reported level of Cr to range between 0.037-0.067 mg/L in Ijana River in Ekpan – Warri. Reily (1991) has reported Cr concentration to vary between 10-15 mg/L in River Irwell, England. Stoepler (1992) reported Cr concentration to 0.001 mg/L in River Rhine, Germany. Similarly, Cr concentration was found to be between 0.1-6.0 µg/L in Eastern Ontario River, Canada (Inhat *et al.,* 1993). Tariq *et al.* (1996) reported Cr concentration to vary between 10-41 µg/L in Indus River, India. The high concentration of Cr in the two rivers was an evidence of high pollution from oil spillage.

Cu: The concentration of Cu in River Otu-Jeremi was 1.776 ± 0.0245mg/L, while that of River Eyara was 1.63 ± 0.00678 mg/L. The Cu concentration of the two rivers were higher than the DPR value of 1.5 (mg/L) for water quality in Nigeria for drinking water and aquatic life. The highest value was recorded in River Otu-Jeremi. Gbem *et al* (2003) recorded mean Cu concentration of 0.02mg/L from Rivers around Jama village, Zaria. In Brazil, Veado *et al.* (1997) reported Cu concentration to be 41µg/L in Das Velhas River.

Fe: The concentration of Fe in River Otu-Jeremi 1.14 ± 0.02449 mg/L and River Eyara 1.236 ± 0.00812 mg/L were above the DPR standards of 1.0mg/L for domestic quality and aquatic life. However, the values obtained are within the range of literature values of 0.408mg/L, 0.80mg/L, 1.90mg/L and 3.80mg/L for River Niger, Warri River, Ogunpa River and Rimi River respectively (Oboh and Edema, 2007). Emoyan *et al.* (2006) reported level of Fe to vary between 0.046 -0.229 mg/L in Ijana River in Ekpan – Warri.

Zn: The Zn concentration of River Otu-Jeremi was 1.07 ± 0.0447 mg/L, while that of River Eyara was 1.026 ± 0.00245 mg/L. The Zn concentrations of the two rivers were above the DPR standards of 1.0mg/L for domestic quality and aquatic life. Gbem *et al.* (2003) recorded low mean Zn concentration of 0.03mg/L from relatively unpolluted River around Jama village, Zaria. Similarly, a low value of Zn concentration (0.02 ± 0.01mg/L) for River Ethiope, Delta State has been reported (Egboh and Emeshili, 2007). Also a high value of 10.3mg/L Zn concentration has been reported for Calabar River (Kakulu and Osibanjo, 1988). Previous (13) study of River Benue water recorded high mean stational concentration of 0.43 ± 0.07mg/L of Zn (Azua 2008).

Comparison of Physico-chemical properties of the sampled rivers

The results of the comparison of the physico-chemical properties of the sampled rivers (rivers Eyara and Otu-Jeremi) with the DPR standards are presented in Tables 3.4 and 3.5.

Table 3.4: Comparison of Physio-chemical Properties of River Out-Jeremi and DPR Standards Using one Sample T-test

One-Sample Test

	Test Value = 0.05					
					95% Confidence Interval of the Difference	
	T	df	Sig. (2-tailed)	Mean Difference	Lower	Upper
PH	3.670	1	.169	10.24000	-25.2103	45.6903
TEMP	26.381	1	.024	31.13000	16.1367	46.1233
EC	4.548	1	.138	256.31000	-459.8117	972.4317
TDS	7.462	1	.085	577.32000	-405.7591	1560.3991
TURB	4.419	1	.142	12.86000	-24.1151	49.8351
TSS	4.284	1	.146	39.07000	-76.8106	154.9506
SALINITY	9.092	1	.070	674.09000	-267.9480	1616.1280
THC	7.104	1	.089	11.58000	-9.1311	32.2911
BOD	4.231	1	.148	13.03000	-26.1051	52.1651
COD	3.571	1	.174	13.82000	-35.3530	62.9930
Fe	14.571	1	.044	1.02000	.1306	1.9094
Cr	-.053	1	.967	-.00100	-.2424	.2404
Cu	11.507	1	.055	1.58800	-.1655	3.3415
Zn	28.143	1	.023	.98500	.5403	1.4297
Pb	1.000	1	.500	.01100	-.1288	.1508

Table 3.5: Comparison of Physio-chemical Properties of River Eyara and DPR Standards Using One Sample T- test

One-Sample Test

	Test Value = 0.05					
					95% Confidence Interval of the Difference	
	t	df	Sig. (2-tailed)	Mean Difference	Lower	Upper
PH	4.104	1	.152	9.85000	-20.6449	40.3449
TEMP	12.609	1	.050	32.53000	-.2520	65.3120
EC	9.112	1	.070	224.60000	-88.6079	537.8079
TDS	19.966	1	.032	526.31000	191.3744	861.2456
TURB	8.370	1	.076	11.30000	-5.8534	28.4534
TSS	10.630	1	.060	33.06000	-6.4563	72.5763
SALINITY	24.921	1	.026	625.03000	306.3584	943.7016
THC	9.432	1	.067	11.13000	-3.8633	26.1233
BOD	10.128	1	.063	11.04000	-2.8098	24.8898
COD	5.129	1	.123	12.36000	-18.2620	42.9820
Fe	9.051	1	.070	1.06800	-.4313	2.5673
Cr	-.212	1	.867	-.00350	-.2132	.2062
Cu	22.642	1	.028	1.51700	.6657	2.3683
Zn	74.077	1	.009	.96300	.7978	1.1282
Pb	1.000	1	.500	.00800	-.0936	.1096

Table 3.5 compares the means of the physico-chemical properties of River Otu-Jeremi with the DPR standards. From the results, only temperature, iron and zinc that did not show significant differences with the DPR standards at P d" 0.05. All other parameters measured showed significant differences with the DPR standards, thereby indicating that they are highly polluted as a result of oil spillage in the area.

Amongst the three elements, chromium had the lowest concentration, having 0.03 mg/L at the DPR limit and a concentration of 0.068 mg/L and 0.063 mg/L in Otu-Jeremi and Eyara Rivers respectively. The concentration of lead was about the same range, having 0.05 mg/L at the DPR limit and a concentration of 0.072 mg/L and 0.066 mg/L in Otu-Jeremi and Eyara Rivers.

Table 3.5 compares the means of the physico-chemical properties of River Eyara with the DPR standards. From the results, only temperature, TDS, salinity, copper and zinc that did not show significant differences with the DPR standards. All other parameters measured showed significant differences with the DPR standards P d" 0.05, thereby indicating that they were highly polluted from the oil spillage in the area.

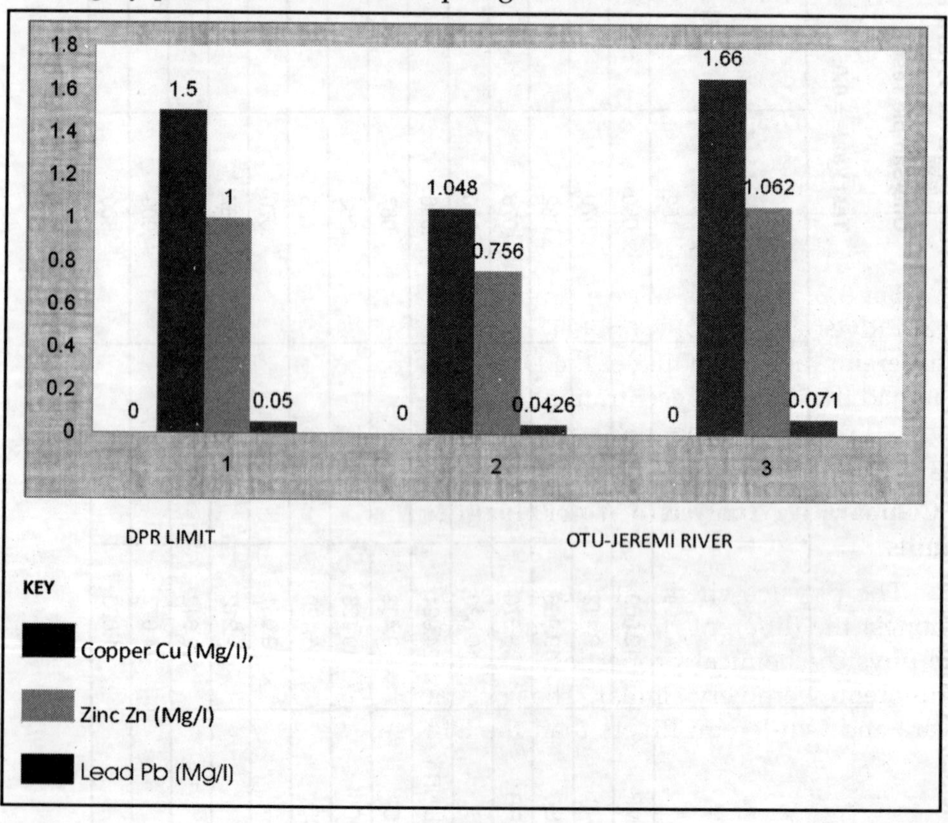

Fig. 3.1

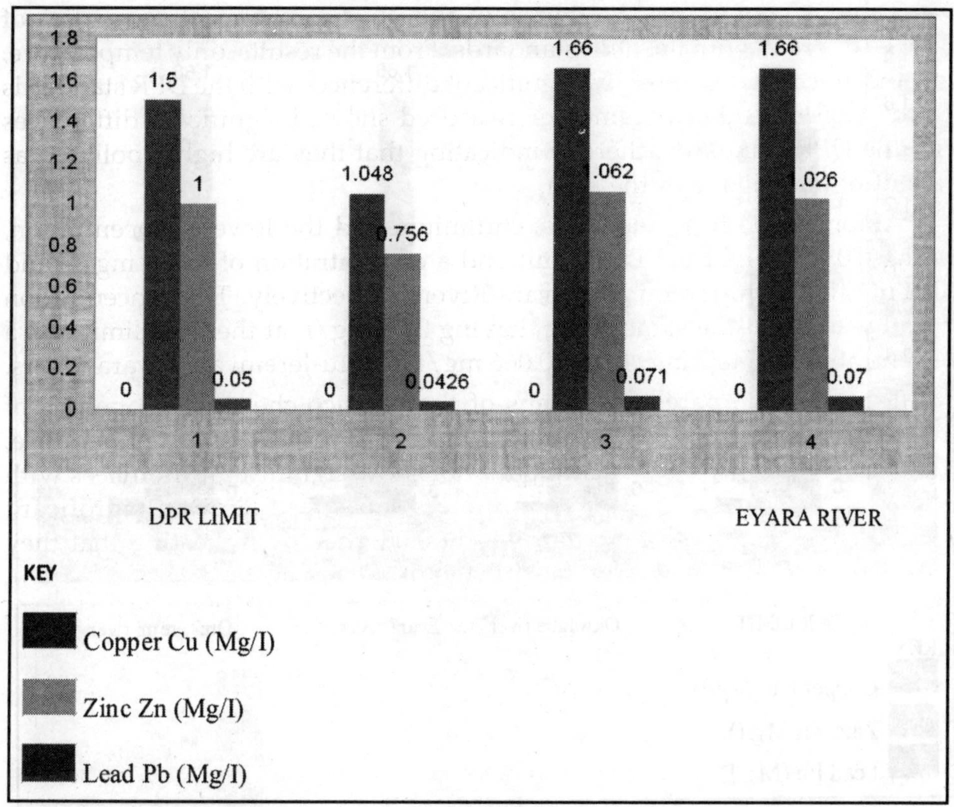

Fig. 3.2

Fig 3.2 compares the concentration of copper, zinc and lead between Eyara River and the DPR limit. The concentrations of copper were higher in Otu-Jeremi River than that of the DPR set limit. Amongst the three elements, lead had the lowest concentration followed by zinc and copper, having 0.066 mg/L, 1.026 mg/L and 1.634 mg/L as at the DPR limit of 0.05, 1.0 and 1.5 mg/L respectively.

A Comparative Analysis of Water Qualities Amongst the Rivers and the DPR Limits

The physico-chemical properties of water for fish production vary amongst the different rivers as well as the DPR limits. The mean values of the physico-chemical properties of water samples from Rivers Eyara and Otu-Jeremi were very similar. The concentrations of acid are higher in both Eyara and Otu-Jeremi Rivers than the DPR standard.

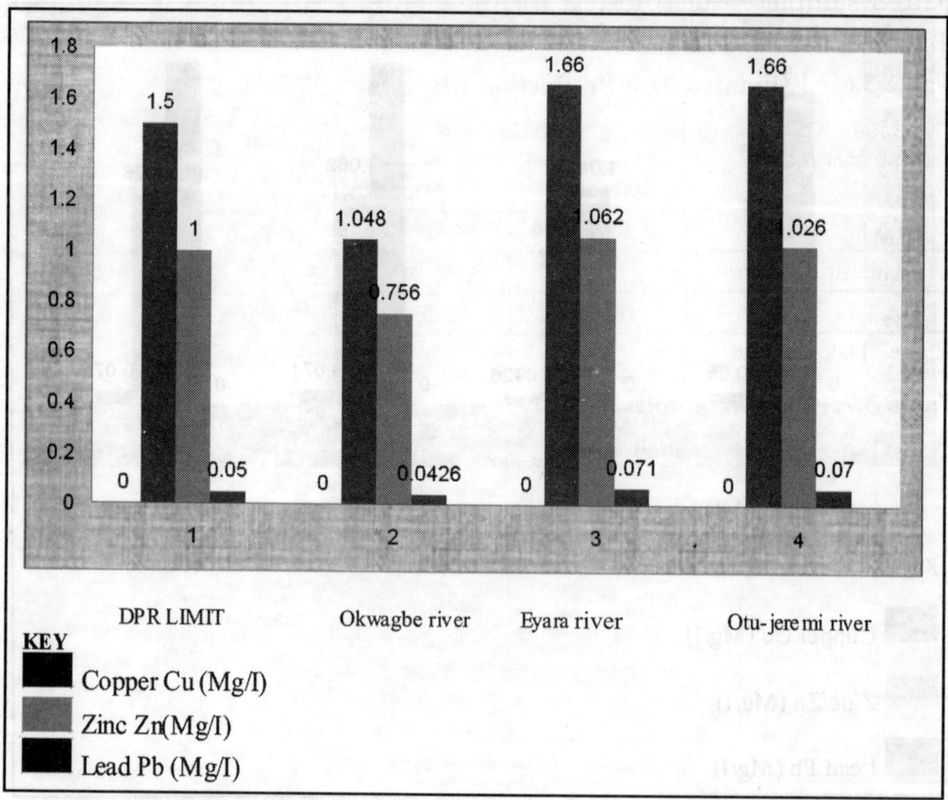

Fig 3.3: DPR Limits/Results of Water Quality from Rivers Okwagbe

Fig. 3.3 compares the concentrations of copper, zinc and lead in all the rivers as well as the DPR limit. The concentrations of copper were higher in Eyara and Otu-Jeremi Rivers than the DPR set limit. Amongst the three elements, lead had the lowest concentrations in all the samples, having 0.05 mg/L at the DPR limit and a concentration of about 0.07 mg/L in Eyara and Otu-Jeremi Rivers. This observed variation in the concentrations of chemical composition of water could be attributed to the effect of oil spill to the Rivers Otu-Jeremi and Eyara respectively. Therefore, it is possible to infer that effective fish production cannot be supported in these rivers which experienced oil spillage over time.

Relationship Between Oil Spillage and Fish Production

From Table 3.6, the results of the study revealed that before oil spillage in the study area, the fish production was estimated at about 1802.5 kg and 1105.5 kg in Otu-Jeremi and Eyara Rivers respectively. However, after the oil spillage, the amount of fish caught per month declined to about 565.5 kg and 321.5 kg in Otu-Jeremi and Eyara Rivers respectively. From the analysis above, the researcher further employed an appropriate statistical test, (the paired sample t - test) to test for the significance of the variation in the quantity of fish caught before and after oil spillage P < 0.05.

Table 3.6: Estimated Fish Production Before and After Oil Spill

Mean Kg of Fish Harvested	Otu-Jeremi		Eyara	
	Before	After	Before	After
75.5 kg.	528.5	201.5	377.5	139.5
91 kg. and Above	1274	364	728	182
Total	**1802.5**	**565.5**	**1105.5**	**321.5**

Source: Fieldwork, 2011.

Table 3.7: Paired Samples Test

		Paired Differences					T	df	Sig. (2-tailed)
		Mean	Std. Deviation	Std. Error Mean	95% Confidence Interval of the Difference				
					Lower	Upper			
Pair 1	Before-After	505.2500	299.2651	149.6325	29.0525	981.4475	3.377	3	.043

Table 3.7 shows there was a significant variation in the total number of fishes harvested before and after oil spillage in the communities at P < 0.05. The decline in the quantity of fishes harvested in Otu-Jeremi and Eyara Rivers could be attributed to oil spillage and pollution of the rivers. This situation brought about not only the loss of household income and fish species caught, but also loss of means of livelihood for these fishing communities.

Perception of the Impact of Oil Spillage on Fish Production

Sex and Marital Status

Table 3.8, revealed that out of 212 respondents 30.5 per cent were male while 65 per cent were female. Also the marital status showed that 25.9 per cent were single, 41.4 per cent married, 12.3 per cent divorced and 16.8 per cent were widows. This means that there are more married people in the area. Also the results of the study showed that there were more females than males in the study area. The result suggested that in these areas of Delta State, women were very much engaged in fish farming like the male counterparts. Women were seen with their canoes on rivers in the study area carrying out fishing activities to cater for the immediate needs of their families and for commercial purposes.

Table 3.8: Sex and Marital Status of Respondents

Sl. No.	Community	Sex		Marital Status			
		Male	Female	Single	Married	Divorce	Widowed
1.	Otu-Jeremi	35	83	33	46	14	23
2.	Eyara	32	62	24	45	13	14
Total		67	145	57	91	27	37
%		30.5%	65%	25.9%	41.4%	12.3%	16.8%

Source: Fieldwork, 2011.

Age of Respondents

The age of respondents as shown in Table 3.9, indicated that out of 212 respondent, 22.2 per cent were within the age of 18-27yrs, those within the age of 28-37 were 36.3 per cent, 38-47years 21.7 per cent and 19.8 per cent were aged 48years and above. This implied that the study area had more of youthful population.

Table 3.9: Age of Respondents in the Study Area

Sl. No.	Community	Age 18-27	Age 28-37	Age 38-47	Age 48 above
1.	Otu-Jeremi	28	40	25	25
2.	Eyara	19	37	21	17
	Total	47	77	46	42
	Percentage	22.2%	36.3%	21.7%	19.8%

Source: Field work, 2011.

Level of Education of Respondents

The findings on educational attainment of the respondent as presented in Table 3.10 showed that 55.7 per cent of the respondents had primary education, 31.1 per cent had secondary education, and 13.2 per cent have tertiary education. This implied that there was a general low level of educational attainment among the respondents. This may not be unconnected with the nature of their occupation as subsistent fishing communities.

Table 3.10: Level of Education in the Study Area

Sl. No.	Name of Community	Primary Education	Secondary Education	Tertiary Education
1.	Otu-Jeremi	68	35	17
2.	Eyara	50	31	11
	Total	118	66	28
	Percentage	55.7%	31.1%	13.2%

Source: Fieldwork, 2011.

Occupational Distribution of the Respondent in the Study Area

The findings presented in Table 3.11, showed that 23.6 per cent of the respondents were farmers, 30 per cent fishermen, 10.8 per cent fishmongers, 19.3 per cent traders and 16.5 per cent civil servants in the study area. This showed that the study area was mostly fishing community, compared to other occupations. This was made possible by the presence of the rivers in the area.

Table 3.11: Occupation of Respondents

Sl. No.	Name of Community	Farmers	Fishermen	Fishmongers	Traders	Civil Servants
1.	Otu-Jeremi	27	36	13	23	19
2.	Eyara	23	27	10	18	16
	Total	50	63	23	41	35
	Percentage	23.6%	30%	10.8%	19.3%	16.5%

Source: Field work, 2011.

Incidence of Oil Spillage in the Study Area

When the respondents were asked if they have experience oil spillage in their communities, all of them responded in affirmative as shown in Table 3.12. When the respondents were asked on the number of oil spillage in their communities, the responses showed that there were 3 incidences of oil spillage at Otu-Jeremi community and 2 incidents at Eyara community.

Table 3.12: Does Oil Spillage Occur in your Area

Sl. No.	Name of Community	(Yes)	(No)	No. of Spill
1.	Otu–Jeremi	117	–	3
2.	Eyara	95	–	2
	Total	212	–	5
	Percentage	100%	0%	

Source: Fieldwork, 2011.

Has There been Decline in Fish Production in the Study Area

When the respondents were asked if they had observed any decline in quantity of fish caught in the study area, about 70.9 per cent of the respondents agreed that there was decline in fish production in Otu-Jeremi community while 65.3 per cent of the respondents at Eyara also agreed that there was decline in fish production in the area.

Table 3.13: Decline in Fish Production

Sl. No.	Community	Yes	No
1.	Otu-Jeremi	83 (70.9%)	34 (29.1%)
2.	Eyara	62 (65.3%)	33 (34.7%)
	Total	145 (68.4%)	67 (31.6%)

Source: Fieldwork, 2011.

Causes of Decline in Fishing in the Study Area

Table 3.14: Is Oil Spill the Cause of Decline in Number of Fish Harvested?

Sl. No.	Name of Community	Yes	No	% of Yes Response
1.	Otu-Jeremi	64	4	94.1%
2.	Eyara	47	2	95.9%

Source: Fieldwork, 2011.

When the respondents were asked to comment on whether oil spillage was the causes of decline in fishing in the study area, 94.1 per cent responded in affirmative in Otu-Jeremi while 95.9 per cent agreed that oil spill was responsible for the decline in fish production in Eyara.

Assessment of Fish Harvest before and After Oil Spillage

Table 3.15: Assessment of Fish Catch Before and After Oil Spillage According to Respondents Opinion

Sl. No.	Name of Community	Assessment of Fish Harvest Before Oil Spill			Assessment of Fish Harvest After Oil Spill		
		High	Medium	Low	High	Medium	Low
1.	Otu-Jeremi	21	–	–	–	3	18
2.	Eyara	13	–	–	–	4	9
	Total	34	–	–	–	7	27
	Percentage	100%				20.6%	79.4%

Source: Fieldwork, 2011.

From Table 3.15, 100 per cent of the respondents (21 at Otu-Jeremi and 13 at Eyara) confirmed that fish harvesting before oil spill was high. While 20.6 per cent says fish harvesting was of medium level after oil spillage, and 79.4 per cent confirmed that fish harvesting was low after oil spillage in the area.

Estimate of Fish Production in the Study Area

This section examines the estimates of fish harvested in kilogram in the study area.

Table 3.16: Estimate of Fish Harvest Before Oil Spill

Sl. No.	Community Name	What is the Estimate of Fish Harvest Before Oil Spill			
		1-30 kg.	31-60 kg.	61-90 kg.	91 kg. Above
1.	Otu-Jeremi			7	14
2.	Eyara			5	8
	Total			12	22
	Percentage			35.3%	64.7%

Source: Fieldwork, 2011.

From Table 3.16, out of 34 respondents, 12 respondents (35.3%) revealed that their fish harvest per day before oil spill was between 61- 90kg, while 22 respondents representing 64.7 per cent revealed that their fish catch was between 91kg and above per day before oil spill.

Table 3.17: Responses to Estimate of Fish Harvest After Oil Spill

Sl. No.	Community	What is Estimate of Fish Harvest After Oil Spill per Day			
		1-30 kg.	31-60 kg.	61-90 kg.	91 kg. and Above
1.	Otu-Jeremi	13	8		
2.	Eyara	9	4		
	Total	22	12		
	Percentage	64.7%	35.3%		

Source: Fieldwork, 2010.

From Table 3.17, out of 34 respondents, 22 respondents representing 64.7 per cent revealed that their fish harvest per day after oil spill is between 1-30 kg., while 12 respondents representing 35.3 per cent revealed that their fish catch is between 31 kg. - 60 kg. per day after oil spill.

DISCUSSION

At Otu-Jeremi River, values of recorded pollutants such as iron, chromium, copper, zinc and lead were as follows; 1.14, 0.068, 1.776, 1.07 and 0.072 while Eyara river recorded values as follows: 1.236, 0.063, 1.634, 1.026, and 0.066 as against DPR (standards) of 1.0, 0.03, 1.5, 1.0 and 0.05 respectively for the various parameters. These rivers exceeded the limit for DPR standard. This implies that the water was polluted and therefore harmful for fish production, thus leading to fish poisoning and increased mortality of fishes in the study area. The pH value recorded in Otu-Jeremi and Eyara rivers, was 13.08 and 12.3 respectively. These are above the safe limit for DPR standard; increase in acidic content in water affects fish existences, metabolism and development which may eventually lead to increase in mortality rate in fish species in the river.

Otu-Jeremi and Environs at the event of oil spill in recent times, has suffered from pollution and contamination of surface water, a major asset where fish production takes place. These have resulted in poisoning and killing of fishes, periwinkle, crabs and other aquatic lives. In the case where some of the fishes survived the pollution, they migrate to other areas where the water is suitable for their existence, thereby causing reduction in the number of fish in the area.

The communities have also suffered reduction in the number and sizes of fish caught in the rivers due to oil spill, the fishermen revealed that the number of fish caught has reduced drastically in the study area as compared to when oil spill has not occurred in the area. The sizes of fish harvested have also been reduced, bigger fishes were caught prior to oil spill in the area. Also, the area now experience absence of some types of fish species that were present in the river before. The communities have also experienced contamination and destruction of fishing materials like boats, nets, hooks, traps and ponds. Commercial sale of commercial fishes have reduced. The communities also suffered deprivation of recreational activities as their swimming and diving activities have been rendered incapacitated due to oil spillage in the area.

Implications of Results

The results as presented in the different section show that both Eyara and Otu-Jeremi Rivers have been impacted upon by oil spill. A comparative analysis of the levels of the physico-chemical prperties and that of the DPR (standard) showed that the oil impacted waters cannot support effective fish production. Thus, the observed low production of fishes in both Otu-Jeremi and Eyara rivers were as expected when compared with the DPR standard. However, the testing of hypothesis II showed that there was significant variation in the number of fish caught before and after oil spill in the study area. This revealed that effects of oil spill had a direct relationship on water quality for fish production in the study area. The result of this study, corroborate Akah *et al.*, (2009) findings in a study on the evaluation of the effects of crude oil on Tilapia *Guineesis* and *Sarothdron melanotheron* in Forcados area. The study findings was also consistent with other studies on the impact of oil spillage on fishing in the Niger Delta area of Nigeria. For example, the oil spillage in Okpoama Kingdom on May 12 or 13, 2009 affected the people greatly ERC/FEN (2009). The volume of crude oil on the surface of the water in the creeks and river was so thick that it was difficult to separate the crude from the water. Many fishing camps were so negatively impacted that they could not go out to fish. Also, apart from the fact that there were no more fish to catch, the fishing nets, hooks and traps were damaged by the spill. The oil spill resulted in the death of aquatic lives and many were seen dead and floating on the surface of the water. Powell (1998) in a study on the impacts of the GENECO barge, Ikata, Okoma and oshika oil spillages on fish and fisheries, reported 50 per cent reduction in fish abundance, total loss of species lacking accessory air-breathing organs and major loss of species without any obvious physiological pattern.

CONCLUSION AND RECOMMENDATION

The study found that the occurrences of oil spills in the study area accounted for the reduction in the number of fishes harvested, thus, oil spills led to poor performance experienced in the production of fish in these fishing communities thereby leading to decline in fishing and income in the study area. The rivers in the communities of Otu-Jeremi and Eyara were polluted and not fit for the production of fishes.

Based on the result of the findings of this study, the following recommendations are hereby presented. Firstly, operators of oil companies should strictly adhere to safety measures and best practices in oil exploration, production and refining to minimize incidence of oil spill during their operation. Secondly, corrosion control/maintenance of oil pipelines and storage facilities should be carried out regularly. Thirdly, equipment used in the oil industries should be inspected to ensure that good and high quality equipments are used in oil exploration activities in the study area.

Environmental awareness and education should be promoted in all aspects of our national lives through public enlightenment campaigns. Jingles in the media houses such as televisions and radios should be aired regularly. Sabotage/vandalizers of oil pipeline and facilities should be discouraged at all levels. The public should be made to know that the effect of oil spill is more deadly and devastating than the compensation and temporal pleasure they achieved in vandalization of oil pipelines. Oil spill prevention target of zero tolerance should be set and enforced, and incentives given to achievers of the set goals. Recouping of rivers with fish fingerlings should be carried out to restock rivers in the study area. This will increase fish population which will enhance fish production in the study area.

REFERENCES

Adakole J.A. and Annune P.A. (2003). Benthic Macro Invertebrates as Indicators of Environmental Quality of an Urban Stream, Zaria, Northern Nigeria. *Journal of Aquatic Science*, 18(2): 85-92.

Agboola, T.A. (1985). 'Review of the Environmental Component in Nigeria's National Development Plans, 1940-1986', Paper Presented at the Policy Seminar on Environmental Issues and Management in Nigerian Development Under the Auspices of the Department of Geography and Regional Planning, University of Benin, Nigeria, 25th - 27th November.

Akah, P.A, Ezike, C.A, Offiah, N and Agbata C.C. (2009) Evalution of the Acute Toxicity of Corexit 95271 Forcados Crude Oil Mixture on Tilapia Guineenses and Sarothedron Melanotheron, *Sustainable Human Development*, Vol. No. 4, pp. 157-178.

Azua E.T. (2008). Studies on Pollution of River Benue in Makurdi Metropolis. Benue State, Nigeria. Ph.D. Thesis. Department of Biological Sciences, University of Agriculture, Makurdi, Nigeria. 317 pp.

Badejo O.T and Nwilo, P.C (2005).*"Management of Oil Spill Along the Nigeria Coast Areas"*. An Article to the Department of Surveying and Geo-informatics, University of Lagos.

Balaram P. (1992). Non-standard Amino Acids in Peptide Design and Protein Engineering. Curr. Opin. Struct. Biology Vol. 2, Issue 6 pp. 845-851. DOI: 10: 1016/0959 – 440X(92) 90110 – S.

Choker, B.A (2004). "Perception and Response to the Challenges of Poverty and Environmental Resources Degradation in Rural Community in Nigeria" *Journal of the Environmental Psychology*, 2(1): 16-29.

Egboh S.H.O. (2010). Water Pollution and Control Chapter 4 in *"Man, His Environment and Sustainable Development"*. University Press, Delsu, Abraka.

Egboh S.H.O. and Emeshili E.M. (2007). Physico-chemical Characteristics of River Ethiope Sources in Umuaja, Delta State. *Journal of Chemical Society of Nigeria* 32(2): 72-76.

Ekekwe, E. (2010). "Environment and Social Economic Impact Oil Spillage in the Riverine Areas of Nigeria" *Proceeding of International Seminar on the Petroleum Industry and the Environmental*, (Lagos: NNPC, FEPA).

Emoyan O.O., Ogbam F.E. and Akarah E. (2006). Evaluation of Heavy Metals Loading of River Ijana in Ekpan – Warri, Nigeria. *Journal of Applied Science and Environmental Management*. 10(2): 121-127.

Environmental Rights Action/Friends of the Earth, Nigeria (2009). Okpoama Oil Spill; Fishing Camps Devastated by the Impact. Environmental Testimonies 2009/04.: www.eraction.org

Eteng, I.A. (2007). The Nigerian State, *Oil Exploration and Community Interest: Issues and Perspective*, Port-Harcourt, University Press.

Federal Ministry of Environment (1992). National Guidelines and Standard for Water Quality in Nigeria. Technical Advisory Committee on Water Quality Criteria, Nigeria. pp. 14-16.

Gbadagesin, A. (1997). *The Impact of Exploration and Production Activities on the Environment: Implications for the Peasant Agriculture"* Seminar Paper on Oil and the Environment Organised by Friedrich Ebert Foundation's in Port Harcourt.

Gbem T.T., Balogun J.K. Lawal F.A., Annunue P.A. and Auta J. (2003). Sublethal Effects of Tannery Effluent on Haematological Indices and Growth of Clarias Gariepinus (Teugels). *Bulletin of Environmental Contamination and Toxicology*. 71: 1200-1206.

Ikporukpo, C.O. (1998). Managing Oil Pollution in Nigeria: Towards an Interactive Approach, pp. 224-229.

Inhat M., Gamble D. S. and Gilchrist (1993). Determination of Trace Elements Level in Natural Fresh Water by Inductively Coupled Plasma Mass Spectrometry. *International Journal of Environmental Analysis and Chemistry*. 53: 63-78.

Isichei, A.O. and Sanford, W.W. (1976). "The Effect of Waste Gas Flares on the Surrounding Vegetation of South-Eastern Nigeria", *Journal of applied Ecology* 13(2): 69-74.

Kakulu S.E. and Osibanjo O. (1998). Trace Heavy Metal Pollution Studies in Sediments of the Niger Delta.

Law A.T. (1980). Sewage Pollution of Kelang River and its Estuary. Pertanika, 3(1): 13-19.

Manilla P.N. and Njoku M.O. (2009). The Chemical Analysis of the Water and Sediments of Nworie River in Owerri, Imo State. *Journal of Chemical Society of Nigeria* 34(2): 94-100.

Manilla P.N. and Frank M.O. (2009). Lakes of the Niger Delta Flood Plain I. Chemical Characterisation of Five Lakes (Akpide, Egbedidi, Esiribi, Aboh and Egbinya) in Bayelsa State. *Journal of Chemical Society of Nigeria* 34(2): 43-49.

Oboh I.P. and C.U. Edema (2007). Levels of Heavy Metals in Water and Fishes from the River Niger. *Journal of Chemical Society of Nigeria* 32(2): 29-34.

Odu, C.T.I. (1987). *"Oil Pollution and the Environmental"*, Business Science Association, 10(2): 30-35.

Ojeh, V.N and Origho, T (2012). Socio-economic Development of Rural Areas in Nigeria Using the Growth Pole Approach: A Case Study of Delta State University in Abraka. *Global Advanced Research Journal of Geography and Regional Planning* Vol. 1(1) pp. 007-015.

Reily C. (1991). Metal Contamination of Food, London: Elsevier Applied Sciences. pp. 3-10.

Staigen, P. (2008). Crude Oil in Water, *The Punch*, Friday, March 7, 2008.

Stoepler M (1992). Cadmium In: Metal and Their Compounds in the Environment: Occurrence, Analysis and Biological Relevance. Merian E. (Ed.) VCH, New York. pp. 803-851.

Tansley, (1935). *The Use and Abuse of Vegetation Concepts and Terms, Forest Ecology and Management* 16, 284-307.

Tariq J., Ashraf M., Jaffar M and Afzal (1996). Pollution Status of Indus River, Pakistan. "Heavy Metal and Macronutrient Contents of Fish, Sediment and Water". *Water Resources* 30(6): 1337-1344.

Veado M.A.R.V., Pinte G, Oliveira A.H. and Revel G. (1997). Application of Instrumental Neuron Activation Analysis and Inductively Coupled Plasma – Mass Spectrometry to Studying the River Pollution in the State of Minas Gerais. *Journal of Radioanalytical and Nuclear Chemistry* 17(1): 101-106.

CHAPTER

Insecticidal Activity of Some Plant Powders Against *Tribolium castaneum* (Herbst) (Coleoptera: Tenebrionidae) on Stored "Acha" (*Digitaria* spp).

M.N. Chukwulobe* B.C. Echezona

ABSTRACT

Ten plant powdered extracts were evaluated in the laboratory for their insecticidal activities against *Tribolium castaneum* (Herbst) on stored "Acha" (*Digitaria* spp). Extracts of *Afromomum meleguetta* K. (seeds), *Annona muricata* L. (leaves and seeds), *Dennettia tripetala* G.Baker (seeds), *Eugenia aromatica* L. Baill. (flower bud), *Gongronema latifolia* Benth. (leaves), *Irvingia gagbonensis* Baill. (leaves),*Monodora myristica* Dunal. (seeds), *Piper guineense* Schum. and Thonn. (seeds) and *Ricinodendron heudelotii* Baill. (leaves) were used. Admixtures of 20g grains to 2g of each extract did not result in any significant mortality of the adult beetle. However, the emergence of F_1 progenies was delayed from 27 days after infestation (DAI) on the untreated check to 35 DAI through 42 DAI on the treated grains. Complete suppression of the F_1 progenies was observed on grains treated with *E. aromatica*, *D. tripetala* and *P. guineense*.

Adult emergence from the unprotected grains on the other hand, did not differ with those of *G. latifolia* and *I. gagbonensis* but was significantly

Department of Crop Science, University of Nigeria, Nsukka, Nigeria.

(P < 0.05) higher compared with those of other protected grains. The highest damage of 10.6% weight loss was sustained by the unprotected grains while the least damage of 0.10% weight loss was suffered by grains treated with *E. aromatica,,* which in turn did not differ with *P. guineense* (0.12%), *D. tripetala* (0.12%), *A. muricata* (seeds) (0.75%) and *R. heudelotii* (0.63%) treated lots. *P. guineense, E. aromatica* and *D. tripetala* were therefore identified as plants with great potentials in the control of *T. castaneum,* and may be exploited in food storage.

Keywords: Adult mortality; F_1 progeny; powdered extract; stored produce; weight loss.

INTRODUCTION

"Acha" or hungry rice *(Digitaria exilis* Kipp. Stapf and *Digitaria iburua* Stapf) belongs to the family Poaceae. It is a minor cereal crop in many countries of West Africa where it is a staple food for several millions of tribal people (Vietmeyer *et al.*, 1996). It is widely grown in Nigeria in the cool region of Plateau state and parts of Bauchi, Kebbi, Taraba, Kaduna and Niger states (Gyang and Wuyep, 2005; Chukwu and Abdul-kadir, 2008). Apart from its nutritional importance, acha is also a crop of high social and cultural value for the local communities traditionally associated with its production. Acha is a cheap source of carbohydrate for man and livestock, particularly in dry, infertile areas of the tropics (Chukwu and Abdul-kadir, 2008). The properties of acha also make it good for use as raw material for several domestic and industrial purposes like making beer, alcoholic drinks and other applications. In medical sector, acha is recommended as a dietary supplement for diabetic patients due to its protein quality (methionine), easily broken-down starch and high fibre content (Chukwu and Abdul-kadir, 2008). Their reports showed that the lipid and ash value of acha are higher than the reported values for most cereal grains. The protein content of acha is high compared with that of other grains. Acha is richer in calcium, magnesium, iron and copper than most cereals. However, because the grains are very tiny (length H" 1.5 mm, width H" 0.9 mm) with an average thousand grain weight (TGW) of 0.59 g (CIRAD, 2004), it is usually infested by the flour beetle (*Tribolium casteneum*) in storage.

The red flour beetle, *Tribolium castaneum* (Herbst) (Coleoptera: Tenebrionidae), is one of the primary pests infesting stored grains. It is widely spread worldwide and very destructive (Levinson and Levinson, 1985; Garcìa *et al.*, 2005). Infestations not only cause significant losses due to the consumption of grains; they also result in elevated temperature and moisture conditions that lead to an accelerated growth of moulds, including toxigenic species (Magan *et al.*, 2003). To reduce the activities of this organism on stored produce, synthetic insecticides have been used for its control. According to Parkin *et al.* (1962); Richards *et al.* (2008); Burril and Collins (2010),

T casteneum has demonstrated resistance to all classes of insecticides used against it especially at the adult stage. Resistance and toxicity problems derived from synthetic insecticides have made it necessary to find more effective, healthier and ecofriendly alternatives.

Plants constitute a rich source of bioactive compound which might act deadly on the insect physiological system. (Daoubi *et al.*, 2005; Kim *et al.*, 2003). Over the past 50 years, more than 2,000 plant species belonging to different families and genera have been reported to contain toxic principles, which are effective against insects (Potenza *et al.*, 2005). Numerous defensive chemicals belonging to various categories (alkaloids, glycosides, tannins, proteic amino acids, steroids, phenols, flavonoids, glucosinolates, quinones, terpenoids etc.), which have behavioral and physiological effects on pests have already been identified (Gonzalo, 2009). Many of these plant parts have also been recognized to be effective as potential health promoters in humans (Khan *et al.*, 2012). These are low in cost, locally available and have proved to be very effective in the control of insect pests (Igbal *et al.*, 2011). Hussain *et al.* (1995) reported that the extract of *Polygonum hydropiper* and *Annona squamosa* had repellent effect against adult *T. castaneum*. According to Lale (1995), the oil extract (10.38 mg/cm^3) of *Syngizium aromaticum* (*Eugenia aromatica*) applied on filter paper showed 70% repellency against *T. castaneum*. Ravi and Gayatri (2007) found out that *Piper nigrum* essential oil is highly repellent and toxic to adults and growing larvae of *T. castaneum*. Therefore, evaluating and using botanical pesticides, either as crude or formulated extracts, has proved an alternative strategy of insect pest management.

The objective of this study therefore was to assess the efficacy of ten powdered plant extracts as protectants to stored *Digiteria* grains against *Tribolium castaneum.*

MATERIALS AND METHODS

This study was conducted in the Department of Crop Science laboratory of the University of Nigeria (06° 52□ N, 07° 24□ E; 447.26 m a.s.l.) Nsukka, Nigeria from September to October 2010.

Tribolium castaneum culture

Initial stock of *Tribolium castaneum* was obtained from infested *Digiteria iburua* grains purchased from Jos main market, Plateau state, Nigeria and was reared in *Digiteria iburua* grains in the laboratory at 30 ± 5 °C, 75 ± 5% relative humidity and 12 hrs light and dark regime. The grains were mixed with yeast at the standard ratio of 19:1 (grain: yeast). The insects were reared in a plastic container (12cm diameter, 14.5cm height), which was covered with muslin cloth for aeration and to prevent insects from escaping. The *Tribolium* were sexed as pupa by examining the genital lobe or papillae under a light microscope. At the very end of the pupa are two pointed structures called urogomphi. The genital lobes are two finger-like structures just anterior to the pointed urogomphi. This papillae are much larger, longer and prominent in females while they appear like finger tips in males (Ludovic *et al.*, 2001). Males and females were kept separately until used.

Plant Material Collection

Plant materials used for this study were collected from various locations within Nigeria. Some of the plant materials selected for this study have been reported by local people as good for the treatment of various body ailment (*G. latifolia*, *I. gagbonensis*, *A. muricata* and *R. heudelotii*), while some have been reported by researchers as being lethal to pests (*P. guineense*, *E. aromatica*, *D. tripetala*, *A. melegueta* and *M. myristica*). These samples were taken to appropriate taxonomists for proper identification. The plant materials assayed are shown in Table 4.1. The plant materials were air dried in well ventilated room for about one week except *E. aromatica* flower buds and *P. guineense* seeds, which were purchased in dry form. They were thereafter milled into fine powder using Thomas Wiley Laboratory mill, Model 4 with 1mm sieve, made by Arthur, H Company, Philadelphia PA, USA. The plant powders were stored in polyethylene bags and used within 24 hours of milling to avoid loss of potency. *Digiteria iburua* grains were sourced from the germplasm collection of Department of Botany University of Jos, Nigeria.

Table 4.1: Plant Materials Evaluated for Insecticidal Activities

Scientific Name	Common Name	Family	Part Used
Afromomum melegueta. K.	Alligetor pepper ("ose oji" Igbo)	Zingiberaceae	Seeds
Annona muricata. L.	Sour sop	Annonaceae	Leaves
Annona muricata. L.	Sour sop	Annonaceae	Seeds
Dennettia tripetala. Baker.	"Mmimi" (Igbo)	Annonaceae	Seeds
Eugenia aromatica Baill.	Cloves ("kanumfari" Hausa)	Myrtaceae	Flower bud
Gongronema latifolia Benth.	"Utazi" (Igbo)	Asclepiadaceae	Leaves
Irvingia gagbonensis. Baill.	Bush mango ("Ugiri", Igbo)	Irvingiaceae	Leaves
Momodora myristica Dunal.	African nutmeg ("Ehuru", Igbo)	Annonaceae	Seeds
*Piper guineense.*Schum, Thonn	Black pepper ("Uziza", Igbo)	Piperaceae	Seeds
Ricinodendron heudelotii Baill	African woodnut tree ("okwe", Igbo)	Euphobiaceae	Leaves

Mortality, Progeny Production and Damage Assessment

Digiteria iburua (acha or Hungry rice) was disinfested by drying in the oven for 24 hrs at 60°C. Twenty grams each of the disinfested grains was weighed into eleven plastic containers (5.5 cm height, 7.5 cm diameter), which were perforated at the sides and the openings covered with muslin cloth for aeration. Two grams each of the powdered plant part was weighed into each container already containing the grains. The content of each container was thoroughly mixed and allowed to stand. Six adult *T. castaneum* (1-7 days old) comprising 3 males and 3 females were introduced into each container. The eleventh container without plant powder served as check or control. The set up was replicated 3 times and arranged in a completely randomized design on a laboratory bench. Mortality counts were taken on day 2 and day 7 after infestation (Emeasor, 2004). After the mortality count on the 7th day, the adults were removed from the containers and the content left undisturbed until 21st day after infestation (DAI). From the 21st day, daily adult emergence counts were taken until the 42nd day to estimate the 1st filial generation (F_1) population. Counting was stopped after 42 days to avoid overlapping of generations. The total number of adults emerged from each container was recorded and the weight of the remaining acha grains taken on the 42nd day to estimate the extent of damage. Data on adult mortality and emergence counts were transformed using square root method. The percentage mortality was obtained using the formula:

$$\% \text{ Mortality} = \frac{\text{No of dead insects}}{\text{No of insects introduced}} \times \frac{100}{1}$$

The percentage mortality calculated was corrected using Abbott's formula (Abbott 1925).

$$\frac{\% \text{ Test mortality '' } \% \text{ control mortality}}{100 - \% \text{ control mortality}} \times \frac{100}{1}$$

Percentage weight loss was calculated using the formula:

$$\frac{\text{Initial weight of acha '' Final weight of acha}}{\text{Initial weight}} \times \frac{100}{1}$$

Statistical Analysis

Data obtained were subjected to analysis of variance (ANOVA) using Genstat System for Window Discovery edition 3, 7.22 DE, 2009. Differences amongst treatment means were separated using F-LSD as outlined by Obi (2002).

RESULTS

Mortality of Adult Insects

All the plant powders tested had little or no effect on the mortality of adult insects 2 DAI when compared with the control (Table 4.2). The mortality caused by some plant powders were not significant (p□ 0.05), though

M. myristica, P. guineense, A. muricata leaves and seeds, *E. aromatica* flower bud and *R. heudelotii* leaves caused slight mortality compared to other powders and the control, which did not register any appreciable mortality during the sampling period. At 7 DAI, the mortality count increased slightly with some powders (Table 4.2). Insect mortality on grains treated with *A. muricata* leaves was appreciably higher relative to the control, although not significantly different from the other plant powders. Generally, *P. guineense, E. aromatica* and *A. muricata* leaves showed the highest mortality effect. These were closely followed by *M. myristica, A. muricata* seeds and *R. heudelotii* leaves.

Table 4.2: Toxicity of Different Plant Powders Against *T.castaneum* Infestation on *Digitaria* spp at Day 2 and Day 7 After Infestation

Treatment	Corrected % Mortality Day 2	Corrected % Mortality Day 7
Afromomum melegueta	1.13	1.13
Monodora myristica	3.26	3.26
Gongronema latifolia	1.13	1.13
Piper guineense	3.26	8.77
Dennettia tripetala	1.13	1.13
Annona muricata (leaves)	3.26	9.79
Annona muricata (seeds)	3.26	5.51
Irvingia gagbonensis	1.13	1.13
Eugenia aromatica	3.26	8.77
Ricinodendron heudelotii	3.26	5.51
Control	1.13	1.13
Mean	13.35	15.12
F – LSD	6.238	8.448
Fpr	0.87	0.193

Adult Emergence

The various plant powders tested significantly suppressed the emergence of the adults when compared with the control except *I. gagbonensis* leaves, which had little effect on adult emergence (Table 4.3). Grains that recieved *P. guineense, D. tripetala* and *E. aromatica,* significantly ($p < 0.05$) suppressed the emergence of *T. castaneum* adults, such that no adult or larva emerged from the samples as is the case with *R. heudolotii,* A. muricata leaves and seeds. The control significantly (p 0.05) produced the highest adult emergence (72), which did not however differ significantly with counts obtained from *G. latifolia, A. meleguata* and *M. myristica.* Adults emerged earlier

(27days) from untreated grains compared to the treated grains (Table 4.3). Adult emergence from grains treated with *R. heudelotii* were significantly (p< 0.05) prolonged (42 days) more than those of the control but not more than those treated with *A. muricata* seeds (41 days) and *A. muricata* leaves (41 days). Grains treated with *P. guineense, E. aromatica,* and *D. tripetala* on the contrast, had no adult or larvae emergence within the sampling period.

Table 4.3: Effects of Various Plant Powders on the Emergence of Adult *T. castaneum* 42 Days of Infestation

Treatment	Mean Mumber of Adults Emerged	Mean Days to Adult Emergence
Afromomum melegueta	33.70 (5.17)	37.67 (6.17)
Monodora myristica	44.70 (5.83)	36.33 (6.06)
Gongronema latifolia	41.30 (6.10)	36.67 (6.09)
Piper guineense	0.00 (0. 71)	0.00 (0.71)
Dennettia tripetala	0.00 (0.71)	0.00 (0.71)
Annona muricata (leaves)	4.70 (2.06)	40.83 (6.43)
Annona muricata (seeds)	3.00 (1.79)	41.00 (6.44)
Irvingia gagbonensis	65.70 (8.03)	35.33 (5.98)
Eugenia aromatica	0.00 (0.71)	0.00 (0.71)
Ricinodendron heudeloti	1.30 (1.18)	42.00 (6.52)
Control	72.00 (8.51)	27.00 (5.243)
Mean	24.20 (3.71)	23.20 (4.64)
F – LSD	35.30 (3.237)	17.50 (0.2635)
Fpr	□ 0.001	□ 0.001

Note: The numbers in parentheses are square root transformed values to which ANOVA was applied.

Weight Loss

Weight loss as a result of *T. castaneum* infestation of untreated grains was significantly (p <0.05) higher compared with those of other treated grains except those admixed with *G. latifolia* and *I. gagbonensis* (Table 4.4). Grains admixed with *P. guineense, D. tripetala* and *E. aromatica* however recorded the least weight losses of 0.12%, 0.12% and 0.10% respectively.

DISCUSSION

The result of this study revealed that the ten plant powders have varying degrees of insecticidal activities. Plant powders assayed did not have significant effects on the mortality of *T. castaneum* adult. The inability of these plant powders to have significant mortality effect on the adult insects may be attributed to either the use of lower dosage or the ability of

Table 4.4: Effects of Various Plant Powders on % Weight Loss of Acha 42 Days After Infestation

Treatment	Mean % Weight Loss
Afromomum melegueta	7.05
Monodora myristica	5.68
Gongronema latifolia	7.80
Piper guineense	0.12
Dennettia tripetala	0.12
Annona muricata (leaves)	2.18
Annona muricata (seeds)	0.75
Irvingia gagbonensis	8.47
Eugenia aromatica	0.10
Ricinodendron heudelotii	0.63
Control	10.57
Mean	3.95
F – LSD	2.413
Fpr	□ 0.001

T. castaneum adult to resist the powdered extracts. This result is in agreement with the work of Shaaya *et al.* (1997), which showed that when plant extracts from various spices and herb plants were assessed for their activities against several major stored-product insects, *T. castaneum* was found to be more resistant than *Sitophilus oryzae, Rhyzopertha dominica* and *Oryzaephilus surinamensis*, to most of the essential oils tested.

Richards *et al.* (2008) also noted that *T. castaneum* possesses chemo-sensing and detoxifying genes capable of detoxifying most insecticides and therefore has the ability of developing resistance to most insecticides used against them. The only promising plant was *A. muricata* leaves which had the highest adult mortality relative to the untreated with the least mortality. *P. guineense, D. tripetala* and *E. aromatica* however, completely prevented the emergence of new adults from the grains when compared with the other treatments or the control. They appreciably reduced the number of adult emergence from the grains. This result suggests that the plant extracts may either have some ovicidal properties or are capable of preventing egg deposition by the adult since no sign of larvae or adult was evident. This agrees with the observation of Adedire and Lajide (1999) who had earlier reported that *E. aromatica* powder has significant contact and fumigant action against *Callosobruchus maculates;* and its mechanism of action is by inhibition of oviposition and direct toxicity to eggs (ovicidal).

The effects of *P. guineense* on adult emergence also agrees with the report of Adedire and Lajide (2003), which indicated that the plant family piperaceae to which *P. guineense* belongs possesses some form of insecticidal properties against eggs of cowpea storage bruchids, which are capable of suppressing various developmental instars. Oliver (1959) and Su (1977) reported that *P. guineense* contains Piperine and Chavicine which are insecticidal to crop pests and act on direct contact with the pests. Umeozor and Pessu (2003) also reported that *D. tripetala and P. guineense* were effective in the control of *Callosobruchus maculatus* at the egg stage. According to their report, virtually no emergence occurred when treatment of both peppers were applied within the first three days of oviposition.

Fasakin and Aberejo (2002) have reported that pulverized plant material from *P. guineense* inhibited egg hatchability and adult emergence of *Dermetes maculatus* in smoked catfish during storage. These three plant powders significantly gave better protection than the other plant powders but are statistically similar with *R. heudelotii*. When compared with the other treatments, *R. heudelotii* recorded the least adult emergence within the sampling period of 42 days. Higher doses of *R. heudelotii* however, may give complete protection against *T. castaneum.* This is likely to be true because according to previous reports, higher doses or concentration of extracts or powders produced better results (Arora *et al.* 2011).

The loss of weight showed almost a direct linear relationship with the number of adult emergence as weight loss may be due to the number of larvae that fed until they develop to pupa stage. This therefore followed a simple principle, which shows that the higher the number of adult emergence, the higher the weight loss. The unprotected grains suffered the highest weight loss, having also recorded the highest adult emergence. It was however followed by *I. gagbonensis;* while *E. aromatica, P. guineense,* and *D. tripetala* recorded the lowest weight loss. These weight losses did not glaringly differ with those of *A. muricata* seeds and leaves and *R. heudelotii.* This loss evaluation clearly showed that "Acha" infested by *T. castaneum* when left untreated can incure serious damage.

CONCLUSION

In conclusion, this study provides evidence that *P. guineense, D. tripetala,* and *E. aromatica* could effectively be used against *T. castaneum* as ecofriendly, less hazardous material for the protection of "Acha" in storage. However further investigation need to be carried out to ascertain how long each treatment can carry the products in the store and the best dosage for each to prevent wastage of material and encourage economy of use.

REFERENCES

Abbott W.S. (1925). A Method of Computing the Effectiveness of an Insecticide. J. Econ. Entomol., 18: 256-267.

Adedire C.O. and L. Lajide (1999). Toxicity and Oviposition Deterrency of Some Plants Extracts on Cowpea Storage Bruchid, *Callosobruchus maculatus* (F). J. Plant Dis. Protect. 106: 647-653.

Adedire C.O. and L. Lajide (2003). Ability of Extracts of Ten Plant Species to Protect Maize Grains Against Infestation by the Maize Weevil *Sitophilus zeamais* during Storage. Nigerian J. Experimental Biol. 4: 175-179.

Arora M., J. Sharama, A. Singh and R.S. Negi (2011). Larvicidal Properties of Aqueous Extracts of *Withania somnifera* on *Tribolium castaneum*. Indian J. Fundamental Applied Life Sci. 2: 32-36.

Chukwu O. and A.J. Abdul-kadir (2008) Proximate Chemical Composition of "Acha" (*Digitaria exilis* and *Digitaria iburua*) Grains. J. Food Sci. and Technol. 6: 214-216.

CIRAD 2004. An African Cereal Crop. French Agricultural Research Centre for International Development http://www.cerealcrops/African.Agric-res/html.

Daoubi M., A. Deligeorgopoulou, A.J. Macias-sanchez, R. Hermamdez-galan, P.B. Hitchcock, J.R. Hanson and I.G. Collado (2005). Antifungal Activity and Biotrans Formation of Diisophorone by Botrytiscinerea. J. Agric. and Food Chemistry 53: 6035-6039.

Emeasor K.C., R.O. Ogbuji and S.O. Emosairue (2005). Insecticidal Activities of Some Seed Powders Against *Callosobruchus maculatus* (F) on Stored Cowpea. J. Plant Dis. and Protect. 112: 80-87.

Fasakin E.A. and O. Aberejo (2002). Effect of Some Pulverized Plant Materials on the Developmental Stages of Fish Beetle, *Dermestes maculatus* Degeer in Smoked Catfish (*Clarias gariepinus*) during Storage. Bio-resource Technol. 85: 173-177.

Garcìa M., O. J. Donael, C.E. Ardanaz, C.E. Tonn and M.E. Sosa (2005). Toxic and Repellent Effects of *Baccharis salicifolia* Essential Oil on *Tribolium castaneum*. Pest Management Sci. 61: 612-618.

Gonzalo S. (2009). Botanical Insecticides. Faculty De Agronomia, University de-concepcion Avenida Vicente Mendez Chile 595.

Gyang J.D. and E.O. Wuyep (2005). "Acha" The Grain of Life. A Bi-annual Publication of the Raw Material Research and Development Council. 6: 39-41.

Hussain M.A., A. Puttaswamy and C.A. Viraktamath (1996). Effect of Botanical Oils on lantana bug, *Or-thezia insigni* Browne Infesting Crossandra. Insect Environment 2: 85-86.

Iqbal M.F., M.H. Kahloon, M.R. Nawaz and M.I. Javaid (2011) Effectiveness of Some Botanical Extracts on Wheat Aphids. The Journal of Animal Plant Sciences, 21(1): 114-115.

Khan M.A., M. Ajab. Khan, G. Mujtaba and M. Hussain (2012) Ethnobotanical Study About Medicinal Plants of Poonch Valley Azad Kashmir. The Journal of Animal and Plant Sciences, 22(2): 493-500.

Kim S.L., J.Y. Roh, D.H. Kim, H.S. Lee and Y.J. Ahn (2003). Insecticidal Activities of Aromatic Plant Extracts and Essential oils Against *Sitophilus oryzae* and *Callosobruchus chinensis*. J. Stored Product Res. 39: 293-303.

Lale N.E.S. (1995). An Overview of the Use of Plant Products in the Management of Stored Product Coleoptera in the Products. Post Harvest News Information 6: 69-75.

Levinson H.Z. and A. Levinson (1985). Storage and Insect Species of Stored Grain and Tombs in Ancient Egyptian. *Zeitschrift fuir angewandte entomologie* 100: 321-339.

Magan N., R. Hope, V. Cairns and D. Aldred (2003). Post Harvest Fungal Ecology: Impact of Fungal Growth and Mycotoxin Accumulation in Stored Grain, Europian J. Plant Pathol. 109: 723-730.

Obi I. U. (2002). Statistical Method of Detecting Differences Between Treatment Means and Research Methodology Issues in Laboratory and Field Experiment. A.P. Express Publishing Company Ltd. Nsukka. Nigeria 8-22.

Okonkwo E.O. and W.I. Okoye (2001). Insecticidal Activity of *Dennettia tripetala* Baker (F.) and *Piper guineense* Schum. and Thonn against *Dermestes maculatus* Degeer. and *Necrobia rufipes* Degeer. on Dried Fish. Nigerian J. Entomol 18: 109-117.

Oliver B. (1959). Nigeria's Useful Plants Part 2. Medicinal Plants (4) Nigerian Field Journal 24: 160-162.

Parkin E.A., E.I.C. Scott and R. Foster (1962). Increased Resistance of Stored-product Insects to Insecticides. The Resistance of Field Strain of Beetle *Tribolium castaneum*. Pest Infestation Res. 34-35.

Potenza M.R., J. Justi Junior and J.N. Alves (2005). Evaluation of Contact Activities of Plant Extracts Against Sitophilus Zeamais Motschulsky. Alternative Methods to Chemical Control. 9th International Working Conference on Stored Product Production. Instituto Biologico/APTA. Av. Conselheiro Rodrigues Alves, Paulo-Brazil 7-19.

Ravi K.U. and J. Gayatri (2007). Evaluation of Biological Activities of *Piper nigrum* Oil Against *Tribolium castaneum*. Bulletin of Insectology 60: 57-61.

Richards S., R.A. Gibbs, G.M. Weinstock, S.J. Brown, R. Denell, R.W. Beeman, R. Gibbs, R.G. Bucher, M. Friedrich and C.J.E. Grimmelikhuijzen (2008). The genome of the Model Beetle and Pest. *Tribolium castaneum*. Nature 452: 949-955.

Shaaya E., M. Kostjukovski, J. Eilberg, and C. Sukprakarn (1997). Plant Oils as Fumigants and Contact Insecticides for the Control of Stored Product Insects. J. Stored Products Res. 33: 7-15.

Su C.F.H. (1977). Insecticidal Properties of Black Pepper to Rice Weevils. J. Economic Entomol., 70: 18-21.

Umeozor O.C. and P.O. Pessu (2003). Insecticidal Effects of *Dennettia tripetala* (bak.f.) and *Piper guineense* (thonn,) Against Immature *Callosobruchus maculatus* (Fab.) on Stored Cowpea, *Vigna unguiculata* (L) Walp. Indian J. Agric. Res. 37: 169-174.

Vietmeyer N.D., N.E. Borlaugh, J. Axtell, G.W. Burton, J.R. Harlan, and K.O. Rachie (1996). Fonio (Acha). In: Vietmeyer ND Edition, Lost Crops of Africa. BOSTID, National Academic Press, Washington, DC, USA.

CHAPTER

Integrating Agriculture, Land Use and Climate Action Programmes to Reduce Green House Emission and Enhance Food Security at National and Local Landscape Levels in Sub-saharan Africa

[1]Ezeaku P.I.*; [2]Asadu, C.L.A. [3]S.C. Eze

ABSTRACT

Agricultural sector of most countries in Sub-saharan Africa (SSA), with Nigeria been no exception, is highly vulnerable to climate change due to the countries' geographic location at the southern edge of Sahara desert. The strong dependence of the population of most SSA countries on rainfed agriculture and livestock, land degradation and desertification, poor infrastructure for crop production, handling, and marketing as well as the myriad interactions between climate variability and food systems have caused fluctuations in food availability (food insecurity) and subsequently loss of human life, malnutrition and diseases including plummeting of national economies.

The aggregate impact of these factors is the biggest challenge to the achievement of the Millennium Development Goals (MDGs) to which

1. United Nations University Institute for Natural Resources in Africa (UNU-INRA) International House, University of Ghana, Legon, Accra.
2. Department of Soil Science; University of Nigeria Nsukka, Nigeria.
3. Department of Crop Science; University of Nigeria Nsukka, Nigeria
* **Permanent address:** Department of Soil Science; University of Nigeria Nsukka, Nigeria.

most countries in SS Africa have subscribed. To attain higher food production implies that agriculture have to be increasingly more productive and more efficient to meet the needs of an increasing population, an indication that emphasis on agriculture supposes to shift from maximizing production to optimizing resource use and sustaining productivity for as long as possible. Strategies for mitigating climate change and increasing diversified agricultural productivity to enhance food security on sustainable basis have become desirous for improving humans' wellbeing, poverty scale-up and economic development.

The objective of this paper was to document some of the mechanisms that could be used to cope with current climate variability, and then contribute to scientific research and technological innovations in addressing the major constraint of drought, land degradation and desertification. The assumption is that if the indigenous resources and technological innovations are effective to cope with current climate variability and other constraints, they will probably be useful to deal with future climate change. To achieve the aim of this paper, the need for climate action on agriculture and land use was examined. Some aspects of technologies with potential for enriching soil carbon, and approaches for creating high-carbon cropping systems and climate-friendly livestock production were discussed. Sustainable strategies for protecting existing carbon stores in natural forests and grasslands as well as restoring vegetation in degraded zones; including market incentives for climate-friendly agriculture and land use were x-rayed.

Finally, in order to respond efficiently and effectively to the implications of climate change for food security and provide knowledge gap, some specific steps i.e public policies to support the needed transition by integrating agriculture, land use, and climate action programmes were recommended.

INTRODUCTION

Current efforts to address climate change have so far focused on the response strategies: mitigation and adaptation. Mitigation seeks to reduce greenhouse gas emissions (GHG) to avoid further warming of the globe, while adaptation, on the other hand, aims to cope with the problem of climate impacts when they materialize (IPCC, 2007). This has been strongly stated in the UN Framework Convention on Climate Change (UNFCC) and the Kyoto Protocol.

More natural systems and many human activities are sensitive to the changing climate. The extent to which these systems will be harmed by climate change depends both on the magnitude of the change and the capacity of the natural or human system to adapt. Society's capacity to adapt is dependent on the prevailing socioeconomic situation through time. Consequently, understanding the evolving socioeconomic situation is important for knowledge of the likely future climate in identifying vulnerable elements of society.

The climate impacts programmes as demonstrated in some countries exemplify the indigenous responses to climate variability.

The northern part of Nigeria, which was badly hit during the desiccation years, has been a fertile ground for some socio-economic and anthropological studies investigating the vulnerability and adaptive capacities of the Sahelian farming communities (Adams and Mortimore, 1997; Mortmimore and Adams, 1999; Mortimore and Adams, 2001). These authors identified 5 categories of crisis and described some elements of strategic adaptation farmers have relied upon in response to these crises (Table 5.1). One important aspect of the farmers' survival strategies in the Sahel resides in their ability to 'negotiate the rain', which goes beyond the simple objective of managing a drought event. Owing to the inter-annual variability of rainfall, farmers have to show enough wits and flexibility every year in the timing of the various farming operations (clearing, planting, weeding and harvesting) and in the management of household labor. They use a combination of local climate indicators including tree fruit and flower production, duration and intensity of cold and hot periods, bird and insect behaviour, movement of stars and the moon to predict precipitations (Roncoli *et al.*, 2002). For example, in a good rainfall year, farm households, which are limited by labour, may decide to reduce the cultivated area, use more manure and focus on weeding to maximise yield while households that have more labour can expand the cultivated area to make maximum use of good rainfall conditions. In a drier year, the behaviour of both sets of households would be different.

Table 5.1: Crises and Farmers' Strategic Adaptations in the Sahel (Mortimore and Adams, 1999)

Perceptions of 'Crisis'	Strategic Adaptations by Farmers
A drought crisis	Negotiating the rains
A food crisis	Managing biodiversity
A stocking crisis	Integrating animals
A degradational crisis	Working the land harder
A coping crisis	Diversifying livelihood

Maintaining a high level of plant biodiversity within the farm boundaries and in the agricultural landscapes has also been a recognized strategy to reduce food insecurity as exemplified in southeastern Nigeria (Ezeaku, 2009). Simultaneous growing, mixing or intercropping different types of crops (or cultivars of the same crops) is not uncommon in northern Nigeria and in many other areas of the Sahel. This strategy seeks to avoid risks of total crop failure rather than maximizing yields of a particular crop. Despite the dry conditions, inventories have shown a surprisingly high number of non-domesticated species (trees, shrubs, herbs) in the Sahelian landscapes, each of them playing useful roles.

The unrelenting conversion of natural systems to croplands is no doubt reducing the plant populations, but plant diversity is not as significantly affected as one would expect since many indigenous tree species are well conserved through a system of selective clearing. The tradition of maintaining or nurturing key useful tree species on farmlands (the parkland farming systems) is a well established feature of the Sahelian farming systems. This practice not only helps conserve biodiversity but also buffers against production risks. While harvesting food, medicine, fodder, resins and building material from these multipurpose trees is a normal occurrence (Joet *et al.*, 1998; Ong and Leakey, 1999), the farmers' reliance on indigenous trees becomes more important during times of acute food shortages (Mortimore and Adams, 2001).

The internal capacity of the rural populace to innovate and readjust their farming systems in the face of adverse conditions has also been demonstrated in the Senegalese groundnut basin. In the 1980s, the Sahel drought was at its peak, but this also coincided with a period of important political reforms in the agricultural sector (Worldwatch Institute, WI, 2009). The New Agricultural Policy (NPA) was brutally put into effect as part of the structural adjustment programmes (SAPs) prescribed by the donor community and the international financial institutions. The subsequent removal of government subsidies on agricultural inputs such as seeds and fertilizers had disastrous consequences on the groundnut industry, which had provided a lifeline to the farming communities for several decades. One way in which farmers responded to the crisis (the demise of the groundnut industry) was to introduce the cultivation of water melon. Before 1987, hardly a farmer in Senegal grew water melon, but by 1999, national production reached almost 300,000 tonnes (WI, 2009). Yet, involvement from the governmental agricultural services in this transformation was minimal. This happened virtually through a process of passive farmer-to-farmer dissemination, fuelled by the high demand in the local market. The water melon crop spread rapidly within the farming communities thanks to its high drought tolerance, its earliness (it matures before the traditional crops) and its capacity to produce in years where many other crops fail.

The study of the dynamics of land use in the village territory of Yomboli, northern Burkina Faso, between 1945 and 1991, provides another example of strategic adaptation by farmers when confronted with changing climatic conditions (Reenberg *et al.*, 1998; Reenberg, 2001). The combined use of aerial photos, satellite imagery and GPS measurements has helped to detect the gradual shift that has occurred in the agricultural landscape. Until 1945, crop production was almost exclusively concentrated on the pediplains (more fertile and finer-textured soils). When the climate was becoming increasingly dry in the following decades, farmers progressively abandoned the pediplains and moved to the dunes. Further investigation showed that this shift from fertile to more sandy soils has been triggered, not by declining soil fertility as many tended to believe, but rather by the farmers realizing that the reduced rainfall no longer allows sufficient yields from these finer textured soils (Mazzucato and Niemeijer, 2000; Reenberg, 2001). Farmers understood the disadvantage of heavy soils in drought years and therefore, where land availability allowed it, field reallocation has been used as a strategic response to reduced rainfall. However, since 1991 (rainfall had come back to near long-term average) the Yomboli farmers have been diversifying cultivation and dispersing their fields on both soil types to reduce the risk associated with variability in precipitation. This risk-spreading strategy has also been observed in other areas of the Sahel such as the Fandou Béri in Niger (Warren, 2002).

These few illustrations represent but a small portion of the myriad adaptive strategies of the Sahelian farmers. Nonetheless, they give an idea of the flexibility of rural households' vis-à-vis the management of their agricultural and natural resources. Obviously, these strategies have their own strengths and have helped rural dwellers withstand some of the pressure posed by climatic variability. Their actions not only enriched their landscapes and enhanced food security; they also helped to "cool" the planet by cutting greenhouse gas emissions and storing carbon in soils and vegetation. If their actions could be repeated by millions of rural communities around the world, climate change would slow down.

Indeed, climate change and global food security are inextricably linked. This was made abundantly clear in 2008, as rioters from Haiti to Cameroon protested the global "food crisis". The crisis partly reflected structural increases in food demand from growing and more-affluent populations in developing countries and short-term market failures, but it was also in part a reaction to increases in energy costs, new biofuel markets created by legislation promoting alternative energy, and climate-induced regional crop losses. Moreover, food and fibre production are leading sources of green house gas (GHG) emissions – they have a much larger "climate footprint" than the transportation sector, for example. Degradation and loss of forests and other vegetative cover puts the carbon cycle further off balance. Ironically, the land uses and management systems that are accelerating GHG emissions are also under mining the ecosystem services upon which long-term food and fibre production depend—healthy watershed, pollination, and soil fertility.

The objective of this paper is to document some of the mechanisms that could be used to cope with current climate variability. In other wards, the paper explains why actions on climate change must include agriculture and land systems and to highlight some promising ways to reduce climate change effect through land use changes. Indeed, there are huge opportunities to shift food and forestry production system as well as conservation area management to mitigate climate change in ways that also increase sustainability, improve rural incomes, and ease adaptation to enhance food security and a warming environment.

Consequently, this paper is structured into nine parts with part one being introduction. Part two examines climate and food security and the need for climate action on agriculture and land use. Part three examines how to make agriculture and land use climate—friendly and resilient. Part four looks at some aspects of technologies with potential for enriching soil carbon, and approaches for creating high-carbon cropping systems. Part five examines factors for promoting climate-friendly livestock production. Part six elucidates sustainable strategies for protecting existing carbon stores in natural forests and grasslands as well as restoring vegetation in degraded zones. Part seven looks at the market incentives for climate-friendly agriculture and land use. Part eight suggests specific steps i.e public policies to support the needed transition by integrating agriculture, land use, and climate action programmes.

Climate Change and Food Security

Although there is no general consensus on the direction changes in precipitations will take in the future, climate change may have negative consequences on agricultural production and food security in the Sahel region (Chamberlin and Diop, 2003; Ezeaku, 2009). Arid conditions are likely to be exacerbated even in places where an increase in precipitation is predicted because of a higher evapotranspiration regime due to higher temperatures. Extremes in the form of droughts and floods will be more frequent, putting an additional pressure on already stressed systems.

While global food supplies may not be affected by future shifts in climate due to gains in arable land from boreal and temperate areas, many projections show Africa losing a significant part of its arable land and the Sahel will be among the worst affected regions. A climate sensitivity analysis of agriculture concluded that three African countries will virtually lose their entire rain-fed agriculture by 2100 (Mendelsohn *et al.*, 2000) and two of them are Sahelian countries: Chad and Niger. A recent simulation exercise in Mali (assuming a temperature rise of between 1 and 2.75 degree C and no adaptation measures applied) suggests that, by the year 2030, reduced precipitation will induce a decline in cereal harvest of 15-19 per cent causing a doubling of food prices. The combined effects of lower production on farming household and higher prices on the Consumer's access to food raises the risk of hunger from its present baseline of 34 per cent to 64-70 per cent of the Malian population by 2030 (Butt *et al.*, 2003).

The Need for Climate Action on Agriculture and Land Use

Land is one of Earth's surfaces and it holds three times as much carbon as the atmosphere does. About 1,600 billion tons of this carbon is in the soil as organic matter and some 540-610 billion tons is in living vegetation (Leifeld, 2006). Although the volume of carbon on Earth's surface and in the atmosphere pales in comparison to the many trillions of tons stored deep under the surface as sediments, sedimentary rocks, and fossil fuels, surface carbon is crucial to climate change and life due to its inherent mobility.

Surface carbon moves from the atmosphere to the land and back, and in this process it drives the engine of life on the planet (Hume, 2001; Blanco-Canqui *et al*, 2008). Plants use carbon dioxide (co_2) from the atmosphere to grow and produce food and resources that sustain the rest of the biota. When these organisms breathe, grow, die, and eventually decompose, carbon is released to the atmosphere and the soil. Carbon from this past life provides the fuel for new life. Indeed, life depends on this harmonized movement of carbon from one sink to another. Large scale disruption or changes on land drastically alter the harmonious movement of carbon.

Land use changes and fossil fuel burning are the two major sources of the increased co_2 in the atmosphere that is changing the global climate. Burning fossil fuel releases carbon that has been buried for millions of years, while deforestation, intensive tillage, and over grazing release carbon from living plants and soil organic matter. Some land use changes affect climate by altering regional precipitation patterns (Hengsdijk *et al*, 2003). Overall, land use and land use changes account for about 31 per cent of total human induced greenhouse gas emissions into the atmosphere. Carbon dioxide (77%), nitrous oxide (8%), and methane (14%) are the three main greenhouse gases that trap infrared radiation and contribute to climate change. Of all the three of these GHGs, land use changes contribute to their release. Worldwatch (2009) note that of the total annual human-induced GHG emissions in 2004 of 49 billion tons of carbon-dioxide equivalent, roughly 31 per cent—15 billion tons—was from land use. Other sources are as shown in Table 5.2.

Yet other types of land use can play the opposite role. Growing plants can remove huge amounts of carbon from the atmosphere and store it in vegetation and soils in ways that not only stabilize the climate but also benefit food and fibre production and the environment. So it is imperative that any climate change mitigation strategy addresses the sector.

Table 5.2: Land Uses and Their Annual Emissions

Land Use	Annual Emissions (million tons CO_2 equivalent)	GHG Emitted
Agriculture	6,500	
Soil fertilization (inorganic fertilizers and applied manure)	2,100	Nitrous oxide*
Gases from food digestion in cattle (enteric fermentation in rumens)	1,800	Methane*
Biomass burning	700	Methane, nitrous oxide*
Paddy (flooded) rice production (anaerobic decomposition)	600	Methane*
Livestock manure	400	Methane, nitrous oxide*
Other (e.g. delivery of irrigation water)	900	Carbon dioxide, nitrous oxide*
Deforestation (including peat)	8,500	
For agriculture or livestock	5,900	Carbon dioxide
Total	15,000	

* The GHG impact of 1 unit of nitrous oxide is equivalent to 298 units of CO_2; 1 unit of methane is equivalent to 25 units of carbon dioxide.

Source: Worldwatch Institute (2009).

Extensive action to influence land use is also going to be essential to sustain food and forest production in the face of climate change. Agricultural systems have developed during a time of a relatively predictable local weather patterns. The choice of crops and varieties, the timing of input application, vulnerability to pest and diseases, the timing of management practices — all these are closely linked to temperature and rainfall. With climate changing, production conditions will change—and quite radically in some places — which will lead to major shifts in farming systems.

The World Agroforestry Centre (ICRAF) and United Nation Environmental Programme (UNEP) report (2008) show the following climate scenario predictions for some Sahelian countries. Chad, for example, the largest country in the Sahel region, epitomises the tragedy of the 1970s. It is estimated that more than 900,000 people were severely affected by the drought, although the actual number of starvation victims and displaced people is unknown (DMC, 1995). The important shortfall in crop production and massive death of livestock had overwhelming economic implications. In 1973, the gross domestic product (GDP) of Chad had a negative growth of 9 per cent. The loss in real economic growth was a devastating setback for the country since per capita gross national product (GNP) dropped to US$ 120 by 1975, ranking Chad as one of the lowest income countries in the world (DMC, 1995). The 1984 drought had similar impacts on Mali and Niger, who saw their GDP fall by 9 and 18 per cent respectively in the aftermath of the drought (World Conference on Disaster Reduction, WCDR, 1994).

In Cape Verde, prediction shows that a reduction in annual rainfall (-20 to -10%), combined with rising temperatures of up to 2.5° C, will expose a large proportion of the rural people to food insecurity. Cultivation of maize, the major staple food crop, under rainfed conditions will no longer be feasible in many areas (Hume, 2001).

Temperatures are projected to increase by between 0.6 and 1.7° C towards 2023, depending on the model used, the GHG emission scenario and the location considered within the country of Chad. Rainfall will remain at current levels or increase slightly. However, the temporal distribution of the rains will be altered, with more rain falling at the onset of the growing season and less rainfall in the normally more rainy months of July, August and September, which can negatively affect crop development. In addition, increased evapotranspiration as a result of the warming will exacerbate the arid conditions and negatively impact forest, agricultural and water resources.

The government of the Gambia used the 1950-1990 period as baseline. In general mean temperature is projected to rise by 3 to 4.5° C in the 2075 horizon. For the vulnerability assessment, the agricultural sector has been divided into 4 sub-sectors and modelling exercises carried out for each of them:

- *Maize system:* for rainfall, some GCM models show a decrease of (-59 to -15%) while others show an increase of 15 to 29 per cent by 2100. In general, increased runoff (58-98%) and drainage (48-84%) are expected. Total maize biomass production is likely to decrease by 19 to 35 per cent compared to baseline even in the case of increased rainfall due to massive leaching of nitrogen.
- *Late millet system:* rainfall is expected to increase by 28-69 per cent depending on GCM outputs. Runoff (2-26%), drainage (3-31%) and extractable water (9-36%) will also increase. A total biomass decrease of 25 to 44 per cent is expected.
- *Early millet system:* a 5-59 per cent increase in rainfall is expected inducing an increase in runoff (8-56%), drainage (4-57%) and extractable water (4-30%). Total early millet biomass will decrease by 1 to 21 per cent.
- *Groundnut system:* rainfall is expected to increase by 13-25 per cent, runoff by 8-23 per cent and drainage by 9-21 per cent. A higher nitrogen uptake is expected resulting in a total biomass increase of 15-47 per cent compared to a situation without climate change.

Climate change is expected to have drastic consequences in Mali. The drying trend that has already been going on for the last few decades will be exacerbated with the following consequences:

- reduction in cereal yield due to drought and declining soil fertility;
- reduction of livestock numbers due to the shrinking of grazing areas;
- reduction of fauna and fi shing resources;
- expansion of cultivated areas to compensate for low yields with encroachment in low potential areas.

Vulnerability and adaptation studies have been carried out on the cereal crops, mainly sorghum. Different temperature rise scenarios (1° C, 2° C, 3° C, 4° C), coupled with rainfall reduction in relation to the 1961-1990 period, have been used to predict the behaviour of sorghum crop at the 2025 horizon. The results show that sorghum yield will drop by 2-26 per cent depending on the scenario and model considered (De Rouw, 2004).

In Mauritania GCM models show that temperatures could rise by up to 1-2° C. Rainfall is expected to decline by 15-30 per cent in the South and 2 per cent in the North with the high warming scenario. In the low warming scenario, rainfall reduction will be less than that without climate change. The vulnerability assessment and adaptation exercise of Mauritania focused on the cereal producing area in the Brakna region, where millet and sorghum are the major crops. Since 1971, the area has experienced declining annual rainfall, a higher frequency of dry spells and higher evaporation rates due to rising temperatures. It is understood that climate change will significantly reduce the area suitable for cultivation as well as cereal yields, which will exacerbate food insecurity and poverty.

Senegal based its projections on a 20 per cent reduction in rainfall and a 4° C increase in temperatures, choosing 1961-1990 as baseline. Climate change will thus result in a reduction of potential millet yield (-33 to -25%) and a reduction of the area suitable for the crop. In comparison, the 1972 and 1973 droughts reduced potential yields by 79 to 63 per cent respectively (Chamberlin and Diop, 2003). Under current conditions, a modelling exercise has shown that moderate intensification and slight expansion of agricultural areas can meet the cereal needs of the population and even produce surpluses. With climate change, coverage of food needs will worsen by 38 to 11 per cent in relation to the current situation, exposing an additional 1-4 million people to food insecurity by 2050.

Despite that climate conditions may improve in some places, for example, rain may become more reliable and growing seasons for some crops may expand, many key strategies for agricultural, forest, and other land use systems to mitigate climate change, that is, to reduce GHG emissions or increase the storage of carbon in production and natural systems have become desirous. They also will help rural communities adapt to that change. Mobilizing action for adaptation in these directions rather than relying only on other types of interventions, such as seed varieties or shifts in market supply chains, could have significant success in slowing climate change.

Making Agriculture and Land Use Climate-friendly and Resilient

An agricultural landscape should simultaneously provide food and fibre, meet the need of nature and biodiversity, and support viable livelihoods for people who live there. In terms of climate change, landscape and farming systems should actively absorb and store carbon in vegetation and soils, reduce emissions of methane from rice production, livestock, and burning, and reduce nitrous oxide emissions from inorganic fertilizers. At the same time, it is important to increase the resilience of production systems and ecosystem services to climate change.

Many techniques are already available to achieve climate friendly landscapes. None is a "silver bullet," but in combinations that make sense locally they can help to move decisively forward. This paper describes five strategies that are specially promoting enriching soil carbon, creating high carbon cropping systems, promoting climate friendly livestock production systems, protecting carbon existing stores in natural forests and grasslands, and restoring vegetation in degraded areas (see Figure 5.1). Many other improvements will also be needed for production systems to adapt to climate change while meeting growing food needs and commercial demands, such as adapted seed varieties. But these five strategies are highlighted because of their powerful advantage in mitigating climate change as well as contributing more broadly to sustainable production systems and other ecosystem services.

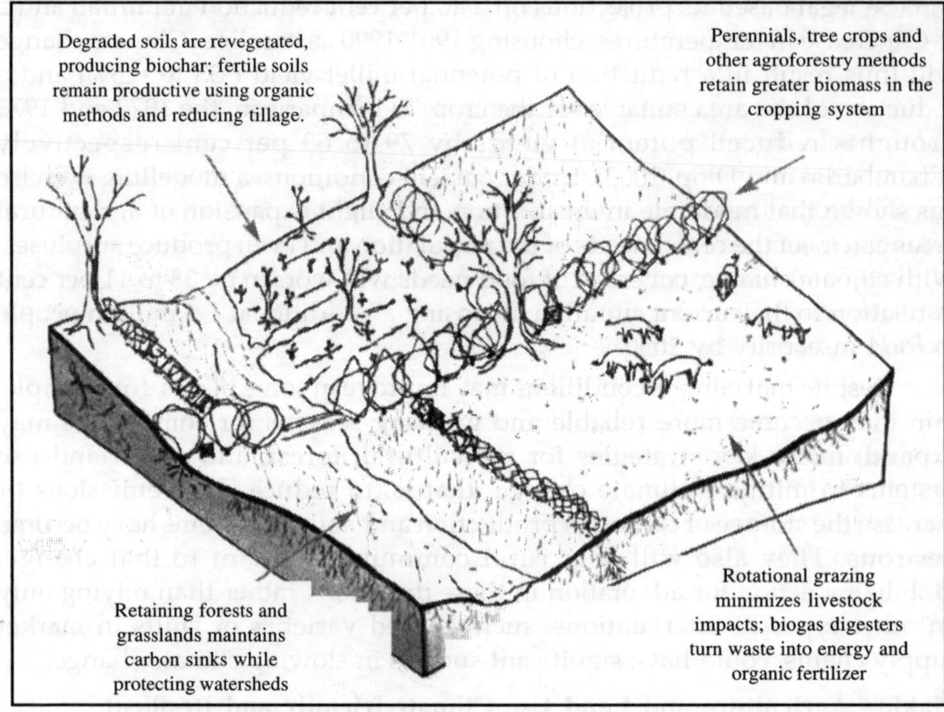

Fig. 5.1: Multiple Strategies to Productively Absorb and Store Carbon in Agricultural Landscapes (*Source*: WorldWatch Institute, 2009)

Moreover, these strategies can help mobilize a broad political coalition to support climate action by meeting the urgent needs of farmers, grazers and rural communities, the food industry, urban water users, resource dependent industries, and conservation organisations. They can help meet not only climate goals but internationally agreed Millennium Development Goals and other global environmental conventions.

Many of these approaches will be economically self sustaining once initial investments are made. It is important to implement this agenda on a large scale in order to have significant impacts on the climate. Key roles that government need to play are to mobilize the financing and social organisation needed for these initial investments, develop additional incentives for activities that have more time consuming or costly yet offer no particular benefits to farmers or land managers, and invest in the development of technologies and management systems that are especially promising but not yet ready for widespread use.

Some Aspects of Technologies with Potentials for Enriching Soil Carbon

(a) Enriching soil carbon

Soil has four components; minerals, water, air, and organic materials – both nonliving and living. The former comes from dead plant, animal, and microbial matter while the living organic material is from flora and fauna of the soil biota, including living roots and microbes. Together, living and nonliving organic materials account for only 1-6 per cent of the soil's volume, but they contribute much more to its productivity (FAO, 2007; World Watch Institute, 2009). The organic materials retain air and water in the soil and provide nutrients that the plants and the soil fauna depend on for life. They are also reservoirs of carbon in the soil.

In fact, soil is the third largest carbon pool on the planet. In the long term, agricultural practices that amend soil carbon from year to year through organic matter management rather than depleting it will provide productive soils that are rich in carbon and require fewer chemical inputs. New mapping tools, such as the 2008 Global Carbon Gap Map produced by the Food and Agriculture Organisation, can identify areas where soil carbon storage is greatest and areas with the physical potential for billions of tons of additional carbon to be stored in degraded soils and need to be fully used.

Enhance soil nutrients through organic methods. Current use of inorganic fertilizers is estimated at 102 million tons worldwide, with use concentrated in industrial countries and in irrigated regions of developing nations. Soils with nitrogen fertilizers release nitrous oxide, a greenhouse gas that has about 300 times the warming capacity of carbon dioxide. Fertilized soils release more than 2 billion tons (in terms of carbon dioxide equivalent) of greenhouse gases every year (World Agroforestry Centre (ICRAF) and UN Environmental Programme (UNEP) 2006 Report. One promising strategy to reduce emissions is to adopt soil fertility management practices that increase soil organic matter and siphon carbon from the atmosphere.

Numerous technologies can be used to substitute or minimize the need for inorganic fertilizers. Examples include composting, green manures, nitrogen-fixing cover crops and intercrops, and livestock manures (Asadu *et al.*, 2004).

Similarly, Lal (2004) notes that the carbon sink capacity of the world's agriculture and degraded soils is about 50 to 66 per cent of the historic loss of 42 to 78 per cent gigatons of carbon. Strategies of soil restoration and wood land regeneration, no-till farming, cover crops, nutrient management, manuring and sludge application, improved grazing, water conservation and harvesting, efficient irrigation, agroforestry practices and growing energy crops on spare or marginal lands increases soil carbon pool. Indeed, an increase of 1 ton of soil carbon pool of degraded cropland soils may increase crop yield by 20 to 40 kg/ha for wheat, 10 to 20 kg/ha for maize, and 0.5 to

1 kg/ha for cowpea. Furthermore, Lal, (2004) notes that carbon sequestration has potential of enhancing food security by offsetting fossil fuel emissions by 0.4 to 1.3 gigatons of carbon per year, or 5 to 15 per cent of the global fossil-fuel emissions. However, the rate of soil organic carbon sequestration with adoption of recommended technologies depend on soil texture and structure, rainfall, temperature, farming system and soil management.

The economics and productivity implications of all these methods vary widely. In some very intensive, high-yield cropping systems, replacing some or all inorganic fertilizer may require costlier inputs, but there is commonly scope for much more efficient use of fertilizer through better targeting and timing. In moderately intensive systems, the use of organic nutrient sources with small amounts of supplemental inorganic fertilizer can be quite competitive and attractive of farmers seeking to reduce cash costs.

Improvements in organic technologies over the past few decades have led to comparable levels of productivity across a wide range of crops and farming systems. The question of whether organic farming can feed the world, as some claim, remains controversial. And more research is needed to understand the potentials and limitations of biological based soil nutrient management systems across the range of soil types and climatic conditions. But there is little question that farmers in many production systems can already profitably maintain yields while using much less nitrogen fertilizer—and with major climate benefits.

Minimize soil tillage: Soil used to grow crops is commonly tilled to improve the conditions of the seed bed and to uproot weeds. But tilling turns the soil upside down, exposing anaerobic microbes to oxygen and suffocating aerobic microbes by working them under. This disturbance exposes nonliving organic matter to oxygen, releasing carbon dioxide. Keeping crop residues or mulch on the surface helps soil retain moisture, prevents erosion, and returns carbon to the soil through decomposition. Hence practices that reduce tillage also generally reduce carbon emissions.

A variety of conservation tillage practices accomplish this goal. In non-mechanized systems, farmers might use digging sticks to plant seeds and can manage weeds through mulch and hand-weeding. Special mechanized systems have been developed that drill the seed through the vegetative layer and use herbicides to manage weeds. Many farmers combine no-till with crop rotations and green manure crops. In Nigeria, farmers have developed organic management systems combined with no-till. No-till plots yielded higher than conventionally ploughed plots and reduced soil erosion by up to 90 per cent (Lal, 1974). No-till has the additional benefit of reducing labour and fossil fuel use and enhancing soil biodiversity—all recycling nutrients and storing carbon (Ohiri and Ezumah, 1990).

The actual net impacts on greenhouse gases of reduced emissions and increased carbon storage from reduced tillage depend significantly on associated practices, such as the level of vegetative soil cover and the impact of tillage on crop root development, which depends on the specific crop and soil type. It is projected that the carbon storage benefits of no-till may plateau over the next 50 years, but this can be a cost-effective option to buy time while alternative energy systems develop (WorldWatch Institute, 2009).

Incorporate biochar: Decomposition of plant matter is one way of enriching soil carbon if it takes place securely within the soil; decomposition on the surface, on the other hand, releases carbon into the atmosphere as carbon dioxide. In the humid tropics, for example, organic matter breaks down rapidly, reducing the carbon storage benefits of organic systems. Another option, recently discovered, is to incorporate biochar—burned biomass in a low-oxygen environment. This keeps carbon in soil longer and releases the nutrients slowly over a long period time. While the burning does release some carbon dioxide, the remaining carbon-rich dark aromatic matter is highly stable in soil. Hence planting fast-growing trees in previously barren or degraded areas, converting them to biochar, and adding them to soil is a quick way of taking carbon from the atmosphere and turning it into an organic slow-release fertilizer that benefits both the plant and the soil fauna.

Interestingly, for years, the farming populations in Nsukka, southeastern Nigeria add incompletely burnt biomass to the soil so that the soils retain high amounts of organic carbon and fertility in stark contrast to the low fertility of adjacent soils. Most crops respond with improved yields for biochar additions without declining productivity. Worldwatch Institute advocates calculate that if biochar additions were applied at rate of up to 183 tons of carbon dioxide equivalent on just 10 per cent of the world's cropland (about 150 million hectares), this method could store 29 billion tons of CO_2-equivalent, offsetting nearly all the emissions from fossil fuel burning.

(b) Creating High Carbon Cropping Systems

Plants harness to energy of the sun and accumulate carbon from the atmosphere to produce biomass on which the rest of the biota depends. The great innovation of agriculture 10,000 years ago was to manage the photosynthesis of plants and ecosystems so as to dependably increase yields. With 5 billion hectares of Earth's surface used for agriculture (69% under pasture and 28% in crops) in 2002, and with half a billion more hectares expected by 2020, agricultural production systems and landscapes have to not only deliver food and fiber but also support biodiversity and important ecosystem services, including climate change mitigation (Worldwatch Institute, 2009). A major strategy for achieving this is to increase the role of perennial crops, shrubs, trees, and palms, so that carbon is absorbed and stored in the biomass of roots, trunks, and branches while crops are being produced. Tree crops and agroforestry maintain significantly higher biomass than clear-weeded, annually tilled crops. Thus achieving a high-carbon cropping system, as well as the year-round vegetative cover required sustaining soils, watersheds, and habitats, will require diversification and the incorporation of a far greater share of perennial plants.

Perennial grains: Currently all arable land is used to grow annual grains. This production depends on tilling, preparing seed beds, and applying chemical inputs. Every year the process starts over again from scratch. This makes production more dependent on chemical inputs (such as nitrogen fertilizer that is a major source of nitrous oxide emissions), which also require a lot of fossil fuels to produce.

In contrast, perennial grasses retain a strong root network between growing seasons. Hence, a good amount of the living biomass remains in the soil instead of being released as greenhouse gases. And they help hold soil organic matter and water together, reducing soil erosion and GHG emissions. Finally, the perennial nature of these grasses does away with the need for annual tilling that releases GHGs and causes soil erosion, and it also makes the grasses more conservative in the use of nutrients. Researchers need to develop perennial relatives of cereals (rice, sorghum and wheat), forages (intermediate wheatgrass, rye), and oilseeds (sunflower) as well as undertake domestication work for a number of lesser known perennial native grasses, and many more perennials that offer unique and exciting opportunities.

Agroforestry intercrops: Another method of increasing carbon in agriculture is agroforestry, in which productive trees are planted in and around crop fields and pastures. The tree species may provide products (fruits, nuts, medicines, fuel, timber, and so on), farm production benefits (such as nitrogen fixation for crop fertility, wind protection for crops or animals, and fodder for animals), and ecosystem services (habitat for wild pollinators of crops, for example, or micro-climate improvement). The trees or other perennials in agroforestry systems sequester and store carbon, improving the carbon content of the agricultural landscape.

Agroforestry is common traditionally in agricultural systems in forest ecosystems and has been introduced into present day subsistence and commercial farming systems in the humid tropics not only in terms of nutrient recycling and soil conservation but also in supplying food and firewood to the small farmers and ensuring overall sustainability of production (IITA, 1986). The highest carbon storage results are found in "multistory" agroforestry systems that have many diverse species using ecological "niches" from the high canopy to bottom-story shade-tolerant crops. Examples are shade-grown coffee and cocoa plantations, where cash crops are grown under a canopy of trees that sequester carbon and provide habitats for wildlife.

Simple intercrops are used where tree-crop competition is minimal or where the value of tree crops is greater than the value of the intercropped annuals or grazing areas, or as a means to reduce market risks. Where crops are adversely affected by competition for light or water, trees may be grown in small plots in mosaics with crops. Research to develop low-light-tolerant crop varieties is desirous though in the Sahel, some native trees and crops have complementary growth patterns, avoiding light competition all together.

While agroforestry systems have a lower carbon storage potential per hectare than standing forests do, they can potentially be adopted on hundreds of millions of hectares. And because of the diverse benefits they offer, it is often more economical for farmers to establish and retain them. A Billion Tree Campaign to promote agroforestry was launched at the U.N. climate convention meeting in Nairobi in 2006. Within a year and a half the programme had shattered initial expectations and mobilized the planning of 2 billion trees in more than 150 countries. Half the plantings occurred in Africa, with 700 million in Ethiopia alone (Pasternak *et al*, 2005). By taking the lead from farmers and communities on the choice of species, planting location, and management, and by providing adequate technical support to ensure high-quality planting materials and methods, these initiatives can ensure that the trees will thrive and grow long enough and large enough to actually store a significant amount of carbon.

Agroforestry research and development needs to be strengthened given the various roles it can play in mitigating the negative effects of climate change. Policies should be put in place to rehabilitate degraded parkland systems and to accelerate the adoption of new technologies that can make a difference, preferably based on indigenous trees and shrubs. Promising technologies include the intensive planting of fodder trees such as *Pterocarpus erinaceus*, live hedges to support the development of off-season market gardening, windbreaks for wind-induced soil erosion control, and improved fallow to enhance soil fertility and reduce soil losses. The Sahel Eco-Farm is a good model of agroforestry system that could be scaled up in the region. The role of trees in improving microclimate, reducing soil erosion and generating income will be more important in the advent of climate change.

Tree crop alternatives for food, feed, and fuel: In a prescient book in 1929, Joseph Russel Smith observed the ecological vulnerabilities of annual crops and called for "A Permanent Agriculture". This work highlighted the diversity of tree crops that could substitute for annual crops in producing starch, protein, edible and industrial oils, animal feed, and other goods as well as edible fruits and nuts—only concerted efforts were made to develop genetic selection, management, and processing technologies.

Exciting initiatives should focus on shifting biofuel production from annual crops (which often have a net negative impact on GHG emissions due to cultivation, fertilization, and fossil fuel use) to perennial alternatives like switchgrass which offers a major new opportunity to use in degraded or low-productivity areas and serves as economically valuable crop with positive ecosystem impacts. But this will require a landscape approach to biofuels planning in order to use resources sustainably, enhance overall carbon intensity in the landscape, and complement other key land uses and ecosystem services.

Promoting Climate-friendly Livestock Production

Domestic livestock—cattle, pigs, sheep, goats, poultry, donkeys, and so on—account for most of the total living animal biomass worldwide. Revolution livestock product consumption is under way as developing countries adopt western diets. Meat consumption in most cities for example, more than doubled in the past 20 years and is projected to double again by 2030 (WI, 2009). This trend has triggered the rise of huge feedlots and confined dairies around most cities and the clearing of huge areas of land for low-intensity grazing. Furthermore, livestock produce prodigious quantities of greenhouse gases: methane (from fermentation of food in the largest part of an animal's stomach and from manure storage), nitrous oxide (from denitrification of soil and the crust on manure storage), and carbon (from crop, animal, and microbial respiration as well as fuel combustion and land clearing).

Livestock now account for 50 per cent of the emission from agriculture and land use change. Remarkably, annual emissions from livestock total some 7.1 billion tons (including 2.5 billion tons from clearing land for the animals), accounting for about 14.5 per cent of emissions from human activities. Indeed, a cow/calf pair on a beef farm is responsible for GHG emissions in a year than someone driving 8,000 miles in a mid-size car (WI, 2009)

Serious action on climate will almost certainly have to involve reducing consumption of meat and dairy by today's major consumers and slowing the growth of demand in developing countries. No such shift seems likely, however, without putting a price on the cost of emission. Meanwhile, some solutions are at hand to reduce emission of greenhouse gases by existing herds.

Intensive rotational grazing: Innovative grazing systems offer alternatives to both extensive grazing systems and confined feedlots and dairies, greatly reducing net GHG emissions while increasing productivity. Conventional thinking says that the current number of livestock far exceeds the carrying capacity of a typical grazing system. But in many circumstances, this reflects poor grazing management practices rather than numbers. However, the best ways to improve the GHG footprint of intensive dairy and meat operations are to improve carbon storage in grass systems, use higher-quality forage, eliminate manure storage, cover manure storage, increase meat or milk production per animal, and use well-managed rotational grazing.

Feed supplements to reduce methane emissions: Methane produced in the rumen (the first stomach of cattle, sheep, and goats and other species that chew the cud) account for about 1.8 billion tons of CO_2-equivalent emissions (WI, 2009). Nutrients supplements and innovative feed mixes have been developed that can reduce methane production by 20 per cent, though these are not yet commercially viable for most farmers. Some feed additives can make diets easier for animals to digest and reduce methane emissions. These require fairly sophisticated management, so they are mainly useful in larger-scale livestock operations (which are, in any case, the main sources of methane emissions). Advanced techniques that can be developed for methane reduction also include removing specific microbial organisms from the animal's rumen or adding other bacteria that actually reduce gas production there.

Biograss digesters for energy: Manure is a major source of methane, responsible for some 400 million tons of CO_2-equivalent. And poor manure management is a leading source of water pollution. But it is also an opportunity for an alternative fuel that reduces a farm's reliance on fossil fuels. By using appropriate technologies like an anaerobic biogas digester, farmers can profit from their farm waste while helping the climate. A biogas digester is basically a temperature-controlled air-tight vessel. Manure (or food waste) is fed into this vessel, where microbial action breaks it down into methane or biogas and a low-odor, nutrient-rich sludge. The biogas can be burned for heat or electricity, while the sludge can be used as fertilizer.

Some communities in developing countries are already using manure to produce cooking fuel. By installing anaerobic digesters, a large pile of manure can be used to produce biogas as well as fertilizer for farms. Even collecting the methane and burning it to convert it to carbon dioxide will be an improvement. And the heat this generates can be used to produce electricity. By thinking creativity, previously undervalued and dangerous wastes can be converted into new sources of energy, cost savings, and even income. Biogas digesters involve an initial cash investment that often needs to be advanced for low-income producers, but lifetime benefits far outweigh costs. This technology could be extended to millions of farmers with benefits for the climate as well as for human well-being through expanded access to energy. Biogas system also contribute to commercial energy; indeed produces sufficient heat to power the digester itself, make hot water, and heat the barns and farm buildings.

Protecting Existing Carbon Stores in Natural Forests and Grasslands

The world's 4 billion hectares of forests and 5 billion hectares of natural grasslands are massive reservoir of carbon—both in vegetation and root systems. As forests and grasslands continue to grow, they remove carbon from the atmosphere and contribute to climate change mitigation. Thus avoiding emissions by protecting existing terrestrial carbon in forests and grasslands is an essential element of climate action.

Reduce deforestation and land clearing: Massive deforestation and land clearing are releasing stored carbon back into the atmosphere. Between 2000 and 2005, the world lost forest area at a rate of 7.3 million hectares per year. For every hectare of forest cleared, between 217 and 640 tons of carbon are added to the atmosphere, depending upon the type of vegetation (Scherr and Franzel, 2002; Worldwatch Institute, 2009). Deforestation and land clearing have many different causes—from large-scale, organized clearing for agricultural use and infrastructure to the small-scale movement of marginalized people into forests for lack of alternative farming or employment opportunities or to the clearing of trees for commercial sale of timber, pulp, or woodfuel. In many cases the key drivers are outside the productive land use sectors—the result of public policies in other sectors, such as construction of roads, and other infrastructure, human settlements, or border control.

Unlike many of the other climate-mitigating land use actions, protecting large areas of standing natural vegetation typically provides fewer short-term financial or livelihood benefits for landowners and managers, and it may indeed reduce their incomes or livelihood security. The solution sometimes lies in regulation, where there is strong enforcement capacity, as with Ethiopia's laws restricting the clearance of natural vegetation. But in many areas the challenge is to develop incentives for conservation for the key stakeholders.

Several approaches are being suggested. One is to raise the economic value of standing forests or grasslands by improving markets for sustainably harvested, high-value products from those areas or by paying land managers directly for their conservation value. Current international negotiations are exploring the possibility of compensating developing countries for leaving their forests intact or improving forest management. During the Conference of the Parties to the climate convention in Bali in December 2007, governments agreed to a two-year negotiation process that would lead to adoption of a mechanism for Reducing Emissions from Deforestation and Degradation (REDD) after 2012. Implementation of any eventual REDD mechanism will pose major methodological, institutional, and governance challenges, but numerous initiatives are already under way to begin addressing these.

A second incentive for conservation is product certification, whereby agricultural and forest products are labeled as having been produced without clearing natural habitats or in mosaic landscapes that conserve a minimum area of natural patches. For example, the Biodiversity and Agricultural Commodities Programme of the International Finance Corporation seeks to increase the production of sustainably produced and verified commodities (palm oil, soy, sugarcane, and cocoa), working closely with commodity roundtables and their members, regulatory institutions, and policymakers. While the priority focus is on conservation of biodiversity, this initiative will have significant climate impacts as well, due to its focus on protecting existing carbon vegetative sinks from conversion, developing standards for sustainable biofuels, and establishing certification systems.

A third approach is to secure local tenure rights for communal forests and grasslands so that local people have an incentive to manage these resources sustainably and can protect them from outside threats like illegal commercial logging or land grabs for agriculture. In this approach, legal arrangements are should be used to strengthen tenure security and local governance capacity.

Reduce uncontrolled forest and grassland burning: Biomass burning is a significant source of carbon emissions, especially in developing countries. Controlled biomass burning in the agricultural sector, on a limited scale, can have positive functions as a means of clearing and rotating individual plots for crop production; in some ecosystems, it is a healthy means of weed control and soil fertility improvement. In a number of natural ecosystems, such as savanna and scrub forests, wild fires can help maintain biotic functions, as in Australia. In many tropical forest ecosystems, however, fires are mostly set by humans and environmentally harmful—killing wildlife, reducing habitat, and setting the stage for more fires by reducing moisture content and increasing combustible materials. Even where they can be beneficial from an agricultural perspective, fires can inadvertently spread to natural ecosystems, opening them up for further agricultural colonization.

Manage conservation areas as carbon sinks: Protected conservation areas provide a wide range of benefits, including climate regulation. Just letting these areas stand not only helps the biodiversity within, it also stores the carbon, avoiding major releases in greenhouse gas emissions. Moreover, due to some early effects of climate change, important habitats for wildlife are shifting out of protected areas. Plants are growing in higher altitudes as they seek cooler temperatures, while birds have started altering their breeding times. Larger and geographically well distributed areas thus need to be put under some form of protection.

Conservation agencies and communities are finding diverse incentive for protecting forested areas, from the sustainable harvesting of foods, medicines, and raw materials to the protection of locally important ecosystem services and religious and cultural values as well as opportunities for nature tourism income. Supporting these efforts to develop and sustain protected area networks, including public, community, and private conservation areas, can be highly effective conservation areas, can be a highly effective way to reduce and store greenhouse gases.

Strategies for Rehabilitating and Protecting Existing Carbon Stores

Restoring Vegetation in Degraded Areas

Extensive areas of the developing world have been denuded of vegetation from large-scale land clearing for annual crops or grazing and from overuse and poor management in community and public lands with weak governance. This is a tragic loss, from multiple perspectives. People living in these areas have lost a potentially valuable asset for the production of animal fodder, fuel, medicines, and raw materials. Gathering such materials is an especially important source of income and subsistence for low-income rural people. Also, the loss of vegetation seriously threatens ecosystem services, particularly watershed functions and wildlife habitat.

Efforts to restore degraded areas can thus be "win-win-win" investments. Although there may be fewer tons of CO_2 sequestered per hectare from restoration activities, millions of hectares can be restored with low opportunity costs and strong local incentives for participation and maintenance.

Revegetate degraded watersheds and rangelands: Hydrologists have learned that "green water"—the water stored in vegetation and filtrating into soils—is as important as "blue water" in streams and lakes. When rain falls on bare soils, most is lost as runoff. In many major watersheds, most of the land is in productive use. Poor vegetative cover limits the capacity to retain rainfall in the system or to filter water flowing into streams and lakes and therefore accelerating soil loss. From a climate perspective, lands stripped of vegetation have lost the potential to store carbon. Landscape that retain year-round vegetative cover in strategically selected areas and natural habitat cover in critical riparian areas can maintain most, if not all, of various watershed functions, even if much of the watershed is under productive uses.

With rapid growth in demand for water and with water scarcity looming in many countries (in part due to climate change), watershed revegetation should be getting serious policy attention. National programmes targeting millions of hectares of forests and grasslands for revegetating would serve as investments to reduce rural poverty and protect critical watersheds. In most cases, very low-cost methods could be used for revegetation, mainly temporary protection to enable natural vegetation to reestablish itself without threat of overgrazing or fire. On highly degraded soils, some cultivation or reseeding may be needed. Two keys to success in these approaches are to engage local communities in planning, developing, and maintaining watershed areas and to include rehabilitation of areas of high local importance, such as productive grazing lands, local woodfuel sources, and areas like gullies that can be used for productive cropping. Extending the scale of such efforts could have major climate benefits, with huge advantages as well for water security, biodiversity, and rural livelihoods.

Reestablish forest and grassland cover in biological corridors: Loss and fragmentation of natural habitat are leading threats to biodiversity. Conservation biologists have concluded that in many areas conservation of biodiversity will require the establishment of "biological corridors" through production landscapes, to connect fragments of natural habitat and protected areas and to give species access to adequate territory and sources of food and water. One key strategy is to reestablish forest or natural grassland cover (depending on the ecosystem) to play this ecological role. These reforestation efforts also have major climate benefits.

In a country's highly threatened Forest, for example, conservation organisations working in the National or State Park can strike a deal with dairy farmers to provide technical assistance to improve dairy-farm productivity in exchange for the farmers reforesting part of their land and maintaining it as a conservation easement. Milk yields will increase and farmers' income be doubled, while a strategic buffer zone would be established for the park.

Market Incentives for Climate-friendly Agriculture and Land Use

All the strategies described in the preceding sections are well within technological reach at far lower cost than many climate solutions such as geological storage of carbon. The challenge is shifting policy and investment priorities and supporting institutions to create incentives for farmers, pastoralists, forest owners, agribusiness, and all other stakeholders within the agriculture and forestry supply chains to scale up best practices and continue to innovate new ones. This will require concerted action by consumers, farmers' organisations, the food industry, civil society, and governments.

The Central players in any response to climate change are the farmers and communities—those who actually manage land—and the food and fiber industry that shapes the incentives for the choice of crops, quality standards, and profitability. Some innovators are already showing the way. For example, the Sustainable Food Lab, a collaborative of 70 businesses and social organisations from throughout the world, has assembled a team of member companies, university researchers, and technical experts to develop and test ways to measure and provide incentives for low-carbon agricultural practices through the food supply chain, mainly by increasing soil organic matter, improving fertilizer application, and enhancing the capacity of crops and soil to store carbon.

A key driver is consumer and buyer awareness. Consumers will take the needed steps once they realize that their choice of meat and dairy products, and their support for natural forests and grassland protection, can have as great an impact on the climate as how far they drive their cars. One immediate action is for consumers, processors, and distributors to adopt greenhouse gas footprint analysis for food and fiber products, addressing their full "life cycle", including production, transport, refrigeration, and packaging, to identify strategic intervention points.

GHG impact is a key metric that can be used for evaluating new food and forest production technologies and for allocating resources and investments. Policymakers can then include incentives for reducing carbon emissions in cost structures throughout the food and land use systems, using various market and policy mechanisms.

Product markets are also beginning to recognize climate values. The last 20 years have seen the rise of a variety of "green" certified products beyond organic, such as "bird-friendly" and "shade-grown," that have clear biodiversity benefits. Various certification options already exist for cocoa and coffee (through the Rainforest Alliance, Starbucks, and Organic, for example). The Forest Stewardship Council's certification principles "prohibit conversion of forests or any other natural habitat" and maintain that "plantations must contribute to reduce the pressures on and promote the restoration and conservation of natural forests," supporting the use of forests as carbon sinks. The rise of carbon emission offset trading could potentially provide a major new source of funding for the transition to climate-friendly agriculture and land use.

Public Policies to Support the Transition

Governments can take specific steps immediately to support the needed transition by integrating agriculture, land use, and climate action programmes at national and local landscape levels. Costa Rica is a leader in these efforts. The government has committed to achieving "climate neutrality" by 2021, with an ambitious agenda including mitigation through land use change. Costa Rica is a participant in the Coalition for Rainforest Nations, a group encouraging avoided-deforestation programmes, and has already increased its forest cover from 21 per cent in 1986 to 51 per cent in 2006. The country is taking advantage of markets that make payments for ecosystem services and ecotourism to support these efforts.

Currently, governments spend billions of dollars each year on agricultural subsidy payments to farmers for production and inputs, and most of these payments exacerbate chemical use, the expansion of cropland to sensitive areas, and overexploitation of water and other resources while distorting trade and reinforcing unsustainable agricultural practices. Some countries are beginning to redirect subsidy payments to agri-environmental payments for all kinds of ecosystem services, and these can explicitly include carbon storage or emissions reduction.

Growth in commercial demand for agricultural and forest products from increased populations and incomes in developing countries and demand for biofuels in industrial nations is stimulating investments by both private and public sectors. In 2003, African governments committed to increase public investment in agriculture to at least 10 per cent a year, although only Rwanda and Zambia have done this so far. The World Bank and the Bill & Melinda Gates Foundation have committed to large increases in funding in the developing world. There is a major window of opportunity right now to put climate change adaptation and mitigation at the core of these strategies.

Paying farmers and land managers to reduce carbon emissions or store greenhouse gases is a critical way to both mitigate climate change and generate ecosystem and livelihood benefits. The carbon market for land use has three main components: carbon emissions offsets for the regulatory market as established by the Kyoto Protocol; offset activities in emerging U.S. regulatory markets operating outside the Kyoto Protocol; and the sale of voluntary carbon offsets coming from land use, land use change, and forestry, primarily to individual consumers, philanthropic buyers, and the private sector.

Paying farmers and land managers to reduce carbon emissions or store GHG is a critical way to both mitigate climate change and generate ecosystem and livelihood benefits. The developing countries can implement afforestation and reforestation projects that count toward emission reduction targets of industrial countries through the Clean Development Mechanism of the Kyoto Protocol. The treaty authorizes afforestation and reforestation but excludes agricultural or forestry management, avoided deforestation and degradation, and soil carbon storage. However, each CDM project must address thorny issues of nonpermanence of carbon uptake by vegetation and soil, risks of potential displacement of emissions as deforestation just moves elsewhere, and sustainable development prospects in the host country that can limit implementation.

A great deal can be done in the short term through the voluntary carbon market, but in the long run it will be essential for the international framework for action on climate change to fully incorporate agriculture and land use.

There are several ongoing initiatives in developed countries to promote diverse types of land-use-based payment (Scherr and Franzel, 2002; Worldwatch Institute, 2009). These initiatives are lessons for African governments and non-governmental organisations (NGOs) to adopt:

1. The World Bank's $91.9-million BioCarbon Fund is financing afforestation, reforestation, REDD, agroforestry, and agricultural and

ecosystem-based projects that not only promote biodiversity conservation and poverty alleviation but also sequester carbon.

2. The Regional Greenhouse Gas Initiative in the northeastern United States includes afforestation and methane capture from U.S. farms.
3. The trading system in New South Wales, Australia—the world's first—provides for carbon sequestration through forestry, including onfarm forest regeneration.
4. The New Zealand government is investing more than $175 million over five years in a Sustainable Land Management and Climate Change Plan to help the agriculture and forestry sectors adapt to, mitigate, and take advantage of the business opportunities of climate change. This scheme include specific cap-and-trade allocations to the dairy sector and incorporate cash grants to encourage new plantings by landowners, increased research funding, technology transfer, and incentives to use more wood products and bio-energy.
5. Rabobank, the world's largest agricultural financier, paid farmers $83,000 to reforest, which will be sold as carbon offsets; the bank intend to use some of these credits to offset its own activities. This is the first transaction of its kind in Brazil's Xingu province, which has the country's highest deforestation rates.

International initiatives to address the interlinked challenge of climate, agriculture and land use are needed in Africa. In other wards, much larger initiatives are needed now to link carbon finance with investments to achieve rural food security by "re-greening" degraded watersheds, promoting agroforestry, restoring soil organic matter, rehabilitating degraded pastures, controlling fires, or protecting threatened forests and natural areas important for local livelihoods. If low-income landowners and managers are to benefit from payments for ecosystem services, they need secure rights, clear indicators of performance, and systems for aggregating buyers and sellers to keep transaction costs low.

A networked movement for climate-friendly food, forest, and other landbased production is needed. This calls for forging unusual political coalitions that link consumers, producers, industry, investors, environmentalists, and communicators. This is beginning to happen in small steps in a country like Brazil, which has began crafting a diverse set of investment programmes to support rural land users who invest in land use change for climate change mitigation and adaptation. The U.N. Environment Programme is initiating dialogues on "greening" the international response to the food crisis, linking goals of international environmental conventions with the Millennium Development Goals (UNDP, 2003).

But much more comprehensive action is needed in Africa. If not, this otherwise positive trend could seriously undermine climate action programmes. A new vision is needed to respond to food crisis and also put the developing countries on a trajectory toward sustainable, climate-friendly food systems.

National policy, however, is not enough. It is essential to invest in building capacity at local levels to manage ecoagricultural landscapes—to enable multi-stakeholders platforms to plan, implement, and track progress in achieving climate-friendly land use systems that benefit local people, agricultural production, and ecosystems.

REFERENCES

Adams, W.M and M.J. Mortimore, 1997. Agricultural Intensification and Flexibility in the Nigerian Sahel. The Geographical Journal 163: 150-160.

Asadu, C.L.A., Ezeaku, P.I. and G.U. Nnaji, 2004. "The Soils of Sub-Saharan Africa and Management Needs for Sustainable Farming". Chapter 1 in: Strategies and Tactics of Sustainable Agriculture in the Tropics – STASAT. (Badejo M.A. and Togun A.O., ds). Published by College Press and Publishers Ltd, Ibadan in Collaboration with ENPROCT CONSULTANTS, Lagos. Vol. 2 Pages 1-27.

Ayuk, E.T., 1997. Adoption of Agroforestry Technology: The Case of Live Hedges in the Central Plateau of Burkina Faso. Agricultural Systems 54: 189-206.

Butt T, B. McCarl, B.J. Angeret, P. Dyke, J. Stutt, 2003. Food Security Implication of Climate Change in Developing Countries: Findings from a Case Study in Mali. Department of Agricultural Economics, Texas A & M University.

Camberlin, P., Diop, M., 2003. Application of Daily Rainfall Principal Component Analysis to the Assessment of the Rainy Season Characteristics in Senegal. Climate Research, 23: 159-169.

DMC, 1995. Natural Disaster: Causes and Effects. Lesson 7: Drought Management Centre, University of Wisconsin. http://dmc.engrwisc.edu/courses/hazards/BB02-07.html

De Rouw, A. 2004. Improving Yields and Reducing Risks in Pearl Millet Farming in the African Sahel. Agricultural Systems 81: 73-93.

Ezeaku, P.I, 2009. Climate Change and Adaptation Strategies: Implications for Sustainable Agricultural Development in Sahel and Sub-humid Areas of Africa. Essay Submitted in Partial Fulfillment of the Award of Certificate of UNU-IC: GCS Course (IC820): Global Climate Change and Sustainability. United Nations University, UN House, Tokyo, Japan, June, 2009.

FAO, 2007. Agriculture and CC – Challenges and Opportunities. http://www.climatechangeprogramme.org/features/article/agri-an-climate Assessed 9th May, 2009.

Hengsdijk, H and H. Van Keulen. 2002. The Effect of Temporal Variation on Inputs and Output of Future Oriented Land Use Systems in West Africa. Agriculture, Ecosystems and Environment 91: 245-259.

Hulme, M. 2001. Climate Perspectives on Sahelian Dessication: 1973-1998. Global Environmental Change 11: 19-29.

Ingram, K.T., Roncoli, M.C., Kirshen, P.H., 2002. Opportunities and Constraints for Farmers of West Africa to Use Seasonal Precipitation Forecasts with Burkina Faso as a Case Study. Agricultural Systems 74: 331-349.

IITA, 1986. IITA Annual Report for 1986. International Institute for Tropical Agriculture, Ibadan, Nigeria.

Lal, R. 2004. Soil Carbon Sequestration Impacts on Global Climate Change and Food Security. Science Vol. 304, No. 5677; pp. 1623-1627.

Lal, R. 1974. No-tillage Effects on Soil Properties and Maize Production in Western Nigeria. Plant and Soil 40: 589-606.

Mazzucato, V., Niemeijer, D., 2000. Rethinking Soil and Water Conservation in a Changing Society. A Case Study in Eastern Burkina Faso. Tropical Resource Mangement Papers, Vol. 32, Wageningen.

Mendelsohn, R., Dinar, A. and Dalfelt, A. 2000. Climate Change Impacts on African Agriculture, Mimeo, Yale University.

Mortimore, M.J., Adams, W.M., 1999. Working the Sahel: Environmental and Society in Northern Nigeria. Routledge, London.

Mortimore, M.J., Adams, W.M., 2001. Farmer Adaptation, Change and 'Crisis' in the Sahel. Global Environmental Change 11: 49-57.

Ohiri, A.C and H.C Ezumah, 1990. Tillage Effects on Cassava (*Manihot esculenta*) Production and Some Soil Properties. Soil and Tillage Research 17: 221-229.

Ong, C.K. and Leakey, R.R.B.: (1999), 'Why Tree Crop Interactions in Agroforestry Appear at Odds with Treegrass Interactions in Tropical Savannahs', *Agroforestry Systems* 45: 109-129.

Pasternak, D., Nikiema, A., Fatondji, D., Ndjeunga, J., Koala, S., Dan Goma, A. and Abasse T., 2005. The Sahelian Eco-Farm. In: G. Omanya and D. Pasternak (eds). *Sustainable Agriculture Systems for the Drylands*. ICRISAT, Patancheru, pp. 286-296.

Reenberg, A., 2001. Agricultural Land Use Pattern Dynamics in the Sudan–Sahel – Towards an Event-driven Framework. Land Use Policy 18: 309-319.

Reenberg, A., Nielsen, T.L., Rasmussen, K., 1998. Field Expansions and Reallocations in a Desert Margin Region Land Use Pattern Dynamics in a Fluctuating Biophysical and Socio-economic Environment. Global Environmental Change 8: 309-327.

Reilly et al 1997. CC and Agricultural Trade: Who Benefits, Who Losses. Global Environmental Change 4(1): 24-36.

Roncoli, M.C., Ingram, K.T., Kirshen, P.H., 2002. Reading the Rains: Local Knowledge and Rainfall Forecasting Among Farmers of Burkina Faso. Society and Natural Resources 15: 411-430.

Scherr, S.J. and Franzel, S., 2002. Promoting New Agroforestry Technologies: Policy Lessons from On-farm Research. In: S. Franzel and S.J. Scherr (eds): Trees on the Farm – Assessing the Adoption Potential of Agroforestry Practices in Africa. CABI Pulishing, CAB International, Wallingford Oxon OX10 8 DE, UK, 1997 pp.

UNDP, 2003. Human Development Report 2003. Millennium Development Goals: a Compact Among Nations to End Human Poverty. 367 pp.

Warren, A., 2002. Land Degradation is Contextual. Land Degrad. Develop. 13: 449-459.

World Conference on Natural Disaster Reduction. 1994. «Disasters Around the World—A Global and Regional View. » Information Paper #4, Yokohama, Japan, 23-27 May.

World Agroforestry Centre (ICRAF) and UN Environmental Programme (UNEP) 2006 Report on "Climate Change and Variability in the Sahel Regions: Impacts and Adaptation Strategies in the Agricultural Sector" Website: http: / / www.unep.org / Themes / Freshwater / doc / Sourced 5th June, 2009.

CHAPTER

Evaluating Soil Fertility and Degradation Rates as Influenced by Land Use Change, Management and Catenary Sequence in North South Eastern Nigeria

Peter. I. Ezeaku[1]*; Ben O. Unagwu[2]

ABSTRACT

Most food crops are grown under rain-fed conditions and in an upland-inland continuum in North SE Nigeria. Increase in population has given rise to increase in land use change, decline in land per capita; and soil degradation that plays major role on decline in soil fertility, nutrient balance, soil quality and productivity of the toposequence. Since soil varies considerably from place to place and its characterization is fundamental to the understanding of soil-landscape processes, a study to detect changes in soil fertility parameters as influenced by land use change and management along the toposequence in the area becomes quite vital.

The present study aims to ascertain the influence of modification to land use and management on associated soil fertility parameters along the catenary sequence. Thirty soil samples were collected in 4 categories of

1. United Nations University Institute for Natural Resources in Africa (UNU-INRA) University of Ghana, Legon, Accra.
2. Department of Soil Science, University of Nigeria, Nsukka.

* **Permanent address:** Department of Soil Science, University of Nigeria, Nsukka.

land use (forest, grassland, fallow and cropped area – annual and plantation crops). Analytical characteristics of the samples were determined and subjected to statistical analysis using SAS. Soil properties, catenary sequence, land use types and management were statistically correlated. Degradation rate of selected soil properties were determined. Results revealed that land use types were located under up-, mid- and low-land physiographies with different management practices. Soil properties varied within these land uses.

Soil bulk density correlation with slope position and management was insignificant but highly significant ($P<0.001$) with land use. Ksat was highest in the upland and midlands and least at the valley bottoms. It was not influenced by either management or land use. The amount of soil organic carbon (SOC) sequestered showed a range from18.1 to 12.5 g/kg, an indication of decline down slope. SOC was not influenced by management ($p=0.184$) and land use ($p=0.252$) but slope position ($P<0.001$). Soil organic nitrogen levels followed similar pattern to that of SOC. CEC values ranged from high (>12cmol/kg) under forest and banana/plantain intercrop, through medium (8-10 cmol/kg) under bush fallow and annuals to low (7cmol/kg) under grasslands. For all slope positions, highest SDR (16.1) was found under grassland soils and least value (SDR = 11.0) obtained under forest soils. Low SDR implies better soil and vice versa for high SDR. Analysis showed that SDR was influenced by slope position as highest SDR (13.8) was found on foot slope and lower SDR at mid- (12.6) and up- (12.9) slopes, indicating greater management requirements for lower slope soils.

Keywords: soil fertility, degradation, land use change, management, catena.

INTRODUCTION

Agriculture plays vital role in the economy of Nigeria, because it contributes to the economic and social well being of the nation through the influence on the gross domestic product (GDP), employment and foreign exchange earnings. Agricultural development is desired because the current race between increasing population and food supply is a real grim.

Land misuse and soil mismanagement, resulting from a desperate attempt by farmers to increase production of food, fibre, fuel wood and feeds for the growing population, has given rise to decline in land per capita, exercabated soil degradation with severe impacts on soil fertility and productivity (Ezeaku, 2011). Decline in soil productivity, especially in cultivated soils; lead to decline in crop yields and it is wide evident. Amana *et al.* (2012) have shown that reduction of crop yields are a major concern in those regions where the attainment of food security is closely related with soil degradation due to nutrient mining. This has posed a great threat to the ability of the nation to support growing rural and urban populations (Ezeaku *et al.*, 2008). Figure 6.1 demonstrates the nexus between land use, productivity and population.

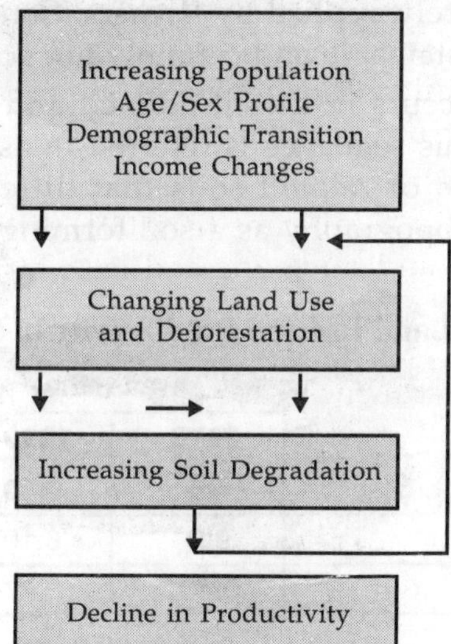

Fig. 6.1: Relationship Between Population, Land Use Change and Productivity

In North southeastern Nigeria, most food crops are produced under rain-fed conditions in an upland-inland continuum. Greater proportions of farmers practice low external-input agriculture (LEIA). On the faces of demographic and environmental pressures and changes in social and political circumstances, this traditional systems are being disrupted (Udoh *et al.*, 2002), particularly when its use is intensified and indiscriminate.

Under LEIA, the choice of land use, allocation and management may not necessarily reflect proper and adequate practices. This problem is further compounded by constraints such as financial status of the farmers, information asymmetry as regards soil properties, suitability and capabilities, etc. This situation has culminated in persistent food crisis in Nigeria as gap between population and food production continue to widen (Udoh et al., 2002). In an effort to increase food production, LEIA depends primarily on expansion of cultivated area at the expense of restorative bush fallow, thereby causing a considerable decline in the length of the cultivation cycle in slash and burn cultivation.

Cultivation over time affects the physical, chemical and biological characteristics of soils. These three characteristics are taken as measures of soil quality, which severally has been defined but centrally reflect the capability to sustain plant and animal productivity, maintain or enhance water and air quality, and promotes plant and animal health (Karlen *et al.*, 1997; NRC, 1993).

In densely populated areas, marginal lands and forest reserves are encroached for crop crop cultivation. Sustainable management practices such as reduced tillage, residue management; proper crop rotations and judicious use of fertilizers through integrated nutrient management (INM) improve soil fertility but are rarely applied by farmers. Consequently, LEIA in most cases is always not sustainable and certainly not economical.

Soil frequently occurs in a well defined and fairly regular sequence related to relief and this sequence is referred to as toposequence, which is defined as a sequence of related soils that differs, one from the other, primarily because of topography as a soil forming factor (Okunsami *et al.*, 1997).

Table 6.1a: Trends in Land Use and Productivity in the Tropics – 1970 to 1999

Land Use	Area (Mha)		Yield ($Kgha^{-1}$)	
	1970	1999	1970	1999
Arable and permanent crops	4.9	6.80	–	–
Forests	9.2	6.10	–	–
Maize	0.26	0.27	821	747

Source: FAO (1970, 1999)

Toposequence could also be described as landforms which occur as catenary sequence (physiography) and developed from the same parent materials in the same climate but under different topographical conditions owing to variation in relief and drainage.

Toposequences in North southeastern Nigeria are heterogeneous in morphology (physiography), soil type, vegetation, hydrology, and agronomic practice. Soil landscape relationships can influence the properties of soils through the summits to the foot slopes and this can be related to soil formation and erosion processes (Ezeaku and Anikwe, 2005).

Evaluation report of the changes in soil properties and productivity along a toposequence has been made elsewhere (USDA, 1996; Mojiri, *et al*, 2011), but the effects of catenary sequence, land use change and management on soil fertility variables under different land use types in Nsukka of north southeastern Nigeria have not received the desired research attention.

The specific objectives are to: *(i)* quantify the amount of soil fertility properties sequestered under different land uses on a hillslope ecosystem; *(ii)* ascertain effects of land use change, management and catenary sequence on soil properties; *(iii)* examine soil property-management-toposequence inter-relationships; and *(iv)* determine soil degradation rates for some measured soil properties, land use types and slope position.

The intended benefits of the study were to provide background assessment that will enhance knowledge of the soil degradation under different conditions of land use as an aid in the rehabilitation through proper management practices of the soils in a fragile soil-landscape continuum; and to further contribute to effective utilization of soil landscape ecologies so as to boost the nation's food production capacity and income growth.

MATERIALS AND METHOD

Site Description

Nigeria is located in the western part of Africa. Nsukka located in Enugu State is situated in north southeastern Nigeria (Fig. 6.2) by latitude 06°51^{1N} and longitude 07°24^{1}E with an elevation of 447.2 m above sea level (Okoibom and Asiegbu, 2006). The area is characterized by a humid tropical climate with wet (April- October) and dry (November-March) seasons, and a mean annual rainfall of 1750 mm bimodally distributed with peaks in July and September; mean annual maximum (day) and minimum (night) temperatures of 31°C and 21°C respectively (UNN Meteorological Station, 2010). The relative humidity ranges between 70 per cent and 80 per cent during the short harmattan period (between December and January) when temperature falls below 22°C.

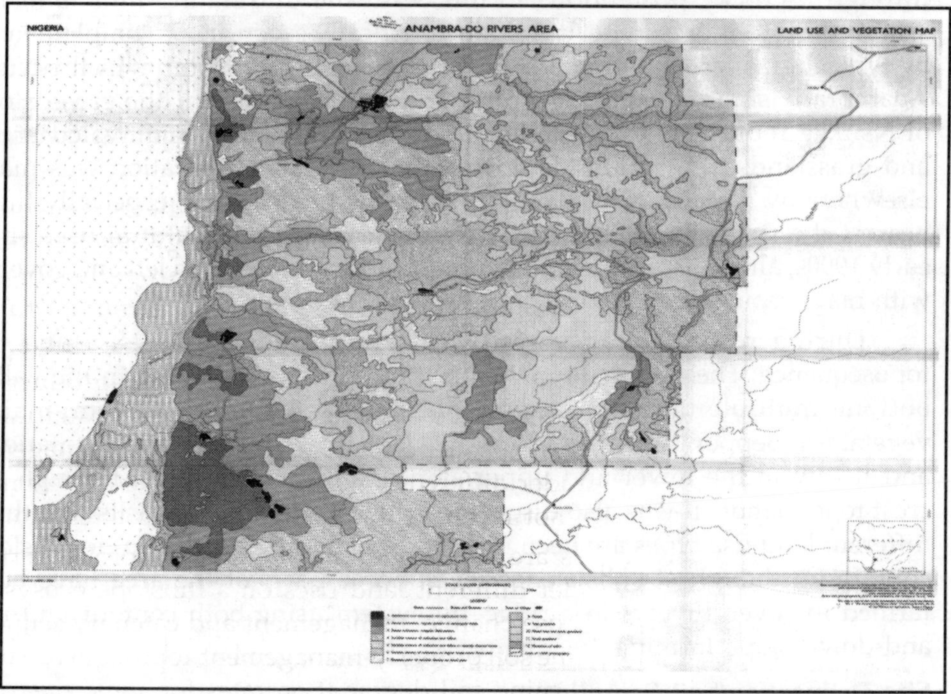

Fig. 6.2: Land Use and Vegetation Map of Anambra-Do River Area, Nigeria

[*Source:* Bawden, 1963: www.eusoils.jrc.ec.europa.eu]

The soils of North SE Nigeria are made up of shallow and stony lithosols found on the slopes of the cuesta and often left uncultivated as typical grassland. The ferrallitic soil, also called red Earth or Acid sands, are found on the plateau, and the hydromorphic soils on the floodplains (www.google.com/Online Nigeria, 2003). The soil color matrix of the mid- and upper-slopes is deep red to brownish red and derived from sandy deposits of false bedded sandstone. They are well-drained ferallitic sandy clay loam classified at the order level as Ultisol and sub-order of Typic kandiusult (Ezeaku, 2000). Lower slopes are reddish brown to brownish black in an order of Alfisol and sub-group of Typic Kandiaquults (Soil Survey Staff, 1999).

Geomorphology/Vegetation/Land Uses

The geomorphology of NSE Nigeria is of the highlands stretching through the undulating hills to plain lands. The vegetation is characteristically Derived savanna (Savanna-mosaic) agroecology, which represents different land uses such as forestry, cultivated areas, and grasslands in a soil-landscape system.

The vegetation on the highlands of southeastern Nigeria and stretching through its rocky promotions to link with the undulating hills is of the semitropical rainforest type. It is characteristically green and is complemented by typical grassy vegetation. Fresh water swamp forest occurs in the Niger Anambra Basin (www.eusoils.jrc.ec.europa.eu) (Fig. 6.2). The agro-ecology of Nsukka represents different land uses such as forestry, cultivated areas, and grasslands in a soil-landscape system. Similar observation was made elsewhere by Neris *et al.* (2012) (Fig. 6.3). The green forest, especially those nearest the small populated parts, were cleared for agricultural uses since early 1990s, although a large number of these have since been left and covered with herbaceous plants and grasses as bush fallow.

During reconnaissance visits, different land uses exist along the toposequence. These include low land traditional rice farming in the valley bottom; multiple (annual) cropping (cassava, plantain, cocoyam, maize, vegetables, pepper, melon seed and beans); citrus and oil palm plantations, and fallow in the lower and upper slopes; and natural forest through the crest to lowlands. It was also discovered during preliminary visits that these different land use types are been utilized over decades in the up-down slope continuum though at subsistence level. Some parts of the area have been farmed for over 15years in a ridge–till system using both contour and up-and-down slope farming.

Site Delineation/Soil Sampling

The length of each hill to foot slope in this study was delineated following the categorization approach by Brubaker *et al.* (1994). Slopes on the site therefore were demarcated into different physiographic units and slope shapes; upper slope (US) (convex), middle slope (MS) (convex) and foot slope (FS) (concave) landscape position (Fig. 6.4).

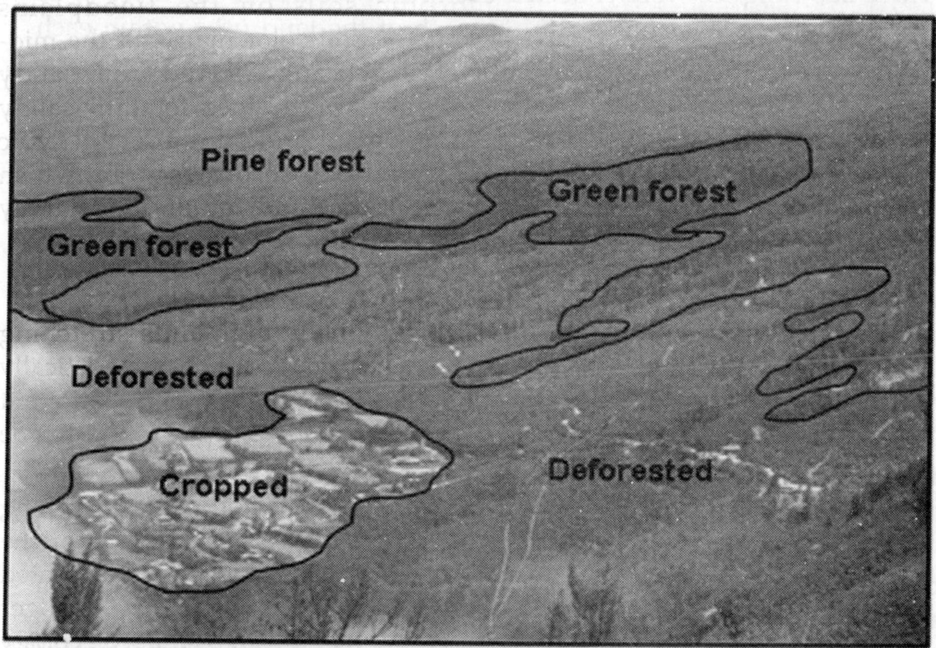

Fig. 6.3: Vegetation Distribution and Land Use (Neris *et al.*, 2012) Typical of the Study Area

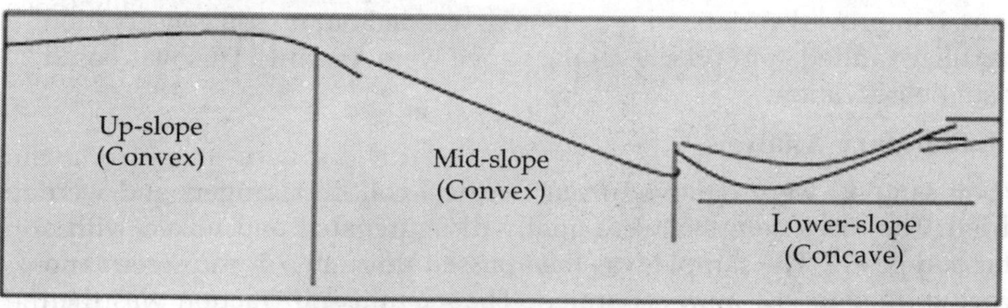

Fig. 6.4

Two transects (1 and 2) were established on the physiographic units. Transect1 was 126 m long with 8 m intervals, while Transect 2 was 98 m long with 6 m intervals. These two transects constituted the sampling sites. Sampling was conducted along the catenary sequence with techniques that ensure that soil types were comparable.

Soil Sampling/Laboratory Analysis

(a) Soil Sampling

Three sub-samples were collected each from the upper soil layer (0-20 cm) and sub-surface layer (20-40 cm) on each of the land uses within each transect and were then mixed to obtain a homogenous sample. The depths (0-40 cm) were chosen because most arable and vegetable crops are surface feeders and zone where most changes are expected to occur. Auger with an internal diameter of 86 mm was used along the same two transects in October 2009, and again in September 2010 and September 2011. For the 3 crop years, a total of thirty samples were collected with augers at 8 m intervals for the 126 m long Transect 1, and at 6 m intervals for 98 m long Transect 2 cutting across all land use types. Also soil core ring (of a known volume - 96.6 cm^3) samples was taken randomly from undisturbed soils at 0-10 cm depth for soil bulk density and soil saturated hydraulic conductivity (Ksat) determinations.

Prior to sampling, the cylinder was fitted with a dolly that protected the rim from being distorted and enabled the corer to be driven easily into the ground with a sledge hammer until it was flush with the soil surface.

At each sampling point, information on the level of management was collected from a mini survey of the farmers in the study area. The level of management was considered to be high if the field was weeded, mulched (to conserve moisture and control erosion), or pruned with application of integrated pest management (IPM) (in case of plantation trees) or if improved varieties were planted, weeded and fertilizer added (for cultivated crops); medium if improved varieties were planted, weeded but no soil conservation and fertilizer added, and poor if all the above were missing. This was based on visual observation.

(b) Laboratory Analysis

Soil samples were removed from the steel collection augers and were air dried. The dried samples were gently disaggregated and mixed with a mortar and pestle. The sample was then passed through a 2-mm screen and the coarse fraction (>2 mm) separated. The <2 mm soil fraction was then ground in a mill to a fine powder. All samples were stored in suitable polythene receptacles.

The analytical characteristics of the soil samples were determined in the following manner.

The percentage by weight of gravel, sand, silt, and clay (particle size diameter <2 mm) were obtained by hydrometer method (Gee and Bauder, 1986). The hydrometer method of silt and clay measurement relies on the effects of particle size on the differential vertical velocities of the particles through a water column (i.e. the sedimentation rate). Sedimentation rate is dependent upon the liquid temperature, viscosity, and the diameter and specific gravity of the falling soil particles.

Soil was dispersed into individual particles after pretreatment with hydrogen peroxide to destroy the organic matter, and addition of sodium hexametaphosphate solution to aid dispersion, then dispersed throughout a water column and allowed to settle. Hydrometer measurements quantified the amount of material remaining in suspension at specific time intervals. This was then related to the amounts of sand, silt and clay in the soil.

Soils on an undisturbed cylindrical core (volume 96.6 cm^3) taken at field-moisture conditions were measured for bulk density on an oven-dried weight basis, and particle density with a pycnometer (Blake and Hartge, 1986).

Soil saturated hydraulic conductivity (Ksat) determination was based on method by Klute and Dickson (1986), in which an undisturbed core sample was collected and saturated over night and mounted on the retort stand after saturation to measure the rate of water drip at consistent hydraulic head of 5 cm. When about three consecutive constant readings are obtained, it is used to calculate the hydraulic conductivity of the soil using an empirical model:

$$\text{Ksat} = \frac{Q \times dz \times 60}{\text{At DH}}$$

Where: Ksat = saturated hydraulic conductivity (cm/s); Q = volume of water obtained (cm^3); T = time; DH = water head; A = Cross sectional area (cm/s), and Dz = height of the core sample (cm)

Soil pH was determined in duplicate both in distilled water and in 0.1N KCl solution, using a soil/liquid ratio of 1:2.5. After stirring for 30 minutes, the pH value was read off using a glass electrode pH meter (Mclean, 1982). Organic carbon (OC) was obtained by the wet dichromate acid oxidation method (Nelson and Sommers, 1982); percentage organic matter was calculated by multiplying the value for organic carbon by the "Van Bermenalen factor" of 1.724, which is based on the assumption that soil organic matter contains 58 per cent Carbon (Alison, 1982).

Total nitrogen was determined using the kjeldhal distillation method as described by Bremmer (1996). The ammonia from the digestion was distilled with 45 per cent NaOH into 25 per cent boric acid and determined by titrating 0.05N KCl.

Available phosphorus was obtained using Bray 11 bicarbonate extraction method as described by Olsen and Sommers (1982). Many extraction techniques for plant-available phosphate have been developed. The modified Olsen extractant is convenient for routine use.

Exchangeable basic cations (Ca, mg, Na and K) were extracted in ammonium acetate (NH_4OA), calcium and magnesium were determined using ethylene diamine tetraacetic acid (EDTA) titration method while potassium and sodium were determined colorimetrically using flame photometer (Rhoade, 1982a). Cation exchange capacity was determined titrimetically using 0.01 N NaOH.

Soil Degradation Rating (SDR)

SDR was determined as a function of SOC, soil bulk density, Ksat, soil texture, rooting depth and soil pH. These properties were weighted as proposed by Lal (1994) with a scale of 1 to 5 (Table 6.1b). A weight of 1 was given when there was no limitation and five was given when the limitation was extreme. In this way, good soils had the least SDR and poor soils had the highest.

Table 6.1b: Rating Scheme for Soil Degradation Rating

Limitation	Relative Weighting Factor
None	1
Slight	2
Moderate	3
Severe	4
Extreme	5

Source: Lal (1994)

Determining the SDR of the selected soil parameters was based on the established critical limits of soil elements from various literatures (Akinrinde and Obigbesan, 2000; Enwezor *et al.*, 1989). The critical limits of some soil properties where crop yield is 80 per cent of the maximum yield was adopted from Aune and Lal (1997) (Table 6.1c).

Table 6.1c: Critical Limits of Soil Properties for Selected Crops

Soil Property	Crop					
	Maize	Groundnut	Cowpea	Sweet Potato	Cassava	Soya bean
Bulk density Mgm^{-3}	1.5	1.39	1.39		1.5	1.39
SOC %	1.08					
pH	5	5.1	4.7			5.1
Al-saturation %	23.5	48.6	38.8	32.4	70.8	20.8
P(mg/kg)	7.6				8.6	10.6
K^+ mmol/kg	0.83		0.7			0.7
Rooting depth (cm)	23	23	22	23	23	22

Source: Aune and Lal (1997).

Statistical Analysis

Data generated was subjected to analysis using SAS (2000). Correlation analysis was carried out to determine the associations between soil fertility variables and the toposequence slopes. The least significant difference ($LSD_{0.05}$) was used to determine the differences between different land use management practices (Hoshmand, 1994) based on the several soil physical and chemical properties.

RESULTS AND DISCUSSION

Soil Physical Properties

The result showed that soil texture varied at the three slope positions and ranged from sandy loam to sandy clay loam. Clay content varied from 8.4 per cent (upslope) through 14.5 per cent (midslope) to 22.6 per cent (downslope), indicating that clay increased down slope. This could be associated with deposition from the upland areas, culminating into enrichment of the lowland slopes due to precipitation event. Analysis reveals that soil texture was influenced more by slope position and not land use and management and could be due to time frame involved as changes are expected after a very long periods of time. In addition, management levels may change from season to season or year to year depending on availability of income, labor and other agro inputs.

Silt content had an opposite trend to sand. It varied from 7.3 per cent at the lower slope through 11.3 per cent (midslope) to 14.2 per cent at the upper slope, indicating more silt upslope. As upslope is a detachment area, it shows that erosion is a selective process and preferentially removes humus and clay fraction leaving the inert and coarse fragments behind. Preferential removal may explain the high clay content in the lower lands (depositional areas) and low clay content uplands (detachment areas).

The results of the present study show that infiltration related property of grass and cropped soils undergo modification when compared to the forest soils: specifically an increase in bulk density. Mean soil bulk density and soil saturated hydraulic conductivity data presented in Table 6.3 ranged from 1.27 MgM^{-3} (Forest upland slope) to 1.50 MgM^{-3} in Grassland foot slope. High mean bulk density values were observed in grassland use at all catenary sequences. Soil bulk density mean values obtained in forested and arable soils (Table 6.2) are below the critical minimum value (1.5 Mg m^{-3}) (Aune and Lal, 1997) capable of impeding crop root growth and development. Yield of crops could be depressed in soils of grassland with high mean bulk density (>1.5 Mg m^{-3}) above the critical limit.

At the uplands and footslopes, there was no difference in bulk density between the cultivated crops and the forest. At the midslope, the bulk density under cultivated (annual crops) was higher than the under forests but not different from other crops. High mean bulk density observed on grasslands could be due to soil compaction resulting from animal trampling while grazing. Also, grasslands were often located on shallow and sometimes stony soils that may not be used for other crop cultivation. This is consistent with Pando *et al.* (2004) who found higher soil bulk density in grasslands and rangelands compared to agricultural sites and attributed the high value to reduction in aggregate stability of soils. Hartemink *et al.* (2008) have shown that a decrease in organic matter and modification of its dynamics impacts negatively on aggregate formation.

Table 6.2: Mean Variation of Soil Bulk Density and Saturated Soil Hydraulic Conductivity with Land Use at the Three Catenary Sequences

Land Use	Bulk Density (Mgm^{-3})			Saturated Hydraulic Conductivity ($cmhr^{-1}$)		
	Upland	Mid Slope	Foot Slope	Upland	Mid Slope	Foot Slope
Forest	1.27a	1.24a	1.18a	2.52a	2.41a	2.38a
Annual crops	1.42a	1.36b	1.33a	3.51a	3.53b	3.56b
Grassland	1.61b	1.53c	1.50b	4.38b	4.47c	4.77c

Note: Mean values followed by the same letter within the same slope position are not statistically different at P = 0.05 level.

Analysis of soil bulk density showed that level of slope position (P = 0.024) and management (P=0.114) did not show significance but the level of land use that showed highly significant ($P<0.001$) effects. It was also discovered that when land use was dropped from the model, slope position did not show significance (P=0.238) but management level became highly significant ($P<0.001$). This shows a high interaction between the variables including those that seem not to be significant. This portends that management effects were masked by land use.

The mean soil saturated hydraulic conductivity (ksat) data ranged from 2.38 to 4.77 cm hr^{-1}. For a tropical soil, to which the study area belongs, this is moderate conductivity following Landon (1984) classification of very rapid (>12.5 $cmhr^{-1}$), rapid (8-12.5 $cmhr^{-1}$), moderately rapid (6-8 $cmhr^{-1}$), moderate (2-6 $cmhr^{-1}$), slow (0.8-2 $cmhr^{-1}$) and very slow (<0.8 $cmhr^{-1}$).

The Ksat was highest in the upland and midlands and least at the valley bottoms. Low water transmissions (infiltration) and hence low Ksat at the lower slopes could have been contributed by clay accumulation and siltation of the pedogenic horizons as well as presence of high water table. This finding corroborates those obtained by Tsui *et al.* (2004) who reported high runoff rates at the foot of a colluvial hillslope implying low infiltration. On the other hand, higher mean Ksat on grass land soils could be attributed to poor soil structural stability due to inadequate accumulation of organic carbon that could improve the soil structure.

Soil saturated hydraulic conductivity variation among slope positions was neither due to the influence by the level of management (which considered weeding, mulching - erosion control and moisture conservation) nor land use but slope position as the only significant factor affecting Ksat.

In general, some studies have shown other effects of land use change and catenary sequence on soil properties to include: (a) the destruction of organomineral complexes and the release of organic matter, which becomes exposed to oxidation (Verde *et al.*, 1993), modification of the soil moisture and temperature regimes (Cerda, 1998b). Nanzyo *et al.* (1993) further noted that isomesic or isothermic temperature regimes under forest vegetation become mesic or thermic under cropping, while the soils' udic moisture regime becomes ustic. In other words, the thermal contrasts increase, as do the wet and dry periods. This favors the irreversible drying with pore-size modification.

Soil Chemical Properties

The results of soil pH showed variation from 5.4 to 6.2 with Banana/ Plantain intercrop having highest mean value (6.2) and the lowest (5.4) under the grasslands. The high pH could be due to returning of crop residues after harvest, while low soil pH may be associated with leaching. Also amount and type of fertilizers normally used and the amount of leaching could contribute to low or high soil pH. Low value of soil pH in the grasslands than in cultivated soils was report by Steenwerth *et al.* (2002).

Soil organic carbon plays an important role in water holding capacity, soil structure and overall soil health (Mojiri *et al.*, 2011). However, the ability to sequester carbon in soil is influenced by the topography of an area in addition to the management practices, initial OC content, soil properties and land use changes (Senthil *et al.*, 2006).

The amounts of soil organic carbon (SOC) sequestered in different physiographic units with different land use types are presented in Table 6.3. The data ranged from 18.1 to 12.5g/kg, an indication of decline downslope. High SOC at the uplands may be associated to its flatness, a characteristic that may offer some natural protection from erosion and hence SOC accumulation. Also, it may be that the movement of SOC is not related to erosion processes because soil carbon concentration is an equilibrium concentration that is more related to hill slope position and carbon inputs both from upslope and the immediate area (Li *et al.*, 2007). They further showed that SOC may be a direct product of mineralization rates rather than being more strongly related to the material deposited and eroded due to enhanced erosion process on disturbed hill slope. Brubaker *et al.* (1993) made similar observation that vegetative grasses in the uplands could have provided cover that protected loss of top soil where most SOC is concentrated.

The result indicates that clay content increases exponentially with SOC. Therefore, high clay content observed on lower lands does not necessarily reflect high SOC seen on uplands. Ayanaba *et al* (1996) and Ayuba (2001) observed little variation in SOC due to clay content.

Table 6.3: Variation of mean SOC within the Catenary Sequence

Landscape Position	Mean SOC	$(SOC)^{-0.5}$	SE	Mean Difference	LSD (.05)	
Upslope	18.12	0.18c	0.0052	Foot-midslope	0.02	0.01
Midslope	15.07	0.20b	0.0029	Footslope-upland	0.03	0.02
Footslope	12.46	0.26a	0.0087	Midslope-upland	0.02	0.02

The result (Table 6.3) showed that SOC was not influenced by management ($p=0.184$) and land use ($p=0.252$) but slope position ($P<0.001$). Lack of differences in SOC between land uses may be the type of carbon stocks available and how it is sequestered in the soil. Ne'emeth *et al.* (1998) found no significant differences in SOC between native vegetation, pasture and plantation land uses in Australia. The highly significant ($P<0.001$) influence by slope position could be associated to minimal erosion phenomena.

Result of soil organic nitrogen (SON) showed a range between 0.96g.kg and 2.46 g/kg (Table 6.4).

Table 6.4: Mean Variation of Soil N (g/kg) Among Different Land Uses Within the Catenary Sequences

Land Use	Soil Organic Nitrogen (g/kg)		
	Upland	Mid Slope	Foot Slope
Forest	2.46a	2.11a	1.59a
Banana/Plantain	1.71a	1.44a	1.16a
Annual crops	1.50ab	1.34ab	1.08ab
Bush fallow	1.38b	1.30b	1.03b
Grassland	1.31b	1.23b	0.96b

Note: Figures followed by the same letter within the same slope position are not significantly different.

The SON level reflects a similar pattern to that of SOC and was corroborated by Kristensen *et al.* (2000). There were variations of SON within land uses, with the highest under forest, banana/plantain and cultivated annuals than others. The high N content under forest could be a result of nutrient recycling since the amount extracted gets returned to the soil as a litter.

Mulching as management practice may have contributed to high N under Banana/Plantain landuse.

When soil organic nitrogen (SON) was analyzed, it showed that it was highly influenced by slope position ($P<0.05$) and land use ($p=0.006$).

Exchangeable basic cations (Ca, Mg, K, Na)

Calcium data ranged from 2.4 to 3.9 cmol/kg. Critical values of 2.0, 0.4 and 0.20 Cmol kg^{-1} for Ca, Mg and K, respectively was reported by Akinrinde *et al.* (2000) in Nigeria. Following the level of Ca in the study, Ca^{2+} is not limiting under all land use types.

When the soil properties were regressed, the result (Table 6.5) showed that Ca^{+2} was influenced by slope position, management level and land use, though it increased with increasing levels of management regardless of the slope position. For the same level of management, exchangeable Ca was highest for upslope and least for the foot slope, indicating slope position had more influence on it than management level. High levels of management on bottom lands were not significantly different from poor levels of management on the uplands and poor management on the midslopes. Upslope and midslope differences were not statistically significant. For all slope positions, the medium and high level of management were not significantly different although they both had higher Ca^{+2} than the footslopes implying that minimal levels of management could result in increased Ca^{+2} levels. No significant differences were found between footlopes with medium slopes or uplands with poor management.

Table 6.5 shows that exchangeable Ca^{+2} varied with land use. Ca^{+2} variation was significantly ($P<0.05$) higher in grassland than cultivated areas and could be associated to high extraction by the grasses. Ayuba (2001) also reported reduced exchangeable Ca in grazed area.

Table 6.5: Comparison of Exchangeable Calcium Among Different Land Use Types

Pair Compared	Mean Difference	LSD (0.05)
Annuals-Banana/Plantain	0.412	0.562 ns
Annuals-Bush fallow	1.226	1.638 ns
Annuals-Grassland	2.240	1.011 *
Annuals-Forest	0.568	1.705 ns
Banana/Plantain-Bush fallow	1.570	1.498 *
Banana/Plantain-Grassland	2.508	0.882 *
Banana/Plantain-Forest	1.200	1.98 ns
Bush fallow-grassland	1.122	1.624 ns
Bush fallow-Forest	0.626	2.288 ns
Banana/Plantain - Bush fallow	2.237	1.549 *
Banana/Plantain - Grassland	3.160	1.148 *
Banana/Plantain - Forest	1.329	2.600 ns
Grassland - Forest	1.538	2.811 ns

Differences between bush fallow and the other land uses were not significant and this lack of variation may be due to fallowing land after it is completely exhausted.

No significant differences were found between Banana/Plantain intercrop and Forest, implying they had similar effect on soil Ca. Exchangeable Ca under all land uses did not vary significantly from the forested areas due to high variation observed under the forest areas.

Results of exchangeable potassium (K^+) varied from 0.17 to 0.42 cmol/kg, corresponding to higher mean K^+ values under forest and cultivated crops than grasslands (Table 6.6). Low K^+ in grasslands could be due to more extensive surface roots for moisture extraction. As grassland areas are mostly located on shallow soils used for grazing, K^+ is bound to decline with time. Leaching could also have contributed to the low K^+ values. Huluggale (1994) reported depleted K^+ values under grazed pasture in Nigeria.

Relationship between K^+ with land use types showed lack of effect by management and slope position but highly significantly ($P<0.01$) influenced by land use.

Table 6.6: Relationship Between Exchangeable K^+ with Land Use Types

Land Use	Exchangeable K ($cmolkg^{-1}$)
Forest	0.42a
Annuals	0.34a
Banana/Plantain	0.32a
Bush fallow	0.21ab
Grassland	0.14c

Note: Figures followed by the same letter within the same slope position are not significantly different.

Exchangeable Mg^{2+} data shows a variation between 0.42 and 2.23 cmol/kg (Table 6.7). The variation of Mg^{2+} content with land use type was similar at all slope positions. Mg^{2+} was highest in the forest followed by Banana/Plantain intercrop and annual crops. The least Mg^{2+} content was found under the grasslands and could be associated to leaching. High content of Mg^{2+} in other land uses could be attributed to litter falls. The results of low and high Mg^{2+} contents obtained in this study corroborates finding by Campo *et al* (2000) who found litter fall to account for 84 per cent Mg^{2+} in Mexico. Mg^{2+} was influenced by both land use and slope position and was higher at the upslope positions and low in the footslopes.

Table 6.7: Relationship Between Exchangeable Mg^{2+} with Land Use Types and Catena

Land Use	Exchangeable Mg^{2+} (cmol/kg)		
	Upland	Mid Slope	Foot Slope
Forest	2.341a	1.823a	1.156a
Annual crops	2.230a	1.621a	1.304a
Banana/Plantain	2.249a	1.726a	1.312a
Bush fallow	1.220b	0.962b	0.436b
Grassland	1.198bc	0.943bc	0.418bc

Note: Figures followed by the same letter within the same slope position are not significantly different.

Mean values of CEC showed lowest value (6.4cmol kg^{-1}) under grassland and highest value (14.2 cmol kg^{-1}) in forest landuse (Table 6.8). Soil CEC has been classified as low (< 6 Cmol kg^{-1}), medium (6-12 Cmol kg^{-1}) and high (> 12 Cmol kg^{-1}) for some Nigerian soils (Ojanuga and Awojuola, 1981). Mean CEC is of the following decreasing order: grassland soils (6.6cmol/kg) < Annuals (9.8 cmol/kg) < Bush fallow (8.2 cmol/kg)(medium class) < Banana/ Plantain intercrop and Forest (>12cmol/kg) considered high. Decrease in CEC suggests decrease in buffering capacity, and is a cause for concern as the land use types with low to medium CEC can be catalogued as unsustainable land use.

Table 6.8: Relationship Between CEC with Land Use Types

Land use	CEC (cmolkg^{-1})
Forest	14.2a
Annuals	9.8a
Banana/Plantain	12.7a
Bush fallow	8.21a
Grassland	6.4b

Note: Figures followed by the same letter within the same slope position are not significantly different.

Low CEC value of tropical soils is due to dominance of kaolinitic clays in the fine earth fraction (Ojanuga *et al.*, 1981). The CEC was not influenced by management and slope position but by land use. The CEC of a soil generally increases with soil pH (Spark, 1984). The low pH (5.4) obtained under grasslands could account for the low CEC of the soils. Low pH, CEC and organic matter imply decrease in biological activities, which has its own adverse effect on productivity of soils.

Phosphorus occurs in soils in both organic and inorganic forms. Inorganic forms are usually more important for crop nutrition (Enwezor *et al.*, 1989). Table 6.9 shows the data for extractable inorganic P. Mean values of P were in the range of 5.92 mg/kg to 16.2 mg/kg with the least obtained in grassland soils. Forest and Banana/Plantain intercrop had highest values.

Table 6.9: Relationship Between Exchangeable P under Different Land Use Types

Land use	Exchangeable P (mgkg^{-1})	Standard Error
Forest	16.18a	0.16
Annuals	9.51ab	0.09
Banana/Plantain	13.22a	0.14
Bush fallow	6.14c	0.16
Grassland	5.92c	0.19

Note: Figures followed by the same letter within the same slope position are not significantly different.

A critical range of 8 to 12 mgkg^{-1} P was reported for Nigerian soils (Enwezor *et al.*, 1989). This shows that except for Forest (16.2 mg/kg) and Banana/Plantain (13.2 mgkg^{-1}), all other land use types were P deficient. The high P availability, especially in Banana/Plantain intercrop soils could be attributed to higher organic materials from mulch materials used as management practice. Buerkert *et al.* (2000) found an increased P availability due to mulch materials in West Africa. In general, phosphorus deficiency in soils has been related to leaching by intense rainfall, high weatherability of the soils, presence of kaolinitic clay as the dominant mineral, and adsorption reaction by soil constituents (Enwezor *et al.*, 1989).

Soil Degradation Rating

Soil degradation rating for the measured soil properties are presented in Table 6.9a. The mean limitation for soil texture and soil organic carbon was moderate (SDR=3.0) and slight for pH (SDR=2.3) and none limiting (SDR=1.3) for soil bulk density eventhough it often poses extreme limitations on hill slopes.

Table 6.9a: Mean Soil Degradation Rating for the Measured Soil Properties

Soil Property	Minimum	Maximum	Mean	Standard Deviation	Standard Error
Soil texture	1.0	5.0	2.7	0.41	0.013
Bulk density	1.0	5.0	1.3	0.57	0.022
Ksat	1.0	5.0	1.2	0.51	0.018
Soil pH	1.0	5.0	2.3	1.30	0.043
SOC	1.0	4.0	2.9	0.27	0.011
SDR	8.0	24.0	10.4	2.36	0.082

Table 6.9b: Soil Degradation Rating Under Land Use Types and Toposequence

Land Use	Soil Degradation Rating (SDR)			
	Upland	Mid Slope	Foot Mean	Slope
Forest	10.6a	10.4a	11.9a	
Banana/Plantain	12.4a	12.2a	11.0a	
Annual crops	12.8ab	12.6ab	13.5a	12.7a
Bush fallow	14.2b	13.5b	14.6ab	
Grassland	17.8b	14.4b	13.3ab	
			15.4b	
			14.4b	
			16.2b	
			16.1b	

Note: Figures followed by the same letter within the same slope position are not significantly different.

The SDR values in Table 6.9b ranged from 10.4 to 17.8. For all slope positions, the highest SDR was found under grassland soils (mean SDR=16.1) and least (SDR=11.0) values obtained in forest. The SDR for banana/plantain intercrop and annual crop soils were intermediate. A low SDR implies a better soil. High SDR in grassland may be associated to a relatively long time it takes to recover the nutrients that are lost during cultivation. This could suggest the soil as of low quality. Sanchez *et al.* (2002) similarly found high degradation levels under grassland and attributed it to soil compaction, an increase in bulk density, low soil depth and high proportions of coarser aggregates in the top soil. The SDR was significant ($P<0.05$) with land use and slope position but not significant with management.

Table 6.9c: Variation of Soil Degradation Rating with Slope Position

Slope Position	Mean Soil Degradation Rating
Up land	12.9ab
Mid slope	12.4b
Foot slope	13.8a

Note: Figures followed by the same letter within the same slope position are not significantly different.

Interaction between SDR and land use types showed a low SDR in forest and banana/plantain intercrop, which can be associated to presence of high litter fall and mulching, hence no significant difference between them irrespective of slope position. Slightly high SDR in annuals relative to forest and banana/plantain intercrop may be due to continuous cultivation and poor protection at the beginning of the rainy season and when there is minimal cover.

The relationship between SDR and slope indicated that SDR was influenced by slope position. Highest SDR was found at the foot slope followed by upslope and lowest at mid slope (Table 9c), though the SDR at the bottom slope was not significant from that of the upland slope. This lack of variation could be attributed to shallow soils on the upland and poor drainage at the foot slope, suggesting further that lower slopes become inundated during the rainy season.

CONCLUSION

The study identified a significant role for topography on SOC storage in soil in addition to other determinant factors such as climate and land use changes. The results revealed that soil properties under different land use types and catenary sequences varied. The land use types were located between upland, midland and lowland physiographies. Management practices varied with land use. Soil physicochemical properties varied within the various LUTs.

The SDR was highly significant with land use and slope position but not significant with management. For all slope positions, the highest SDR was found under grassland soils and least values obtained in forest, annual crop and banana/plantain intercrop soils. A low SDR value implies a better soil and vice versa for a high SDR soil.

The relationship between SDR and slope showed that SDR was influenced by slope position with foot slope having highest SDR and lowest SDR at mid slope, suggesting greater management requirements for the former soils.

RECOMMENDATION

Careful assessment of the land resources is essential to make any change in the natural ecosystem. Encroachment on such areas by agriculture to provide more food may lead to deterioration of soil health through the rapid loss of soil fertility parameters. Appropriate legislation is important to safeguard the biodiversity of our ecosystem against deforestation and other anthropogenic activities by man in the course of meeting human needs.

No-till or reduced tillage practices should be embarked upon to increase SOM in the soil. Increase in residue return, less mixing and less soil disturbance ensures higher moisture control, reduced soil surface temperature, proliferation of root growth and bio-activity and decrease risk of soil erosion and productivity decline. Contrary will accelerate the mineralization of soil organic carbon, which in turn affects negatively the productivity potentials of the soil.

The ridge-furrow system has been suitable for soil and water conservation in structurally unsuitable soils (Lal, 1985). Since it conserves water, and also increases effective root volume on poorly drained soils and on nutrient deficient soils, it is recommended for practical application by rural farmers and agriculturist farming in the upland-inland continuum of north SE Nigeria.

REFERENCES

Ahn PN (1975). West African Soils London Oxford University Press. pp. 232.

Akinrinde, E.A, Obigbesa, GO (2000). Evaluation of Fertility Status of Selected Soils for Crop Production in Five Ecological Areas of Nigeria. Proc. 26th Ann. Conf. Soil Sci. Soc. Nig., Ibadan, Oyo State., pp. 279-453.

Allison F.E. (1982). Organic Carbon. In: Black C.A. (ed). Methods of Soil Analysis Part 2. *American Soc. Agron.* 9: 1367-1378.

Amana SM., Jayeoba OJ., Agbede OO. (2012). Effects of Land Use Types on Soil Quality in a Southern Guinea Savannah, Nasarawa State of Nigeria. *Journal of Soil Science.* Vol. 22(1) pp. 181.

Aune, JB. Lal R (1997). Agricultural Productivity in the Tropics and Critical Limits of Properties of Oxisol, Ultisol and Alfisol. Tropical Agric. 74: 96-103.

Ayanaba, A. Tuckwell SB Jenkinson DS (1996). The Effects of Clearing and Cropping on the Organic Reserves and Biomass of Tropical Forest Soils. Soil Biochem 8: 519-525

Ayuba, HK (2001). Livestock Grazing Intensities and Soil Deterioration in the Semi-arid Rangeland of Nigeria: Effects on Soil Chemical Status. Discov. Innovate 13 (3-4): 150-155.

Bawden, MG (1963). Land Use and Vegetation Map of Anambra-Do Rivers Area, Nigeria Map D.O.S (MISC) 252 www.eusoils.jrc.ec.europa.eu

Blake, GR., Hartge, KH. (1986). Bulk density. In Methods of Soil Analysis, Part 1, A. Klute (Ed.) Agron. No. 9. USA Madison W.I. pp. 370-373.

Bray RH Kurtz NT (1945). Determination of Total Organic and Available form of Phosphorus. Soil Sci. 59: 39-45.

Bremmer, J.M., Mulvaney, C.S (1982). Total N, P. 895-926. In: Page et al (eds) Methods of Soil Analysis. Part2. 2nd ed. Agron. Monog. 9. ASA and SSSA, Madison WI.

Bremmer JM. (199). Nitrogen total. In: Sparks D. L. (eds). Method of Soil Analysis Part 111. Chemical Methods SSSA Book Series No. 5 . *Am. Soc. of Agron.* pp. 1085-1121.

Brubaker, SC., AJ. Jones, DT. Lewis Frank. K (1994). Soil Properties Associated with Landscape Position. Soil Sci. Soc. Amer. J. 57: 235-239.

Buerket, A., A. Batiano K. Dossa K (2000). Mechanism of Residue Induced Cereal Growth Increases in W. Africa. Soil Sci. Soc. Amer. J. 64: 346-358.

Campo, J. Maass, JM., Jaramilo, VJ Yrizar AM (2000). Ca, K and Mg Cycling in a Mexican Tropical Dry Forest Ecosystem. Biogeochemistry 49(1): 21-36.

Cerda, A. 1998b. Soil Aggregate Stability Under Different Mediterranean Vegetation Types. Catena 32: 73-86.

Eludoyin OS. Wokocha CC. (2010). Soil Dynamics Under Continous Monocropping of Maize (*Zea mays*) on a Forest Alfisol in South-western Nigeria. *Asian journal of agricultural sciences.* 3(2): 58-62 (2011) pp. 58-62.

Enwezor, W.O., Ohiri, A.C., Opuwaribo, E.E. Udo EJ (1989). Review of Fertilizer Use on Crops in Southeastern Nigeria. Fertilizer Procurement and Distribution, Lagos, Nigeria. 420 pp.

Ezeaku, P.I., 2011. Methodologies for Agricultural Land Use Planning: Sustainable Soil Management and Productivity. Published by Great AP Express Publishers Ltd., Nsukka, Nigeria. 248 p.

Ezeaku, PI., Alaci, D (2008). Analytical Situations of Land Degradation and Sustainable Management Strategies in Africa. Pakistan J Agric. Soc Sci., 4: 42-52 (http://www.fspublishers.org)

Ezeaku PI Anikwe, MAN (2005). A Model for Description of Water and Solute Movement in Soil-water Restrictive Horizons Across Two Landscapes in South-East Nigeria. Journal of Soil Science 171(6):492-500 (USA).

Ezeaku, PI. (2002). Applicability of Two Concepts of Land Evaluation to the Soils of Southeastern Nigeria. Ph.D., Thesis. University of Nigeria Nsukka. 271 p.

FAO Production Year Book. (1970).

FAO Production Year Book. (1999).

FORMECU, (1998). The Assessments of Vegetation and Land Use Changes in Nigeria. 1976/1978 and 1993/95. Federal Dept. of Forestry, Abuja. 30 pp.

Gee, GW., Bauder, JW (1986). Particle Size Analysis. P. 383-411. In: Klute, A (ed). Methods of Soil Analysis. Part 2, 2nd ed. Agron. Monog. 9. ASA and SSSA, Madison, WI.

Hertemink, A.E., Veldkamp, T Bai, Z (2008). Land Use Change and Soil Fertility Decline in Tropical Regions. Turkish J. of Agric. & Forestry, 32: 195-213.

Hoshmand, RA (1994). Experimental Research Design and Analysis. A Practical Approach for Agricultural and Natural Sciences. CRC Press 408 pp.

Hullugale, NR (1994). Long-term Effects of Land Clearing Methods, Tillage Systems and Cropping Systems on Surface Soil Properties of a Tropical Alfisol in SW Nigeria. Soil Use Mgt 10(1): 25-30.

Karlen, D.L., Mausbach, M.J., Doran, J.W., Cline, R.Q., Harris, R.F., Schuman, G.E (1997). Soil Quality: A Concept, Definition and Framework for Evaluation. Soil Sci. Soc. Amer. J. 61: 4-10.

Klute A Dirksen J (1986). Hydraulic Conductivity and Diffusivity. Laboratory Methods. In: A klute (ed). Methods of Soil Analysis Part 1 2nd ed. pp. 687-734.

Kristensen, H.L., G.W. McCarty, Meisinger JJ (2001). Effects of Soil Structure Disturbance on Mieralization of Organic Soil Nitrogen. Soil Sci. Amer. J 61(1): 371-378.

Lal, R (1985). Soil Surface Management in the Tropics for Intensive Land Use and High and Sustained Productivity. In: B.A. Stewart (ed), Advances in Soil Science. Vol. 5. 1-109.

Lal, R (1994). Methods and Guidelines for Assessing Sustainable Use of Soil and Water Resources in the Tropics. Ohio State Univ. Coumbus, OH, 78 pp.

Lal, R (1999). Soil Quality and Food Security: The Global Perspective. In Lal, R (Ed.) Soil Quality and Soil Erosion. CRC Press, Boca Raton, FL, pp. 3-16.

Landon, J.R (1984). Booker Tropical Soil Manual. Longman Inc. New York. 450 pp.

Li, Y., Zhang, Q.U., Reicosky, D.C. Lindstrom M.J., Bai, L.Y., Li, L (2007). Changes in SOC Induced by Tillage and Water Erosion on a Steep Cultivated Hillslope in the Chinese Loess Plateau from 1898-1994 and 1954-1998. J. of Geophysical Res. 112.

Mclean EO (1982). Soil pH and Lime Requirement. *Agron. 9. SSSA. Madison W.I.* pp 199-224.

Mojiri A., Emami N. and Ghafari N (2011). Effect of Land Use Changes and Hill Slope Position on Soil Qualities. *African Journal of Agricultural Research.* Vol 6(5) pp. 1114-1119.

Nanzyo, M., Shoji, S., Dehigren, R (1993). Physical Characteristics of Volcanic Ash Soils. In: Shoji, S., Nanzyo, M, Dehigren, R (eds). Volcanish Ash Soils. Genesis, Properties and Utilization. Elsevier Sci. Publishers, B.V., Amsterdam. P. 288.

National Research Council, (1993). Soil and Water Quality: An Agenda for Agriculture. National Academy Press, Washinton, DC, 516 pp.

Nelson, D.W., and Sommers, CE (1982). Total Carbon, Organic Carbon and Organic Matters, P. 539- 579. In: A.C. Page and C.A. Black (eds). Methods of Soil Analysis Part 2, 2nd ed. Agron. Monogr. 9 ASA and SSA, Madison, W.I.

Ne'meth,T.P., P. Csatho' Anton A (1998). Soil Carbon Dynamics in Relation to Cropping Systems in Principal Ecoregions of Eastern Europe, with Particular Regard to Hungarian Experiences. P 255-283. In Lal et al (ed) Management of Carbon Sequestration in Soil. *Advances in Soil Science*. CRC Press. New York.

Neris, J., Jimenez, C., Fuentes, J., Morrilas, G., Tejedor, M. (2012). Vegetation and Land Use Effects on Soil Properties and Water Infiltration of Andisols in Tenerife (Canary Islands), Spain. Catena 98: 55-62.

NEST, (1991). *Nigerian Threatened Environment: A National Profile*, Intec Publication, Ibadan, Nigeria.

Oko-ibom G.O. Asiegbu JE (2006). Growth and Yield Responses of Rainy Season Field Tomatoes to Timing and Splitting of Fertilizer Application. Journal of Agriculture, Food, Environment and Extension. Vol. 5 No. 1 pp. 17-25.

Okusami, T.A., Rust, R.H Juo, ASR (1997). Characterization and Classification of Some Soil Formed on Post-cretaceous Sediments in Southern Nigeria. Soil Sci. 140:110-119.

Olsen, S.R., Sommers, L.E (1982). Phosphorus. p. 403-434. In: Page *et al* (eds) Methods of Soil Analysis. Part 2. Agron 9. ASA, SSSA. Madison, W.I.

Ojanuga, AG Awojuola, AI (1981). Characteristics and Classification of the Soils of the Jos Plateau, Nigeria. Nigerian Soil Science, 10: 101-119.

Pando, M.M., E. Jurado, M. Manzano, Estrada E (2004). The Influence of Land Use on Desertification Processes. J. Range Mgt. 57(3): 320-324.

Rhoades, J.D (1982a). Cation Exchange Capacity. In: Page, A.L. (Ed.), Methods of Soil Analysis Part 2. 2nd Edition Agron. Monogr. 9. ASA, Madison, WI, pp. 149-157.

Rossiter L (1994). Lecture Notes: Land Evaluation SCAS Teaching Series. No. T94-1. FAO Soils Bulletin 32.

SAS Institute, (2000). SAS Procedures Guide. Release 8 Edition, SAS, Cary, NC.

Sanchez-Maranon, M., Sriano, M., Delgado, G Delgado R (2002). Soil Quality in Mediterrenian Mountains Environment: Effects of Land Use Change. Soil Sci. Soc. Amer.J 66: 948-958.

Senthil, K.S., Kravchenko, A.N., Robertson, GP (2006). Soil Carbon Sequestration as a Function of Initial Carbon Content in Different Crop Management Systems of a Long-term Experiment. In: Abstracts 18th World Congress of Soil Science, Inter. Union of Soil Science (IUSS), USA. SOM Stabilization and Carbon Sequestration pp. 139-144.

Spark, DL (1995). Environmental Soil Chemistry. Academic Press, Inc. San Diego, California.

Steenwerth, K.L., L.E. Jackson, F.J. Calderon, M.R. Stromberg, and K.M. Scow. 2002. Soil Community Composition and :Land Use History in Cultivated and Grassland Ecosystems of Coastal California. Soil Bio & Biochemistry 34(11): 1599-1611

Tisdell, C (1996). Economic Indicators to Assess the Sustainability of Conservation Farming Projects: An Evaluation. *Agric. Ecosyst.Environ.*, 57: 117-31.

Tsui, C., Chen, ZS Hsier, CF (2004). Relationships Between Soil Properties and Slope Position in a Lowland Rain Forest of Southern Taiwan. Geoderma 123: 131-142.

Udoh, EJ., IC. Idiong Odok GN (2002). Issues in Sustainable and Use and Management in the Rain Forest Belt of Sub-Saharan Africa. *J.Environ. Exten.*, 3: 16-20.

URL: http://www.google.com/Online Nigeria (2003). Soil Distribution Along a Toposequence.

University of Nigeria Meteorological Station, 2010.

Soil Survey Staff (1999). Soil Taxonomy: A Basic System of Classification for Making and Interpreting soil Surveys. N.R.C.S. USDA, Washinton D.C. 869 pp.

Verde, J.R., Camps Arbestain, M. Macias F (2004). Effect de las Practicas Agricolas Sobre Laestabilidad de los complejos organoalumicos en suelos andicos de Galicia. Edafologia 11: 319-328.

World Bank (1992). *World Development Report*. World Bank, Washington D.C.

CHAPTER

Nanotechnology and Crop Protection

Abba, Nathan Yatai; Echezona, Bonaventure Chukwujindu*

INTRODUCTION

Nanotechnology is the creation and use of materials or devices at extremely small scales. These materials or devices fall in the range of 1 to 100 nanometers (nm). One nm is equal to one-billionth of a meter (0.000000001m), which is about 50, 000 times smaller than the diameter of a human hair. Scientist refer to the dimensional range of 1-100 nm as the nanoscales, and materials of this scale are called nanocrystals or nanomaterial (Chinnamuthu and Murugesa, 2009; Yang and Luzzi, 2009).

The nanoscale is unique because nothing solid can be made any smaller. It is also unright because many of the mechanisms of the biological and physical world operate on length scales from 0.1-100 nm. At these dimensions materials exhibit different physical properties, thus scientist expects that many novel effects at the nanoscale will be discovered and used for breakthrough technologies.

A number of breakthroughs have already occurred in nanotechnology. These developments are found in products used throughout the world. Some

---

Dept. of Crop Science, University of Nigeria, Nsukka, Nigeria.

examples are catalytic converters in automobiles that help remove air pollutants, devices in computers that read from and write to the hard disk, certain sun screens and cosmetics that transparently block harmful radiation from the sun, and special coating for sports clothes and gear that help improve the gear and possibly enhance the athlete's performance (Yang and Luzzi, 2009).

CONCEPT OF NANOTECHNOLOGY

The concept of nanotechnology originated with American physicist Richard P. Fayman Dec., 1959.

Nanotechnology began being promoted as a key component of future technology in the late 1970s. The term nanotechnology was first used in 1974 by Japanese Scientist Norio Taniguchi in a paper titled "On the Basic Concept of Nanotechnology. However, the term was also used by American engineer K. Eric Drexler in the book Engines of creation (1986), which had a greater impact and helped accelerate the growth of the field. By this time, major breakthroughs had been achieved in industry, such as the formation of nanoparticles catalyst made of nonreactive metals and used in catalytic converters found in automobiles. These catalysts chemically reduced noxions Nitrogen oxides to benign nitrogen and simultaneously oxidized poisonous carbon nanoxide to form CO_2 (Yang and Luzzi, 2009).

THE TOOLS OF NANOTECHNOLOGY

The scientific community began serious work in nanoscience when tools became available in the late 1970s and early 1980s, first to probe and later to manipulate and control materials and systems of the nanoscale. These tools include the transmission electron microscope (TEM), the atomic force microscope (AFM), the scanning tunneling microscope (STM) (Yang and Luzzi, 2009).

GROWTH AND POTENTIAL BENEFITS OF NANOTECHNOLOGY (NT)

Catherine *et al.* (2013) reported that Nanotechnology is hailed as having the potential to increase the efficiency of energy consumption, help clean the environment, and solve major health problems. They said nanotechnology is able to massively increase manufacturing production at significantly reduced costs. Nanotechnology advocates claim that products of nanotechnology will be smaller, cheaper, lighter yet more functional and require less energy and fewer raw materials to manufacture (Catherine *et al.*, 2013 and Ghomade *et al.*, 2013).

Nanotechnology may provide new solutions for the millions of people in developing countries who lack access to basic services such as safe water, reliable energy, healthcare, etc. The 2004 UN Task force on services, technology and innovation noted that some of the advantages of nanotechnology include production using little labour, land, or maintenance, high productivity, low cost and modest requirements for materials and energy. Inexpensively made, very strong and very light materials are possible with nanotechnology; shatter proof diamond could be produced in precisely the shapes we want and over fifty times lighter than steel of the same length. It is possible to produce a Cadillac of weight fifty kilograms or a full sized sofa you could pick with one hand. Surgical instruments could operate on the cells and even molecules from which we are made, something well beyond today's medical technology. The majority of nanotechnology research and development and patents for nanotechnology and products are concentrated in developed countries including the United States, Japan, Germany, Canada and France. Many developing countries, for example Costarica, Chile, Bangladesh, Thailand and Malaysia are investing considerable resources in research and development of nanotechnologies. Emerging economies such as Brazil, China, India and South Africa are spending millions increasing their scientific output as demonstrated by their increasing numbers of publications in peered reviewed publications. (Ralph, 1997; Ghomade *et al.*, 2011).

NANOTECHNOLOGY AND AGRICULTURE

Nanotechnology has began in agriculture and will continue to have a significant effect in the main areas of breeding new crop varieties, development of new functional materials and smart delivery systems for agrochemical like herbicides, fertilizers and pesticides, SMART systems (i.e. S – Specific, M – Measurable, A. – Achievable, R – Realistic and T – Time-based) integration for food processing, packaging and other areas like remediation of herbicide and pesticide residues from plant and soils, effluent water treatment etc. (Ralph, 1997; Moraru *et al.*, 2003; Susha *et al.*, 2009, Ghormade *et al.*, 2011).

Nanotechnology potentials are increasing day by day with suitable techniques and sensors being identified for precision agriculture, natural resource management and early detection of pathogens and contaminants in food products. (Susha *et al.*, 2009; Chinnamuthu, and Murugesa, 2009).

PRECISION FARMING

The process of maximizing crop yields and minimizing of the usage of pesticides fertilizers and herbicides through efficient monitoring procedures is referred to as precision farming (WILL, 2013). Precision farming utilizes remote sensing devices, computers and global satellite positioning systems to analyse various environmental conditions in order to determine the growth of plant under these conditions and identify problems related to crops and their growing environments. Precision farming also helps determine plant development, soil conditions, and seeding and controls environmental pollution to a minimum extent by reducing agricultural waste (Will, 2013)

The usage of smart sensors in precision farming will result in increased agricultural productivity by providing farmers with accurate information that will enable them to make accurate decisions related to plant growth suitability (Maria, 2009).

PLANT PROTECTION

Plant protection is the science of managing invertebrate pests and vertebrate pests, plant diseases, weeds and other pest organisms that damage agricultural crops and forestry. Agricultural crops include field crops (maize, wheat, rice, etc), vegetable crops (potatoes, cabbages, etc), fruits and horticultural crops. Crop protection encompasses:

- Pesticide- based approaches such as herbicides, insecticides, fungicides, etc.
- Biological pest control approaches such as cover crops, trap crops and beetle banks.
- Barrier-based, approaches such as textiles and bird netting, tranches, etc.
- Animal psychology-based approaches such as bird scarers, etc.
- Biotechnology based approaches such as plant breeding and genetic modification.(Crop Life International, 2013; Dupont, 2013 and Reddy, 2013).

Food crops must compete with 30 000 species of weeds, 3 000 species of nematodes and 10 000 species of plant eating insects (crop life India, 2013). It is a known fact that despite the use of modern crop protection products, 20 - 40 per cent of potential food production is still lost every year to pest. These losses can occur while the crop is growing in the field, when it is in storage and in the home. In short, an adequate, reliable food supply cannot be guaranteed without the use of crop protection products (Crop Life India, 2011; Articlesbase, 2009).

BENEFITS OF CROP PROTECTION IN WORLD FOOD PRODUCTION

The benefits of crop protection in food production as reported by Crop Life India (2011); Crop Life America (2011) and Articlesbase (2009) include:

(a) **Increase food production:** Crop protection technologies allow crop products to increase crop yields and efficiency of food production processes. Up to 40 per cent of world's potential crop production is already loss annually because of the effects of weeds, pests and diseases. These crop losses will be doubled if existing pesticides uses were abandoned.

(b) **Decrease in cost of food:** Because the use of pesticides improves crop yields, crop protection technologies also affect the cost of food. Without crop protection chemicals, food production would decline, many fruits and vegetables would be in short supply and prices would rise. Helping to keep food prices in check for the consumer is another large benefit of crop protection.

(c) **Consumer benefits**: Pesticides allow consumers to consume high-quality produce that is free of insect blemishes and insect contamination. Crop protection chemicals that reduce and, in some cases, eliminate, insect damage allow the consumer to purchase high-quality produce free of insect fragments.

(d) **Household pest control**: Pesticide products are used to control termites, cockroaches, ants, rats and other pests.

(e) **Industry and infrastructural pest control**: Herbicides are used to control vegetation that clogs navigable and other water ways or threatens to obstruct highway, utility and railroad rights.

(f) **Use of crop protection in recreational areas**: Pesticides are used to protect and enhance lawns, gardens, public parks, playing fields, lakes and ponds for public enjoyment.

(g) **Crop protection in Human Health:** many agricultural commodities are vulnerable to attack by afflatoxins and insect control is necessary to prevent it passage from insect to plant. Afflatoxin, a carcinogen, can cause liver and other cancers in humans, lowers the body's normal immune response, and can impair growth in children. Crop protection chemicals are used to control insect damage that leads to afflatoxin contamination.

NANOTECHNOLOGY AND CROP PROTECTION

There is an ever increasing consumption and demand for food. In agriculture new molecular and cellular biology tools are expected to provide disease prevention and treatment in plants eg. Disease diagnosis, Screening and treatment in farming practices involving.

- Vector and pest detection and control.
- Disease, monitoring
- SMART treatment delivery systems at a nanoscale serve as carriers and provide on board chemical detection and decision taking ability for self regulation.

These smart systems deliver precise quantities of drugs or nutrient or other agro-chemicals required. These intelligent systems thus monitor and minimize pesticide and antibiotic use (Maheswar and Madhuri, 2008, Madhuri *et al.*, 2010).

ACTIVE INGREDIENTS AND TRADITIONAL DELIVERY METHODS FOR CROP PROTECTION

Pesticides, herbicides and fungicides, which aid in crop protection, are considered 'active ingredients' in that they destroy, prevent, repel or mitigate any pests, weeds and fungi that attack crops. The delivery of an active ingredient onto the crops is not easy. For example, the molecules that form a pesticide tend to clump together and render it ineffective unless it is combined with the appropriate emulsifiers, dispersing agents, antifreezes (i.e. pesticide is not expected to freezes before it does it jobs), odorants (to indicate volatility), oils such as mineral and soybean oil, solvents (use to dissolve the active ingredient), surfactants (increase solubility of the active ingredient) etc and all the a fore mentioned are chemical additives. Many of these additives are extremely volatile, harmful to the environment and humans and often not as efficient as they should be at delivering the active ingredient. (Robert, 2013; Will, 2013; Maria, 2009)

Nano uses ultra-small, water dispersible particles to effectively encapsulate and deliver non-soluble active ingredients like herbicides, pesticides, and fungicides to crops. The particles function as a small envelope that gets the package (active ingredient) where it needs to go with minimal impact on the soil and the surrounding environment.

Robert (2013) reported that what differentiates Nanotechnology from the traditional delivery methods for active ingredients in crop protection is that its products require no solvents and significantly fewer additives. This could result in benefits for the grower such as reductions in the amount of pesticide to be used, reduced itching and reduced staining.

THE NEED FOR NANO-AGROCHEMICALS AND MATERIAL

Pesticides do not have the best reputation when it comes to the potential impacts on human health and environment. Volatile organic solvents are frequently relied on to deliver crop protection chemicals to farmer's fields. The solvents themselves are often known carcinogens, not the kind of thing we want to our farmlands- that grow our food crops (Tyler, 2012). The pesticides are often not effective as they should be and farmers tend to overspray to make sure enough of the active ingredients in insecticides, fungicides and herbicides are disperse across a field to be effective. Another biggest problems with pesticides is they tend to agglomerate, resulting in uneven distribution on the soil (Tyler, 2012).

Some of the products like nanopesticides have arrived already in the market, while many others are under developing stage and it may take many years before they are commercialized. These applications are largely intended to address some of the limitations and challenges like problems of weed management, slow release fertilizers before weed management, slow release fertilizers conditional release of pesticides and herbicides, precise micro-management of soils, the more efficient and targeted use of inputs and new toxin formulations for pest control (Chinamuthu and Murugesa, 2009; Siddhartha, 2011; Mukhopadhyay *et al., 2013)*

Table 7.1: Nanotechnology and Areas of Application in Agriculture

Technology	Example	Application
Energy storage, production and conversion	• Novel hydrogen storage based on carbon nanotubes • Photovoltaic cells and organic light emitters (Quantum dots) composite film coatings for solar cells and carbon-nanotubes).	• Cheaper and clean energy • Low weight and low cost solar cells. • Improved rechargeable batteries.
Agricultural productivity enhancement	• Nanoporous zeolites for slow release and efficient delivery of fertilizers, nutrients and drugs. • Nanocapsules for pesticide delivery. • Nanosensors for soil quality and plant health monitoring.	• More efficient and sustainable production that requires fewer inputs.
Food processing and storage	• Nanocomposites in plastic film for food packaging • Antimicrobial nanoemulsions for decontamination • Antigen detection at nanoscale.	• Cheaper, safe food products with longer storage life.
Vector and pest ditection and control	• Pest and pathogen detection (nanosensors)	• More rapid deployment of safer control strategies.

(Will, 2013; Chinnamuthu and Murugesa, 2009).

Table 7.2: Nano-agrochemicals and Nano-materials under Development

Types of Product	Product Name and Manufacturer	Nano Content	Purpose
Nano-agrochemicals Super combined fertilizer and pesticide	Pakistan-US science and Technology Cooperative Programme	Nano-clay capsule contains growth stimulants and bio-control agents	Slow release of active ingredients, reducing application rates.
Herbicide	Tamil Nadu Agricultural University (India) and Technologico de monterry (Mexico)	Nano-formulated	Designed to attack the seed coat of weeds, destroy soil seed banks and prevent weed germination.
Pesticides, including herbicides	Australian Common wealth Scientific and Industrial Research Organisation.	Nano-encapsulated active ingredients	Very small size of nanocapsules increases their potency and may enable targeted release of active ingredients.
Nano-materials Nutritional supplement	Nanoceuticals Mycronhydrin powder, RBC life sciences	Molecular cages 1-5 nm diameter made from silica mineral hydride complex	Nano-sized mycrohydrin has increased potency and bioavailability. Exposure to moisture releases H ions and acts as a powerful antioxidant.
Nutritional drink	Oat chocolate Nutritional drink Mix, Toddler Health	300 nm particles of iron (sunActive Fe)	Nano-sized iron particles have increased reactivity and bioavailability.
Food packaging	Adhesive for McDonald's burger containers, Ecosynthetix	50-150 nm starch nanospheres	These nanoparticles have 400 times the surface area of natural starch particles. When used as an adhesive they require less water and thus less time and energy to dry.
Food additive	Aquasol preservative, aqua Nova	Nanoscale micelle (capsule) of lipophilic or water insoluble substances.	Surrounding active ingredients within soluble nanocapsules increases absorption within the body (including individual cell).
Plant growth treatment	Primo Maxx, syngenta	100 nm particle size emulsion	Nano-sized particles increases the potency of active ingredients, potentially reducing the quantity to be applied.

(CopperWiki, 2006; Chinamuthu and Murugesa, 2009; Robert, 2013)

CROP MANAGEMENT

(a) Control of Agricultural Environment

Precision farming is one of the most important areas for increasing the productivity of crops by applying inputs in previously required quantity and at required time (USDA, 2005). Tiny sensors and monitoring systems enabled by nanotechnology will have a large impact on the future precision farming methodologies. Precision farming has been a long-felt goal to maximize output (i.e. crop yield) while minimizing input (i.e. fertilizers, pesticides, herbicides, etc.) through monitoring environmental variables to help reduce the agricultural waste and thus keep environmental pollution to a minimum (Doug, *et al.*, 2003 Maria, 2009; will, 2013).

(b) Crop Nutrition Management

It is observed that yields of many crops have begun to stagnate as a consequence of imbalanced fertilization and decline in organic matter content of soils. Excessive use of nitrogenous fertilizers affects the groundwater and also causes eutrophication in aquatic systems. With nano-fertilizers emerging as alternative to conventional fertilizers, build-up of nutrients in soils and thereby entrophication and drinking water contamination may be eliminated.

SLOW RELEASE OF NANO-FERTILIZERS AND NANO-COMPOSITES.

Slow release fertilizers are excellent alternatives to soluble fertilizers. Nutrients are released at a slower rate throughout the crop growth; plants are able to take up most of the nutrients without waste by leaching. Slow release of the nutrients in the environment could be achieved by using zeolites.

Fertilizer patented can be coated with nanomembranes that facilitate slow and steady release of nutrients. Coating and cementing of nano and subnano composites are capable of regulating the release of nutrients from the fertilizer capsule (Liu, *et al.*, 2006).

A patented nano-composite consists of NPK micro-nutrients, manose and amino-acids that increases the uptake and utilization of nutrients by grain crops has been reported (Jinghua, 2004).

NANOSENSORS IN CROP PRODUCE AND PRODUCT PROTECTION

Efficient detection systems which monitor and detect pathogen invasion, infection nutrition requirement and uptake and contamination have been developed. As the nanosensor enables us to detect and eradicate infectious diseases in plants and animals before visible symptoms appear, the heavy economic losses that occur otherwise are reduced by many folds. Smart delivering systems help in the controlled delivery of nutrients, pesticides, probiotics and neutraceutics.

Nanosensors are already being used by the store keepers to identify food items which have passed their expiry dates. Moreover, post harvest protection of agro-products is also the concern of nanotechnologist by antimicrobial packing of edible food films made with cinnamon or oregano oil, or nanoparticles of zinc, calcium and other materials that kill bacteria. Green packaging using nanofibres made from lobster shells or organic corn both are antimicrobial and biodegradable. (Madhuri *et al.*, 2010; and Siddhartha, 2011).

Improved food packaging needs packaging materials having strength, barrier properties and stability to heat and cold. These are being achieved using nanocomposite materials. Bayer polymers have produced a nanocomposite film 'Durethan'. It is a film enriched with silica nanoparticles which reduce the entrance of oxygen and other gases, and preserves moisture, thus preventing food from spoiling. Incomporation of silver, magenesium oxide, Zinc oxide nanoparticles which can kill harmful microorganisms in food or beer packages will save the contamination. Some nanoscientists have suggested that nanosensors could be used to detect chemicals, pathogens and toxins in food. Use of nanowheels, nanofibers and nanotubes are been tried to improve the quality of food packages. Maria, 2009; Will, 2013; Amy et al, 2010 and Madhuri, 2010).

NANOSCALE BIOSENSORS IN PROTECTING CROP PRODUCT

Involving biological molecules such as sugars or proteins as target-recognition groups could be used as biosensors on foods to detect pathogens and other contaminants. In food industry nanosensors would provide increased security of manufacturing, processing, and shipping of food products through sensors for pathogen and contaminant detection. Benefits of using nanosensors are final, portable, rapid response and processing, specific, quantitative, reliable, accurate, reproducible, robust and stable which can overcome the deficits of present sensors. (Charych et al., 1996 and Madhuri et al., 2010).

NAONLAMINATION IN PROTECTING CROP PRODUCT

Madhuri et al., (2010) reported that the nanolamination technique is another viable option for protecting the food from moisture lipids and gases. Nanolaminates can improve the texture and preserve flavor as well as colour of the food. Nanolaminates consist of two or more layers of nano-sized (1 - 100) thin food grade films which are present on a wide variety of foods: fruits, vegetables, meats, chocolates, candies, baked goods and French fries (Morillon, 2002; Cagri et al., 2004; Cha and Chinnan, 2004; Rhim, 2004).

Nanolaminates are prepared from edible polysaccharides, proteins and lipids. Park (1999) has shown that Polysaccharide and protein based nanolaminates are good barriers against oxygen and carbon dioxide, but poor in protecting against moisture. Trials are on to develop laminates that can protect against all the desired factors. Coating foods with nanolaminates is done simply by spraying it on the food surface (McClements et al., 2005).

NANOPARTICLES IN CONTROLLING PLANT DISEASES

Some of the nanoparticles that have entered into the arena of controlling plant diseases are nano forms of carbon, silver, silica, alumino-silicates, DNA – tagged nanogold, etc (Chakravarthy et al., 2011).

REASONS FOR USING METALLIC NANOPARTICLES IN CROP PROTECTION

Nanoparticles show sharp prejudice from their bulk in many respects which becomes bonus for developing diagnostic tools. Certain nanocrystals (Crystalline nanoparticles) are attractive probes of biological markers because of:

- Small size (1 - 100 nm).
- Large surface to volume ratio (aspect ratio).
- Chemically alterable physical properties.
- Change in the chemical and physical properties with respect to size and shape.
- Strong affinity to target particularly proteins (in case of gold nanoparticles).
- Structural sturdiness in spite of atomic granularity.
- Enhanced or delayed particles aggregation depending on the type of the surface modification.
- Enhanced photo emission.
- High electrical and heat conductivity.
- Improved surface catalytic activity.

McNeil, 2005; Rosi and Mirkin, 2005; Liu *et al.*, 2006; Shrestha *et al.*, 2007; Garg *et al.*, 2008).

ON SITE DIAGNOSIS OF NUTRIENT STATUS

Soil solution can be allowed to react with nano-products that will give accurate measurement of availability of nutrients in the soils. Nanosensors can be used to determine nutrient, moisture and physiological status of plants which assists in taking up appropriate and timely corrective measures. Nanoparticles are mini-laboratories that have the potential to precisely monitor temporal and seasonal change in soil plant system. Nanosensors detect the availability of nutrients and water precisely, which is very much essential to achieve the mission of precission agriculture (Subramanian *et al.*, 2007; Chinnamuthu and Murugesa, 2009).

DIAGNOSIS OF NUTRIENT DISORDERS IN PLANTS

Nanoparticles are used as SMART treatment delivery system for human health, similarly planting nanoparticles in the plant could determine the nutrient status in plants and useful for remedial measures to the malady that causes yield reduction.

SEED MANAGEMENT

Pollen flight is determined by air temperature, humidity, wind velocity and pollen production of the crop. Use of pan sensors specific to contaminating pollen can help alert the possible contamination and thus reduces contamination. The same method can also be used to prevent pollen from contaminating field crops.

Novel genes are being incorporated into seeds and sold in the market. Tracking of sold seeds could be done with the help of nanobarcodes (NiceWarner *et al.*, 2001) that are encedable machine readable, durable and sub-micron sized taggants.

Disease spread through seeds and many times stored seeds are killed by pathogens. Nanocoating of seeds using elemental forms of Z_n, M_n P_t A_u, A_g will not only protect seeds but used in far less quantities than done today. Su-- and Li *et al.*, (2004) developed a technique known as quantumdots as a fluorescence marker coupled with imuno-magnetic separation for *Escherichia coli 0.57:H7* which will be useful to separate in unviable and infected seeds.

Seeds can also be imbibed with nano-encapsulations with specific bacterial strain termed as smart seed. A smart seed can be programmed to germinate when adequate moisture is available that can be dispersed over a mountain range for reforestation. (Nataragan and Sivasubramanian, 2007).

NANOTECHNOLOGY AND WEEDS

Nanotechnology herbicide molecules encapsulated with nanoparticles are aimed for specific receptor in the roots of target weeds, which enter into system and translocated to parts that inhibit glycosis of food reserve in the root system. This will make the specific weed plant to starve for food and gets killed (Chinamuthu et al., 2007 and Green Answers, 2013).

USING NANOTECHNOLOGY TO GROW CROPS IN HOSTILE CONDITIONS

Researchers in both developed and developing countries are developing, crop that are able to grow under hostile conditions, such as fields where the soil contains high levels of salt (sometimes due to climate change and rising sea levels) or low level of water. They are doing this by manipulating the crop genetic material, working on a nanotechnology scale with biological molecules (Catherine et al., 2013 and Siddhartha, 2011).

Green Answers (GA) (2013) also reported that a nanotechnology known as agro-sillica (a highly refined silicate derived from quartz) helps reduce water loss and wilting among plants. The agro-sillica, dissolved in water and sprayed over the plants, is quickly absorbed into the plants epidemic layer, where it forms a thick sillicated skin. This layer slows water loss from the plant, protecting it from high heat and wilting.

PLANT DISEASE DIAGNOSTIC

Diseases are one of the major factors in limiting crop productivity. The problem in the disease management lies with the detection of the exact stage of prevention. Among diseases, viral diseases are the most difficult to control, as one has to stop the spread of the disease by vectors. Nano based diagnostic kits not only increase the speed of detection but also increase the power of detection by being able to detect the exact strain of virus and stage of application. Detection and utilization of biomarkers that accurately indicate disease stages with differential protein production in both healthy and diseased states lead to the identification of the development of several proteins during the infection cycle (Chinnamuthu et al., 2009 and Robert, 2013).

NANOCIDES: PESTICIDE VIA ENCAPSULATION

A more sophisticated approach to formulating nanoscale pesticides involves encapsulation. Packaging the nanoscale active ingredient within a kind of tiny envelop or shell. According to the agrochemical industry, reformulating pesticides in microcapsules can also extend patent protection, increase solubility, reduce the contact of active ingredients with agricultural workers and have environmental advantages such as reducing run off rates.

There are also agrochemicals in the form of an emulsion in which the active ingredient is made up of nanoscale droplets in the range of 10 - 400 nm (micro emulsion concentrate) with advantages such as reduced application rate, a more rapid and reliable activity and extended long-term activity (Chinnamuthu et al., 2009; Madhuri et al., 2010; Maria, 2009; Amy et al., 2010 and Will, 2013).

POST-HARVEST FOOD PROCESSING

Nano-materials help to keep products fresh for a longer period of time by using nansensors placed in food production and distribution facilities, food packing or the food itself which can detect all kinds of food pathogens like *E. coli, Campylobacter* and *Salmonella* by attaching themselves to the pathogen. In food and beverage industry, attempts have been made to add micronutrients and anti-oxidants to food substances, but these anti-oxidants degrade during manufacturing and food storage. Nano-cocohleates delivery system protects these substances from degradation.

Using nanoparticles technology, Bayer has developed an even more airtight plastic packaging that will keep food fresher and longer than plastics, which is hybrid system "as it is enriched with an enormous number of silicate nanoparticles" (Bayer, 2005).

NANOPARTICLES FOR ENVIRONMENTAL REMEDIATION

Chinnamuthu and Murugesa, (2009) reported that research has shown that nanoscale iron particles are very effective for the transformation and detoxification of a wide variety of common environmental contaminants, such as chlorinated organic solvents, organochlorine pesticides and PCBs. Modified iron nanoparticles, such as catalyzed and supported naoparticles have been synthesized to further enhance the speed and efficiency of remediation. Recent research has suggested that as a remediation technique, nanoscale iron particles have several advantages; i.e.

- Effective for transformation of large variety of environmental contaminants;
- Inexpensive; and
- None toxic.

Utilization of "magnetic" bacterial seems useful for metallic ion and heavy metal removal from aqueous solutions. (eg $A_{g,}$ $H_{g,}$ P_{b}, C_{u}, Z_{n} S_{b} $M_{n,}$ F_{e}, A_{s}, $N_{i,}$ Al $P_{t,}$ P_{d} and R_{u}). In the presence of magnetic ions such as ion sulphide, heavy metal precipitates onto bacterial cell walls, making the bacteria sufficiently magnetized for removal from suspension by magnetic separation procedure.

DETOXIFICATION OF HERBICIDE RESIDUES

Excessive use of herbicides leave residue is soil and cause damage to the succeeding crops. Residual problems due to the application of atrazin herbicide pose a threat towards widespread use of herbicide and limit the choice of crops in rotation. Application of silver modified with naoparticles of magnetite stabilized with carboxymethyl cellulose (CMC) nanopaparticles recorded 88 per cent degradation of herbicide atrazine residue under controlled environment (Susha et al., 2009).

Endosulfan is a stable pesticide and it is frequently on soils. It has the potential to cause health problems including genetic disorders. This pesticide residue can be detected in PPM levels using gold nanoparticles and is absorbed onto the nanoparticles surface. After long interaction, nanoparticles precipitate from the solution, which can be detected and selectively extracted by nobel metal nanoparticles. This process can be used for field detection of pesticide residues, environmental decontamination and drinking water purification. (Amy, *et al.*, 2010).

Advantages of Nanotechnology in Crop Protection

There is possibility to fabricate sensors to monitor pathogens on crops and measure their productivity.

Disadvantages

Nanotechnology increases the ability of potentially toxic substances to penetrate deep layers of the soil and travel large distances (Amy, *et al.*, 2010).

Table 7.3: Common Environmental Contaminants that can be Transformed by Nanoscale ion Particles

Chemical	Chemicals
Chlorinated methanes	Trihalomethanes
Carbon tetrachloride (CCl_4)	Bromoform (CHB_{r3})
Chloroform ($CHCl_3$)	Dibromochloromethane ($CHBr_2Cl$).
Dichloromethane (CH_2Cl_2)	Dichlorobromomethane ($CHBrCl_2$).
Chlorinated benzenes	**Chlorinated ethenes**
Tetrachlorobenzenes ($C_6H_2 Cl_4$)	Tetrachloroethene (C_2Cl_4)
Trichlorobenzenes ($C_6H_3 Cl_3$)	Trichloroethene (C_2HCl_3)
Dichlorobenzenes ($C_6H_4 Cl_2$)	*cis*—Dichloroethene ($C_2H_2 Cl_2$)
Chlorobenzene ($C_6H_5 Cl$)	*trans*- Dichloroethene ($C_2H_2Cl_2$)
Pesticides	1.1—Dichloroethene ($C_2H_2Cl_2$)
DDT ($C_{14}H_9Cl_5$)	Vinyl chloride (C_2H_3Cl)
Lindane ($C_6H_6Cl_{16}$)	**Other polychlorinated hydrocarbons**
Organic dyes	PCBs
Orange II ($C_{16} H_{11}N_2 N_aO_4S$)	Dioxins
Chrysoidine ($C_{12}H_{13}C_1N_4$)	Pentachlorophenol (C_6HCl_5O)
Tropaeolin O ($C_{12}H_9N_2N_aO_5S$)	Other organic contaminants
Acid orange	N-nitrosodimethylamine (NDMA) ($C_4H_{10}N_2O$)
Acid Red	TNT ($C_7H_5N_3O_6$)
Heavy metal ions	**Inorganic anions**
Mercury (Hg^{2+})	Dichromate ($Cr_2O_7^{-7}$)
NICKEL (Ni^{2+})	Arsenic (AsO_3^{-4})
Silver (Ag^+)	Perchlorate (ClO^-_4)
Cadmium(Cd^{2+})	Nitrate (NO^-_3)

(Chinnamuthu and Murugesa, 2009)

RISK OF NANOTECHNOLOGY FOR DEVELOPING COUNTRIES

A range of emerging technologies, including biotechnology, nanotechnology and synthetic biology, are expected to transform society. Handling the development and regulation of those promising technologies is a daunting task as the risks presented will not be understood until the technologies are fully developed. (Gregory, 2004).

Concerns are frequently raised that the claimed benefits nanotechnology will not be evenly distributed and that any benefits including technical and/ or economic) associated with nanotechnology will only reach affluent nations (Invernizzi et al., 2008). The majority of nanotechnology research and development and patents for nanomaterials and products is concentrated in developed countries including the United States, Japan, Germany, Canada and France.

Most patents related to nanotechnology are concentrated amongst few multinational corporations, including IBM Micro technologies, Advanced Micro devices and Intel. This has led to fears that it will be unlikely that the developing countries will have access to the infrastructure, funding and human resources required to support nanotechnology research and development, and that is likely to exacerbate such inequalities (Scrinis and Lyons, 2007).

The agriculture and food industries demonstrate the concentration of nanotechnology related patents. Patents over seeds, plant material, animal and other agric-food techniques are already concentrated amongst a few corporations. This is anticipated to increase the cost of farming, by increasing farmers input dependence. This may marginalized poorer farmers, including those living in developing countries (Scrinis and Lyons, 2007).

Producers in developing countries could also be disadvantaged by the replacement of natural products (including rubber, cotton, coffee and tea) by development in nanotechnology. These natural products are important export crops for developing countries, and many farmers' livelihoods depend on them. It has been argued that their substitution with industrial nanoproducts could negatively impact the economics of developing countries that have traditionally relied on these export crops (Invernizzi *et al.*, 2008).

It is speculated that people who work in unskilled labor jobs for a livelihood may become the first human workers to be displaced by the constant use of nanotechnology in the workplace, noting that lay offs often affect the jobs based around the lowest technology level before attacking jobs with the highest technology level possible (Kurzweil, 2005).

It has also been speculated that nanotechnology may give rise to nanofactories which may have superior capabilities to conventional factories due to their small carbon and physical footprint on the global and regional environment. The miniaturization and transformation of the multi acre conventional factory into the nanofactory may not interfere with their ability to deliver a high quality product; the product may be of even greater quality due to the lack of human errors in the production stages (Invernizzi, *et al.*, 2009).

Nanofactory system may use precise atomic procisioning and contribute to making superior quality products that the "bulk chemistry' method used 20th century and early 21st century cannot produce. Those advances might shift the computerized workforce in an even more complex direction, requiring skills in genetics, nanotechnology and robotics (Ralph, 1997).

CONCLUSION

Indiscriminate use of pesticides and fertilizers causes environmental pollution, emergence of agricultural pests and pathogens and loss of biodiversity. Nanotechnology, by virtue of nanomaterial related properties, had potential agro-biotechnological applications for alleviation of these problems. The role of nanotechnology in plant and soil systems demonstrates that nonmaterials may assist in

(a) The controlled release of agrochemicals for nutrition and protection against pests and pathogens.
(b) Delivery of genetic material.
(c) Sensitive detection of plant disease and pollutants.
(d) Protection and formation of soil structure.

Affordability and would wide adoption of nanotechnology in crop protection will lead to the actualization of world food security.

REFERENCES

Amy, C., Tony, G. and Ana, D. (2010) Nanotechnology in Agriculture. Texas A and M Engineering. http://www.scribd.com/doc/7640458/Nanotechnology-and-its-Application-in-Crop-Improvement.

Articlesbase (2013) *Crop Protection methods Increase Agricultural Productivity manifold.* ©2005 – 2013 Free ArticlesBase.com. All rights reserved. Accessed 1/3/2013.

Bayer (2005) *Securely* Wrapped: Service for a Better Life. http//www.research.bayer.com/median/pages/2999/Polyamides.pdf. Accessed- 17th/11/2012.

Cagri, A.; Ustunol, Z. and Ryser, E.T. (2004) "Antimicrobial Edible Films and Coatings": *A review J. Food Protect.*, 67: 833-838.

Catherine, B. and Mikas. (2013) "What is Nanotechnology and what can it do"? Nanomeasure, University of Warsaw, Warsaw, Poland. Accessed – 22nd/4/2013.

Cha, D.S. and Chinnan, M. S. (2004) "Biopolymer-based Antimicrobial Packaging": *Review. Crit, Rev. Food Sci.-Nutri.* 44: 223-237.

Chakravarthy, A.K.; Atanu, B.; Shashank, P.R.; Timothy, T.E.; Doddabasappa, B. and Swanpan, K.M. (2012) "DNA – tagged nano Gold: A New for the Control of Armyworm, *Spodoptera litura* Fab. (Lepidopter: Noctuidae)". *African Journal of Biotechnology* Vol. 11 (38), pp. 9295-9301. Accessed – 24th/11/2013.

Charych, D.; Ceng, Q.; Reichert, A.; Uziemko, G.; Stroh, N.,; Nagy, J.; Spevak, W. and Stevens, R. (1996) "Principle of Formation of Clay Monolayer Containing Nanocomposites". *Chem.Biol.3:113.*

Chinnamuthu, C.R and Kokiledevi, (2007). Weed Management Through Nanoherbicides. In *Application of Nanotechnology in Agriculture,* Chinnamuthu, C.R., Tamil Nadu Agricultural University, Coimbatore, India.

Chinnamuthu, C.R. and Murugesa, P.B. (2009) "Nanotechnology and Agroecosystem". *Madra Agric J.*, 96 (1-6): 17-31.

Copper Wiki (2006) Nanotechnology in food. http://www.copperwiki.org/index.php. Accessed - 22/4/2013.

Croplife America (2011) *Benefits of pesticides, Insecticides and Crop Protection Chemicals.* Croplife Communications 1156 16th Street, NW. Washinton, DC 2005. Accessed – 1/3/2013.

Croplife India (2011) *Crop Protection*. Croplife India/Croplife International.

Croplife International (2013) *Crop protection Horticulture* stubs/crop. Accessed 1/3/2013.

Doug, R.; Luvall, J.C.; Joey, S.; Paul, M.; David, K. and Dana, S. (2003). *Precision Agriculture: Changing the face of farming.* http://www.agiweb.org/geotimes/novo3/feature-agric.html. Accessed- 17th/11/2012.

Dupont (2013) *Protecting Plants to Feed the World.* Crop Protection, United States. Accessed – 1/3/2013.

Garg, J., Poudel, B., Chiesa, M. (2008). "Enhanced Thermal Conductivity and Viscosity of Copper Nanoparticles in Ethylene Glycol Nanofluid". *Appl. Phys;* 103: 074301.

Ghormade, V., Deshpande, M.V., and Paknikar, K.M. (2011), Nanotechnology in Crop Protection. *Biotechnol Ad.* 29 (6): 792-803 Centre for Nano Bioscience, Agharkar Research Institute, India. Accessed – 19/11/12.

Green Answers (GA) (2013) *How can Nanotechnology help Crops Damaged by Weather Change?* Copyright © 2013. Green Answers.com.LLC.All rights reserved.

Gregory, J.M, (2004) *Virtual vineyard. Accenture*: http://www.accenture.com/xdoc/en/ideas/outlook/3-2004/pdf/case-sensor.pdf. Accessed- 17th/11/2012.

Invernizzi, M., Foladori, G and Maclurcan, D. (2008) "Nanotechnology's Controversial Role for the South." *Science Technology and Society* 13 (1): 123-148. Doi: 10.1177/097172180701300105.

Jinghua, G. (2004). Synchrotron Radiation, Soft X-ray Spectroscopy and Nanomaterials. *J. Nanotechnol*, 1: 193-225.

Kurzweil, R. (2005). The *Singularity is near.* Penguin Books.

Liu, X., Feng, Z.; Zang, J.; Xiao, Q. and Wang. Y. (2006). "Preparation and Testing of Cementing Nano-subnano Composites of Slow or Controlled Release of Fertilizers". *Scientia Agricultura Sinica*, 39: 1598-1604.

Madhuri, S. Ajoy, K. C. and Rolif, K. (2010). "Nanotechnology in Agricultural Disease and Food Safety". *Journal of Phytology 2(4):* 83-92. Research Centre for Nanotechnology and Bionanotechnology, Maharashtra, India.

Maheshwar, S. and Madhuri, S. (2008). *Carbon Nanomaterials. Applications in Physico-chemical and Biosystems;* Defence *Science Journal 58 (4): 5491-5516, 2008.*

Maria, D. (2009) "*New Opportunities in Nanotechnologies*". Carleton University, Canada. Accessed – 22nd/4/2013.

McClements, D.J. Decker, E.A. and Weiss, J. Investors; University of Massachussetts, Assignee. (2005). UMA 05-27: *Novel Procedure for Creating Nanolaminated Edible Films and Coatings,* U.S. Patent Application (2005).

McNeil, S. (2005). "Nanotechnology for the Biologist". *J. Leukoc Biol.* 78: 585-94.

Moraru, C.I. Panchapankesan, C.P.; Quingrong, H., Takhistov, P., Sean, L. and Kokini, J. L. (2003). *Nanotechnology: A Frontier in food Science Technology*, 57: 24-29.

Morillon, V.; Debeaufort, F.; Blond, G.; Capelle, M. and Voilley, A. (2002) Factors Affecting the Moisture Permeability of Lipid-based Edible Films: *A Review Crit.Rev.Food Sci. Nutri.*, 42: 67-89.

Mukhopadhyay, Siddhartha Sankar (2013). *Agriculture Nanotechnology's Green Field.* Available from Nature Proceedings http://dx.doi.org/10.1038/npre.2012.6900.1(2012).

Nataragan, N. and Sivasubramanian, K. (2007). *"Nanotechnology in seed management" Chinamuthu*, C.R., Chandraskaran, B. and Ramasamy (Eds), Tamil Nadu Agricultura; University, Coimbatore, India,

Nicewarmer – Pena, S.R.; Freeman, R.G.; Keiss, B.D.; He, L.; Pena, D.J.; Walton I.D.; Cromer, R., Keating, C.D. and Natan, M.J. (2001) "Submicrometer Metallic Barcodes' *Science* 294: 137-41.

Park, H.J. (1999) "Development of Advanced Edible Coatings for Fruits". *Trends Food Sci. Technol.* 10: 254-260.

Ralph, C.M. (1997). *It is a Small, Small, Small, Small World.* Xerox PARC 3333 Coyote Hill Road Palo Alto, Ca 94304.

Reddy, P.P. (2013) "Recent Advances in Crop Protection". *Life Sciences – Plant Sciences.* Springer. 259 p.

Rhim, J.W. (2004) "Increase in Water Vapour Barrier Property of Biopolymer-based-edible Films and Coating by Compositing with Lipid Materials". *Trends Food Sci. Technol.* 10: 254-260.

Robert, P. (2013) *Startup Profile: Vive Nao: Bringing Nanotechnology to the farm.* Nanomeasure, University of Warsaw, Poland. Accessed – 22/4/2013.

Rosi, N.L. and Mirkin, C.A. (2005). *"Nanostructures in Biodiognostics" Chemical.* Rev; 106: 1547-62.

Scrinis, G. and Lyons, K, (2007)" The Emerging Nano-corporate Paradigm and the Transformation of Agri-Food Systems" *International Journal of Sociology of Agriculture and Food* 15(2).

Shrestha, S., Yeung, C.M. Y., Nunnerley, C.; and Tsang, S.C. (2007). "Comparison of Morphology and Electrical Conductivity of Various Thin Films Containing Nano-crystalline Praseodymium Oxide Particles". *Sens. Actuators A: Phys* 136, 191.

Siddhartha, S.M. (2011) Nanotechnology in Agriculture: Propagating, Perpetuation, and Protecting Life". *Electron microscopy and Nanoscience Lab. Punjab Agric. University,* Ludhiana, India. Accessed – 20/11/2012.

Su, X.L. and Li, Y (2004) "Quantum dot Biolabelling Coupled with Immuno-magnetic Separation for Detection of *Escherichia Coli*". *Anal Chem* 76: 4806-10.

Subramanian, K.S., Paulraj, C. and Natarajan, S. (2007) Plant Nutrient Management Through Nanofertilizers. An Application of Nanotechnology in Agriculture. Chinnamuthu, C.R.; Murugesa, P.B. (Eds). Tamil Nadu Agricultural University, Coimbatore, India.

Susha, V.S., Chinanuthu, C.R. and Pandian, K. (2009). "Remediation of Herbicide Atrazine' Through Metal Nanoparticles". Paper Presented in the International Conference on Magnetic Materials and Their Applications in the 21st Century, October 21-23, 2008. Organized by *The Magnetic Society of India,* National Physical Laboratory, New Delhi.

Tyler, H (2012) *"Vive Crop Protection"* Canadian Chemical News.

United States Department of Agriculture (USDA) (2005) Nanoscale Science and Engineering for Agriculture and Food Systems. Report of Cooperative State Research Education and Extension Service, USDA, National Planning Workshop, November 18-19, 2002, Washington, DC.

Will, S. (2013) *Nanotechnology in Agriculture.* AZoM.com.pty.Ltd. Accessed – 2013.

Yang, P. and Luzzi, D.E. (2009) "Nanotechnology". *Mircrosoft®Encarta(R)(DVD).* Redmond, W.A: Microsoft Corporation, 2008.

CHAPTER

Best Performance of Menthol Mint Cultivars Under Different Dates of Transplanting

Sandeep Sharma[1]; G.S. Panwar[2]; Saudan Singh[3]

ABSTRACT

A field experiment was conducted to evaluate the best performance of different dates of transplanting for four menthol mint (*Mentha arvensis L.*) cultivars (Kushal, Himalaya, Saksham and Kosi) were transplanting on 15th March, 30th March and 15th April respectively. The Randomized Block Design (RBD) was used in experiments. The study revealed that showed highest plant height (75cm) and fresh herb yield (228.6q/ha) from Saksham cultivar transplanted on 15th March, lowest plant height (25cm) and fresh herb yield (176.6q/ha) from Kushal cultivar, when it was transplanted on 15th April. However, highest oil content (0.7%), oil yield (147.7kg/ha) and menthol yield (104.8kg/ha) was recorded in cultivar Kosi when it was transplanted on 15th March. The study concluded that cultivar Kosi it was transplanted on 15th March is the optimum date of transplanting of menthol mint for higher growth and yield.

Key word: Menthol mint, cultivar, transplanting, growth, yield and oil.

1. Project Directorate for Farming System Research, Modipuram, Meerut - 250110, India.
2. Bihar Agriculture University, Sabour, Bhagalpur, India.
3. Central Institute of Medicinal and Aromatic Plants, Lucknow - 226015, India.

INTRODUCTION

Mint belonging to genus Mentha (family Lamiaceae) varying in their aroma and end use have been known as useful plant species from the time immemorial. Mints are commonly used as the source of fragrance and flavour especially for culinary preparations. Although many species of mints are being cultivated world over, only four species are predominantly cultivated in India. These incluade Menthol mint (Mentha arvensis L. var. *piperascens*), Pepper mint (M. *piperita*), Bergamot mint (M. *citrata*) and Spearmint (M. *spicata*). Among these, menthol mint (also referred as Japanese mint) is the most popular species commercially cultivated in India.

It is extensively cultivated in India, China, Brazil, Japan, USA, France, Australia, Thailand, Angola and Argentina (Srivastava et al., 2000). In India, Menthol mint is cultivated in tarai and central regions of Uttar Pradesh, Punjab and Haryana, where it has proved a boon to growers and fitted well in some of the existing cropping systems. The area under this crop in the country is estimated to be about 1.5 lakh hectare with annual production of 14000 tonnes of oil (Khanuja et al., 2006). At present the production of menthol mint oil in the country accounts for about 80 per cent of the total world production. About 30 years ago though the demand of menthol mint oil as well as menthol was being met through import, however, presently India is the first largest producer as well as exporter of menthol mint oil and its derivatives (menthol, menthone and terpenes) to the world market.

To cope with the ever increasing demand of menthol mint oil and its derivatives in domestic as well as in overseas markets, there is a need to increase the production of oil in the country at lower cost of production to meet the internal/external demand and also to compete in the international market. One of the possible was to increase the oil production in the country is to popularize the cultivation of mint among small holders who constitute for the majority of mint growers. Since mint is a labour intensive crop, it is highly desirable proposition for small holders, and it also fits well in different cropping systems. Generally, menthol mint is planted in the second fortnight of January which neither falls under rabi nor the summer season, however, manipulation in cultivation practices allows growing of menthol mint after harvest of rabi crops which attracts majority of small holders to venture in to mint cultivation. Possibilities of transplanting menthol mint after rabi crops by using nursery raised plantlets has also been well established and give good yield. (Ram, 1985; Singh et al., 1998).

Studies carried out by Saini et al (2002) revealed that 15th March is the optimum date of transplanting for cultivar Kosi. But Himalaya, Kushal and saksham are the other important high yielding cultivars of menthol mint developed by CIMAP. The information on optimum time of planting with respect to different cultivars of menthol mint is not available. Hence present investigation on "Best performance of menthol mint (Mentha arvensis L.) Cultivars under different dates of transplanting" was carried out with following objectives:

1. To find out optimum date of menthol mint transplanting.
2. To evaluate yields potential of different menthol mint cultivars under different dates of transplanting.

MATERIAL AND METHODS

The experiment was carried out at Central Institute of Medicinal and Aromatic Plants, Lucknow. Situated at 26.5ºN latitude 80.5ºE longitude and altitude of 120 meter mean sea level during 2008 using cultivars Kushal, Himalaya, Saksham and Kosi. The The annual maximum and minimum temperature are 41.8ºc and 6.6ºc, respectively. The experimental field was well drained and leveled. Composite soil samples from 0-15 cm depth were collected before planting for physical and chemical analysis before fertilizer application. The details of physical-chemical properties of soil have been presented in (Tables 8.1 & 8.2) which indicate that soil of experimental plot was sandy loam in texture, poor in organic carbon and available N, and medium in available phosphorus and potassium.

Table 8.1: Physical Properties of Experimental Field

Particulars Method Employed Partical size distribution:	Value
Sand (%)	70.5
Silt (%)	9.0
International pippet method (Piper, 1950)	
Clay (%)	20.5
Texture of soil	Sandy loam

Table 8.2: Chemical Properties of the Experimental Field

Particulars	Values	Methods Employed
Soil pH (1:2.5)	7.7	Glass electrod/Elico/pH meter (Jackson,1973)
EC (dsm -1) (1:2.5)	0.45	
Organic Carbon (%)	0.50	Walkley and Black method (Black, 1965)
Available N (kg/ ha)	177.00	Alkaline Permanganate method (Subbaih and Asija, 1973)
Available P (kg/ha)	13.7	Olsen method (Olsen et. al; 1954)
Available K (kg/ha)	168.00	Flame Emission Spectrophotometry (Jackson, 1973)

A Factorial Randomized Block Design (FRBD) was used with three dates of transplanting (15th March, 30th March and 15th April) and four cultivars (Kushal, Himalaya, Saksham and Kosi). The experimental treatments were replicated three times.

TREATMENT

Date of transplating: 03	Cultivars: 04
D1: 15th March	V1: Kushal
D2: 30th March	V2: Himalaya
D3: 15th April	V3: Saksham
	V4: Kosi

EXPERIMENTAL CROP CULTIVARS

Four cultivars of Menthol mint (Mentha arvensis L.) were used in this study. All these are developed by Central Institute of Medicinal and Aromatics Plants, Lucknow. The brief details of all cultivars are given below:

Kushal: Fast growing cultivar with high yield of essential oil and menthol. Suitable for delayed planting conditions.

Himalaya: Tall growing and spreading type of growth habit. Suitable for direct planting conditions of sub-tropical plains.

Saksham: Hardy variety. Comparatively better for water stress and excess water conditions. Suitable for delayed harvesting in rainy season.

Kosi: The genotype possesses light green leaves, whitich flowers and branching providing a globular canopy allowing equal distribution of sun light, early maturing habit, robust growth habit, high leaf density and wide synchronous growth. Early maturing period 90-100 days as against other varieties like Kosi and Himalaya. Better tolerance of leaf spot, rust and powdery mildew diseases. It yields higher biomass (250 q/ha to 400 q/ha) and synthesizes more oil percentage (0.71-1.0%) and menthol content (81-83%) with oil yield above (200 kg/ha). This is an advantage to fit this genotype in the cropping system in the country for the conventional crops. For instance, in respect to the food crops like potato, chickpea or wheat which are extensively grown in north Indian plains and harvested during March – April, their cultivation can be relayed well with the cultivation of Kosi.

IMPORTANT CULTURAL OPERATIONS

Raising of Plantlets in Nursery Bed

For raising of plantlets, suckers of menthol mint variety Kosi, Kushal, Saksham and Himalay were chopped in small pieces of 2-3 cm length and planted in the nursery beds in rows 15 cm apart at 1 cm deep and covered with mixture of fine soil and Farm Yard Manure and a light irrigation was given just after planting for proper sprouting. The sucker were planted in nursery bed before 40 days before transplanting in each date.

FIELD PREPARATION

Before transplanting the field was deep ploughed with soil turning plough. This was followed by a harrowing then one pre sown irrigation was given when the field came in condition. Final beds were prepared by two or three cross harrowing and planting.

FERTILIZER APPLICATION

Nitrogen, Phosphorus and potassium were applied at 150, 60 and 60 kg/ha through, urea, diaammonium phosphate (46% P_2O_5 and 18% N) and muriate of potash (60% K_2O), respectively. One third of the total nitrogen and full amount of phosphorus and potassium were placed as basal and mixed well in the soil, remaining two third does of N was top dressed in two equal splits after 30 and 45 days of transplanting.

TRANSPLANTING OF SEEDLINGS

About 40 days old seedling having 8-10 leaves were transplanted at 50 cm. row spacing , 15cm apart as per treatment i.e., on 15th March, 30th March and 15th April 2008.

IRRIGATION

To obtain luxuriant growth, menthol mint requires frequent irrigation during summer months. As a result, 09 irrigation were given during crop growing seasons.

HARVESTING

Menthol mint crop was harvested 100 days after transplanting when 2-3 lower leaves become yellow. Plant was cut at 5cm from ground level with the help of sickles and weighed immediately harvest to record the fresh weight per plot. The plant growth, herb yield and oil quality were recorded and essential oil content on v/w basis was extracted by hydro distillation using Clevenger glass apparatus at each harvest.

RESULTS AND DISCUSSION

Effect of different menthol mint cultivars and dates of planting on various growth, yield and quality parameter are presented in this chapter.

Plant Height: Data recorded on plant height as influenced by different dates of transplanting and cultivars on menthol mint at various stages of crop growth and at harvest are presented in (Table 8.3).

Effect of Cultivar

Data presented in (Table 8.3) revealed that significant differences in plant height due to different cultivars were observed irrespective of different stages of crop growth. Cultivar Saksham registered significantly higher plant height, closely followed by Himalaya, Kosi and Kushal, irrespective of different stages of crop growth. Cultivar Saksham regeistard 23.3 cm height as against 21.7, 18.3 and 16.7cm, recorded from cultivars Himalaya, Kosi, and Kushal, respectively at 30 days after transplanting. There was a 39-43 per cent increase in plant height in a interval of 15 days up to 60 days after transplanting. There after increasing trend in plant height reduced up to 22-25 per cent. Maximum plant height of cultivar Saksham was recorded as 58.3 cm as against 54.2, 44.7 and 41.7cm recorded in cultivar Himalaya, Kosi and Kushal, respectively, at harvesting stage. The differences in plant height of different cultivars might be due to their different nature of growth. Kumar *et al.*,(1999) also observed significant differences in various cultivars of menthol mint.

Table 8.3: Plant Height (cm) of Menthol Mint Cultivars as Influenced by Planting Time at Various Stages of Crop Growth

Treatments	Days After Transplanting			
	30 DAT	45 DAT	60 DAT	At Harvest
Cultivars				
Kushal	16.70	23.30	33.30	41.70
Himalaya	21.70	30.30	43.30	54.20
Saksham	23.30	32.70	46.70	58.30
Kosi	18.30	25.70	36.70	44.70
SEm±	0.25	0.35	0.51	0.90
CD at 5%	0.74	1.04	1.49	2.63
Dates of Transplanting				
15 March	25.00	35.00	50.00	62.50
30 March	20.00	28.00	40.00	49.10
15 April	15.00	21.00	30.00	37.50
SEm±	0.22	0.31	0.44	0.78
CD at 5%	0.64	0.90	1.29	2.28

DAT- Days after transplanting

Effect of Dates of Transplanting

Remarkable differences in plant height were observed in menthol mint due to different dates of transplanting at various stage of crop growth. Highest plant height of 25, 35, 50 and 62.5cm was recorded at 30, 45 and 60 days after transplanting and at harvest, respectively when menthol mint was planted of 15th March. The crop planted on 15th March registered lowest plant height i.e. 15, 21, 30 and 37.5 cm at 30, 45, 60 days after transplanting and at harvest respectively. Appreciable differences in plant height due to different dates of transplanting may be due to prevailing atmospheric conditions particularly increasing air temperature and decreasing relative humidity under extended date of transplanting. Delay in date of transplanting causes reduction in overall growth and plant height of menthol mint. Similar observation were recorded by many other workers (Singh et al., 1995; Singh et al., 1997; Ram et al., 1999; Patra et al., 2002 and Ram et al., 2004).

Plant Spread

Data recorded on the plant spread in menthol mint as affected by different cultivars and date of transplanting is set out in (Table 8.4). Data revealed that both the treatment cultivars as well as date of transplanting exhibited notable differences in plant spread.

Table 8.4: Plant Spread (cm) of Menthol Mint Cultivars as Influenced by Planting Time at Various Stages of Crop Growth

Treatments	Days After Transplanting			
	30 DAT	45 DAT	60 DAT	At Harvest
Cultivars				
Kushal	7.00	13.80	24.60	44.30
Himalaya	7.30	14.40	26.00	46.70
Saksham	7.50	14.70	26.60	47.70
Kosi	7.20	14.10	25.20	45.30
SEm±	0.06	0.15	00.15	00.26
CD at 5%	0.19	0.44	00.44	00.76
Dates of Transplanting				
15 March	7.80	15.00	27.20	48.50
30 March	7.60	14.70	26.60	47.50
15 April	6.40	12.90	23.00	42.00
SEm±	0.06	0.13	00.13	00.23
CD at 5%	0.17	0.38	00.38	00.66

DAT- Days after transplanting

Effect of Cultivar

Cultivars brought about significant differences in plant spread. Maximum plant spread up to 7.5 cm was recorded with cultivar Saksham as against 7.3 cm with Himalaya, 7.2 cm. with Kosi and 7.0 cm with Kushal at 30 days after transplanting. Similar trend in plant spread was noticed in later stages of crop growth as well as at harvest. Cultivar Saksham regeisterd 14.7 cm plant spread as against 14.4 cm with Himalaya, 14.1cm with Kosi and 13.8 cm with cultivar Kushal at 45 days after transplanting. Appreciable increase in plant spread was registered with increase in time and about 80 per cent increase in plant spread was recorded in a period of next 15 days irrespective of different cultivars. Maximum plant spread of 47.7 cm was recorded in cultivar Saksham at harvest which was significantly superior over other cultivars. The next cultivar with respect of plant spread was Himalaya which registered 46.7 cm. Plant spread at harvest followed by 45.3 cm in Kosi and 44.3 cm in Kushal.

The marked variation in the plant spread could be attributed to the basic physiological differences in different cultivars. It was observed that cultivar Saksham was more spreading in nature whereas Kosi was compact type.

Effect of Date of Transplanting

Data presented in (Table 8.4), revealed that there was a significant decrease in plant spread at all the stages of crop growth. The crop transplanted on 15th March remained significantly superior with respect of plant spread at all the stages of crop growth. Fifteen March transplanted crop registered 7.8, 15.0, 27.2 and 48.5 cm plant spread at 30 days after transplanting, 45 days after transplanting, 60 days after transplanting and at harvest, respectively. There was a significant decrease in plant spread due to delay in transplanting and about 2-3 per cent decrease in plant spread was observed when crop was transplanted on 30 March over 15th March transplanted crop, irrespective of stages of crop growth. Plant spread decrease by 13-18 per cent in 15th April transplanted crop, over 15th March transplanted crop irrespective of different growth stages. Main causes for decreasing trend in plant spread may be prevailing environment condition and specially rise in temperature, and fall in relative humidity.

Fresh Herb Yield

Data on fresh herb yield as affected by different cultivars and date of transplanting is set out in (Table 8.5).

Effect of Cultivar

Data revealed that different cultivars could not make any significant difference in fresh herb yield. However cultivar Kosi produced highest (206.8 q/ha) herb yield closely followed by Saksham (205.6 q/ha), Kushal (202.5 q/ha) and Himalaya (199.5 q/ha). Contrary to above finding, Kumar et al., (1999) reported significantly higher yield in cultivar Kosi as compared to other high yielding cultivar.

Effect of Date of Transplanting

Data on fresh herb yield as influenced by date of transplanting is given in (Table 8.5). Data revealed that crop planted on 15th March yielded significantly higher fresh herbage yield over 30th March planted crop and 15th April transplanted crop. Yield recorded on 15th March planted crop was 226.5 q/ha as against 203.3q/ha in 30th March transplanted crop and 181.0q/

ha in 15th April transplanted crop. Decreasing trend in herbage yield due to delay in date of transplanting was attributed to prevailing weather conditions. Balyan and Singh 1975, Singh et al.,1979, Singh and Nand 1979, Singh et al.,1986, Singh et al.,1998, Patra et al.,2002 and Ram et al.,2004 also reported similar trend in yield while working on menthol mint under different agro-climatic conditions.

Oil Content (Fresh Weight Basis)

Data recorded on oil content on fresh weight basis as affected by different cultivars and dates of transplanting is recorded in (Table 8.5).

Table 8.5: Fresh Herb Yield, Oil Content and Oil Yield of Menthol Mint Cultivars as Influenced by Planting Time at Various Stages of Crop Growth

Treatment	At Harvest		
	Fresh herb yield (q/ha)	Oil content (FWB) %	Oil yield (kg/ha)
Cultivars			
Kushal	202.5	0.7	127.8
Himalaya	199.5	0.6	122.8
Saksham	205.6	0.6	120.2
Kosi	206.8	0.7	137.5
SEm±	2.955	0.002	1.763
CD at 5%	NS	0.01	5.16
Dates of Transplanting			
15 March	226.5	0.6	137.0
30 March	203.3	0.6	127.0
15 April	181.0	0.7	117.3
SEm±	2.569	0.002	1.527
CD at 5%	7.483	0.006	4.466

FWB: Fresh weight basis

NS: Non Significant

Effect of Cultivar

There was a significant difference in oil content of different cultivars. Cultivar Kosi regeisterd significantly higher oil content over other three cultivars, cultivar Kushal ranked as second with respect of oil content and produced significantly higher oil content over Himalaya and Saksham. Himalaya also found significantly superior over Saksham with respect of essential oil content on fresh weight basis. Kumar et al.,1999, Dwivedi et al.,2000 and Kumar et al.,2000 also reported significant variation in the oil content of the different cultivars of mentha species.

Effect of Date of Transplanting

Data presented in (Table 8.5) on essential oil content as influenced by different dates of transplanting revealed that date of transplanting brought about significant differences in the essential oil content in menthol mint. Essential oil content increase significantly with delaying date of transplanting. 15th March transplanted crop registered lowest (0.6%) essential oil content as against (0.6%) in 30th March transplanted crop and (0.7%) in 15th April transplanted crop. Significant variation in essential oil content due to date of transplanting may be due to differences in leaf: stem ratio as essential oil remains in leaves only. Thus increasing proportion of leaves could improve oil content. Similar observation were also reported by Singh et al.,1995 in spearmint , Singh et al., 1997 in peppermint and Ram et al.,1998 in menthol mint. Ram et al., 2004 also reported similar result in menthol mint.

Oil Yield

Data recorded on essential oil yield and affected by different cultivars and dates of transplanting is reported in (Table 8.5). Data revealed that different cultivars as well as dates of transplanting brought about remarkable differences in the essential oil yield.

Effect of Cultivar

It is cleared from the data given in (Table 8.5) that cultivar Kosi registered highest essential oil yield of 137.5 kg/ha which was significantly superior over other cultivars. Yield level of cultivar Kushal and Himalaya remained statistically at par whereas essential oil yield of cultivar Himalaya was statistically at par with cultivar Kushal as well as Saksham. Chauhan et al., 2000, Patra et al., 2002 and Singh et al., 2002 also study essential oil yield potential of different cultivars of menthol mint under different climatic conditions and reported significant variations.

Effect of Date of Transplanting

Data recorded in (Table 8.5), on essential oil yield of menthol mint as influenced by different dates of transplanting, clearly revealed that highest essential oil yield of 137 kg/ha was recorded on 15th March transplanted crop. The yield potential of the menthol mint decrease significantly with delay transplanting and a reduction in yield about 10kg/ha due to 30th March planted crop and 20kg/ha due to 15th April transplanted crop was recorded over 15th March transplanted crop. Similar result on essential oil yield as affected by different dates of transplanting were recorded by Singh et al., 1995, Singh et al., 1997 and Ram et al., 2004.

Quality of Menthol Mint Oil

Menthol Content

Data recorded on effect on cultivars, effect on dates of transplanting and interaction effect of cultivar and dates of transplanting on menthol content in essential oil of menthol mint is presented in (Table 8.6).

Table 8.6: Menthol Content, Menthyl Acetate and Menthone Content of Menthol Mint Cultivars as Influenced by date of Transplanting

Treatment	Menthol content (%)				Menthyl Acetate Content (%)				Menthone Content (%)			
	Date of Transplanting				Date of Transplanting				Date of Transplanting			
	15 March	30 March	15 April	Mean	15 March	30 March	15 April	Mean	15 March	30 March	15 April	Mean
Cultivars												
Kushal	73.9	74.8	69.8	72.8	1.0	1.8	2.6	1.8	9.9	8.1	11.4	9.8
Himalaya	72.5	73.1	65.8	70.5	1.2	5.2	7.3	4.6	11.1	5.7	7.9	8.2
Saksham	73.7	72.8	62.0	69.5	1.1	1.8	3.2	2.0	10.5	8.6	10.6	9.9
Kosi	71.2	75.5	72.6	73.1	2.1	1.5	1.4	1.7	9.3	7.5	10.1	8.9
Mean	72.8	74.1	67.6		1.4	2.6	3.6		10.2	7.5	10.0	
	SEm ±	CD at 5%			SEm ±	CD at 5%			SEm ±	CD at 5%		
V	0.18	0.52			0.03	0.09			0.03	0.09		
D	0.15	0.45			0.03	0.08			0.03	0.09		

V- Varieties
D- Dates of transplanting

Effect of Cultivar

Data presented in (Table 8.6) revealed that highest menthol content of 73.1 per cent was recorded in cultivar Kosi followed by 72.8 per cent in cultivar Kushal. However differences in these to cultivar remained statistically at par. Cultivar Himalaya and Saksham produced significantly lower menthol content over Kushal and Kosi. Differences in menthol content in different cultivars was due to their genetic character and same was reported by Kumar et al., 1999, Singh et al., 2000 and Khanuja et al., 2001.

Effect of Date of Transplanting

Data presented in (Table 8.6), on the effect of different dates of transplanting on the menthol content in essential oil of menthol mint clearly revealed that highest menthol content was recorded in 30th March transplanted crop. The crop transplanted before or after this date registered lower menthol content. However lowest menthol content was by recorded in 15th April transplanted crop. These finding are also in conformity with the finding of Singh et al.,1997, Shah et al., 1999 and Ram et al., 2004.

Menthyl Acetate

Data recorded on effect of different cultivars, effect of different dates of transplanting and interaction effect on cultivar with date of transplanting on menthyl acetate content is presented in (Table 8.6).

Effect of Cultivar

Data presented in (Table 8.6) revealed that highest menthyl acetate (4.6%) was recorded in cultivar Himalaya, followed by cultivar Saksham, Kushal and Kosi.

Effect of Date of Transplanting

Data of the different dates of transplanting given in (Table 8.6) revealed that menthyl acetate content increased with delay in the date of transplanting. It was reported 1.4 per cent in 15th March transplanted crop, 2.6 per cent in 30th March transplanted crop and 3.6 per cent in 15th April transplanted crop.

Menthone Content

Data recorded on menthone content in essential oil of menthol mint as influenced by different cultivars, different dates of transplanting and interaction effect on cultivars with dates of transplanting is reported in (Table 8.6).

Effect of Cultivar

Data presented in (Table 8.6) on the effect of cultivar on the menthone content revealed that there was a significant difference in the menthone content in essential oil of different cultivars. The highest menthone content

(9.9%) was recorded in cultivar Saksham closely followed by cultivar Kushal (9.8%). Himalaya gave lowest menthone content (8.2%) whereas menthone content recorded from Kosi was (8.9%).

Effect of Date of Transplanting

Data presented in (Table 8.6), on menthone content in essential oil of menthol mint revealed that date of transplanting had considerable effect on menthone content.

Lowest menthone content (7.5%) was recorded from 30th March transplanted crop whereas it increases either advancing the date of transplanting or delaying the date of transplanting. In 15th March transplanted crop menthone content was (10.2%) and in 15th April transplanted crop it was (10.0%).

Menthol Yield

As menthol is the one of the major and most essential components of the essential oil of menthol mint, data on total menthol yield was also developed and presented in (Table 8.7 & Fig. 8.1).

Effect of Cultivar

Data presented in (Table 8.7 & Fig. 8.1) clearly revealed that Kosi yielded 99.9 kg/ha menthol as against 92.2 kg/ha in Kushal, 86.2 kg/ha in Himalaya and 83.3 kg/ha in Saksham. The differences in all the cultivars for menthol yield were statistically significant. Kumar et al., 1999, Singh et al., 2000 and Ozel and Ozguven 2002, also reported great variation in the quality of the essential oil of mint species.

Table 8.7: Menthol Yield (kg/ha) of Menthol Mint Cultivars as Influenced by Date of Transplanting

Treatment	15 March	30 March	15 April	Mean
Cultivars				
Kushal	100.6	94.6	81.2	92.2
Himalaya	95.6	89.4	73.5	86.2
Saksham	94.8	86.50	68.6	83.3
Kosi	104.8	102.9	91.9	99.9
Mean	98.9	93.4	78.8	
	SEm ±	CD at 5%		
V	1.26	3.68		
D	1.09	3.18		

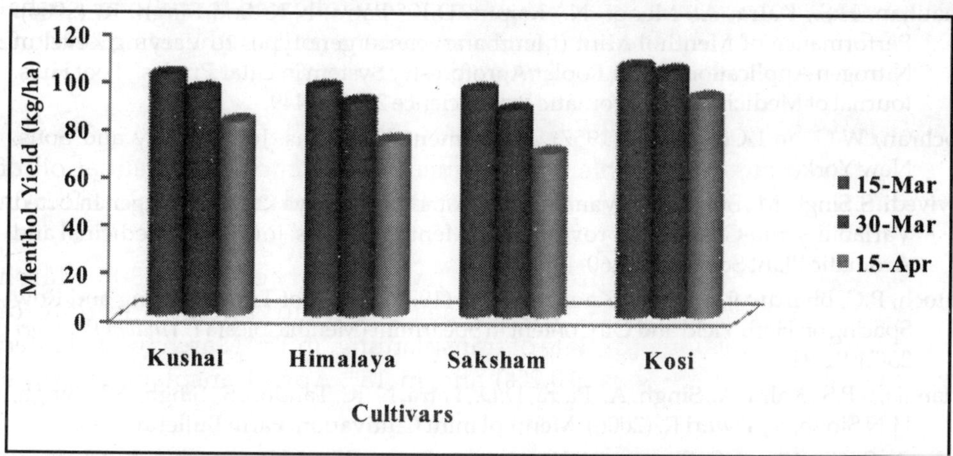

Fig 8.1: Menthol Yield (kg/ha) of Menthol Mint Cultivars as Influenced by Date of Transplanting

Effect of Date of Transplanting

Data presented in (Table 8.7 & Fig. 8.1) also revealed that date of transplanting had significant effect on total menthol yield. Menthol yield decrease significantly with delay in the date of planting. Highest menthol yield (99 kg/ha) was recorded from 15th March transplanted crop followed by 93.4 kg/ha, from 30th March transplanted crop and 78.8 kg/ha from 15th April transplanted crop. Variation in menthol content in essential oil caused significant differences in the total menthol yield due to different dates of transplanting. Similar result were also reported by *Ram et al.,1998, Ram et al., 2001 and Ram et al.,2004.*

CONCLUSION

Results of the present investigation indicate that for optioned higher productivity of good quality menthol mint oil under sub- tropical condition of central Uttar Pradesh. Menthol mint cultivar Kosi may be recommendation for its commercial cultivation. Results of the present studies also suggest that there is a need of conducting more dates of transplanting experiment with advancing the dates of transplanting as highest oil yield and net returns in optioned on first date (15th March) of transplanting.

REFERENCES

Balyan, S.S.and Singh, A. (1975). Studies on Optimum Time of Planting in Mentha. *Indian J. Agron*. 20: 192-193.

Bhardwaj, S.D., Katoch, P.C., Kaushal, A.N., Raina, V. (1978). Effect of Time of Planting and Spacing in Relation to Herbage Yield and Oil Content in Menthapiperita Linn. In Himanchal Pradesh. *Indian J. Agric. Sci.* 48(8): 463-466.

Black, C.A. (1965). Methods of Soil Analysis. Part 2 Am. Soc. Agron. Medison. Wisconsin, U.S.A.

Chauhan, H.S., Kalra, A., Mengi, N., Rajput, D.K., Patra, N.K. and Singh, K. (2000). Performance of Menthol Mint (Mentha arvensis) genotypes to Varying Level of Nitrogen Application Under Poplar Agroforestry System in Uttar Pradesh Foot Hills. Journal of Medicinal and Aromatic Plant Science 22, 447-449.

Cochran, W.G. and Cox, G.M. (1957). Experimental Designs. John Willey and Sons, New York.

Dwivedi, S. Singh, M., Singh, A.P. Vandana Singh and I.B. Maurya (2000). Mutagen Induced Variability and Genetic Improvement in Mentha Species. Journal of Medicinal and Aromatic Plant Science 22, 460-463.

Katoch, P.C; Bhardwaj, S.D. and Kaushal, A.N. (1979). Effect of Time Planting and Row Spacing on Herb Yield and Oil Content in Spearmint (Menthaspicata L.) *Indian Perfumer* 23(2): 91-94.

Khanuja, S.P.S., Kalra, A., Singh, A., Patra, D.D., Patra, N .K., Tandon, S., Singh, A.K. Singh, H.N Singh, S., Tiwari R. (2006). Menthol mint Cultivation. Farm Bulletin. 45-5.

Khanuja, S.P.S., Kumar, S., Shasany, A.K., Dhawan, S., Darokar, M.P., Naqvi, A.A., Dhawan, O.P., Singh, A.K., Patra, N.K., Bahl, J.R., Bansal, R.P. (2001). A menthol Tolerant Variety Saksham of Mentha Arvensis yielding High Menthol. Journal of Medicinal and Aromatic Plant Science, 23(2): 110-112.

Kumar, S., Bahl, J.R., Bansal, R.P., Kukreja, A.K., Garg, S.N., Naqvi, A.A., Luthra, R. and Sharma, S. (2000). Profiles of the Essential Oils of Indian Menthol Mint Mentha Arvensis Cultivars at Different Stages of Crop Growth in Nortern Plains. Jour. Med. Arom. Pl. Sci. 22: 774-786.

Kumar, V and Sood, M., (2011). Effect of Transplanting Time, Spacing and Fertilizers on Herbage and Oil Yield of Menthapiperita L. *International Journal of farm sciences* 1(2): 68-74.

Kumar, B. Ram, P. Sharm, S. and Ranjan, V. (1999). Status of Menthol mint (Mentha arvensis L.) Cultivation in India: A Survey Report on Haryana and Punjab. Indian Perfumer 43: 83-87.

Mekonnen, S.A. and Kassahun, B.M., (2011). Effect of Inter Row Spacing and Harvesting Time on Growth and Essential Oil Yield of Spearmint (Menthaspicata l.). *International Journal of Sustainable Agriculture* 3(2): 39-43.

Ozel, A., Ozguven, M.(1999). Effect of Different Planting Time on Yields and Agricultural Charaters of Differents mint (Mentha spp.) Varieties under Harran Plains Condition. *Journal of Agriculture and Forestry* 23; 921-928.

Ozel, A., Ozguven, M. (2002). Effect of Different Planting Time on Essential Oil Components of Different Mint (Mentha spp.) Varieties. *Turkish Journal of Agriculture and Forestry* 26(5): 289-294.

Patra, N.K., Singh, V.R., Ram, P. and Kumar, B. (2002). Yield Appraisal of Menthol Mint (Mentha arvensis L.) Varieties Under Late Transplanted Cropping Programme. Indian Perfumer 46(1) : 21-23.

Ram, M., Ram, D., Singh, S., Roy, S.K., Kumar, S. (2001). Effect of Planting Time on the Growth and Essential Oil Yield in Different Varieties of Menthol Mint (Menthaarvensis). *Journal of Medicinal and Aromatic Plant Science* 22/23.

Ram, P. Kumar, B., Negi, M.S., Yaseen, M., Singh, V.R., and Patra, N.K. (2004). Impact of Plantlet Age and Planting Time on Yield of Transplanted menthol mint. *Indian Perfumer* 48(3): 299-303.

Shah, B.N., Baruah, A.K.S. and Baruah, B.C. (1999). Effect of Planting Date and Spacing on Yield of Herb and Essential Oil of Menthapiperita. *Indian J. Agronomy* 44(4): 851-856.

Singh.,K., Rao, B.R.R.; Singh, C.P.; Kaul, P.N.; Mallavarapu, G.R.; Ramesh, S. (2002). Comparative Performance of Menthol Mint (Mentha arvensis L.f. Piperacens Malinvaud ex homs) Cultivar in semi- arid Tropical Climate. Journal of Spices and Aromatic Crops 11(1): 67-69.

Singh, K., Kaul, N.P., Bhattacharya, A.K. and Singh, C.P. (1999). Effect of Planting Dates and Spacing on Performance of Menthaarvensis L in Semi arid Climate of Hyderabad. *Indian Perfumer* 43(1): 29-34.

Singh, M., Singh, A., Singh, S., Tripathi, R.S., ingh, A.K. and Patra, D.D.(2010). Cowpea (*Vignaunguiculata L.*) as a Green Manure to Improve the Productivity of a Menthol Mint (*Menthaarvensis L.*) inter Cropping System. Industrial Crops and Products 31: 289-293.

Singh, M., Singh, V.P. and Singh, D.V. (1995). Effect of Planting Time on Growth Yield and Quality of Spearmint (Menthaspicata L.) Under Sub-tropical Climate of Central U.P. *J Essential Oil Res*. 7: 621-626.

Singh, N.P. and Nand, K. (1979). Influence of Planting Time and Row Spacing on the Yield of Spearmint. *Indian Perfumer* 23(1): 53-54.

Singh, N.P., Saxena, M.C. and Nand, K. (1977). Effect of Dates of Planting, Row Spacing and Rates of Nitrogen Application on the Herb Yield of Menthaarvensis L. *Indian Perfumer* 21: 83-85.

CHAPTER

Effect of Growth and Yield Performance of Selected Accessions on *Jatropha curcas L.*

Sandeep Sharma[1]; Bajrang Singh[2]

ABSTRACT

Jatropha curcas L. internationally and locally known respectively, as Physic nut, is a highly promising species for biodiesel production in Brazil and other countries in the tropics. *Jatropha curcas* arise from greek word "Jatros"which mean a 'Doctor'and "trophe"means nutrition, Jatropha curcas is a stress-resistant perennial plant growing an marginal soils. *Jatropha curcas* is a wellestablished plant in India. This plant offers the option both to cultivate wastelands and to produce vegetable oil suitable for conversion to biodiesel. *Jatropha* can act as environmental friendly alternative feedstock for bio-diesel production. *Jatropha curcas* is gaining global popularity as a potential feedstock of biodiesel. Although the oil yield of the species is better than any other non-edible oil yielding plants, the lack of agronomic defame this species for further exploitation. Furthermore, there is paucity of data on the growth and yield performance of *Jatropha curcas* plantations.

1. Project Directorate for Farming Systems Research, Modipuram, Meerut (UP), India.
2. National Botanical Research Institute, Lucknow (UP), India.

Oil content in the seeds was 31 per cent, ranging from 16 to 35 per cent. The *Jatropha* oil can be easily processed to fully replace Petroleum based diesel fuel. Thus, the use of this plant for large scale biodiesel production is of great interest with regard to solving the energy shortage, reducing green house gas emissions, rural employment generation and increasing the income of farmers. An evaluation of 24 accessions selected of *Jatropha curcas* were screened, based growth and yield parameters was carried out at National Botanical Research Institure, Lucknow, and field. The aim of this study was to determine the best growth and yield performance of the selected accessions. The experiment was conducted using Randomized Block Design (RBD) with four replication and 24 selected accessions. The study was carried out to investigate the effect of growth and yield performance of selected accessions on *Jatropha curcas* L.

Key words: Jatropha curcas, Growth performance, Yield performance, rural development, Bio-fuel, Energy, Petroleum.

INTRODUCTION

It has been increasingly apparent that the production of befouled must originate from non-food crops dedicated solely to energy production. These crops should not compete with food crop production. *Jatropha curcas* originated in Central America. It is a perennial softwood shrub or small tree that is now fairly well established in most tropical and subtropical areas of the world. It is commonly referred to as physic nut or American Purging out. It belongs to the family of Euphorbiaceae. It can grow almost anywhere and it is a drought resistant perennial soil. In India total wasteland are estimated to be 63.85 mha (ICAR 2010). Among these saline (21,989 ha) and sodic (1346.97 lha) soils occupy about 1.35 mha alone in U.P. state (Sharma et al).

It is easy to establish, grows relatively quickly and lives for 40-50 years. Its productive life is from 30-40 years. The hardy *Jatropha curcas* is resistant to drought and pests and produces seeds containing 40 per cent. When the seeds are crushed and processed, the resulting oil can be used in a standard diesel engine, while the residue can also be processed into biomass to power electricity plants and it is the one of the best candidates of future bio-diesel production (Heller, 1996). Normally, it grows between three and five meters in height but can attain a height of up to eight or ten meters under favorable conditions. It has large green to pale green leaves, alternate to sub opposite, three to five lobed with a spiral phyllotoxix. Flowers are formed terminally individually female usually slightly larger and occurs in the host season. *Jatropha curcas* groes almost anywhere even on gravel, sandy and saline soils. It can thrive on the poorest stony soil and can grow even in the crevices of rocks. *Jatropha* oil has a very high saponification value and is being extensively used for making soap in some countries. Also the oil is used as an illuminant as it burns without emiting snake.

The latex of *Jatropha curcas* contains an alkaloid known as Jatrophine which is believed to have anti-cancerous properties. It is also used as an external application for skin disease and rheumatism and for sores on domestic livestock. The bark of *Jatropha curcas* yield a dark blue dye which is used for colouring cloth, fishing nets and lines (Griffiths *et al* 1989). Its leaves are used as food for silkworm. A number of industrial companies have launched plans and have started to develop new industries based on the *Jatropha* oil (Biofuel production). The main objective of the study was to find out superior accessions of *Jatropha curcas* degraded sodic lands in terms of growth, yield and oil per cent which could be economically exploited on such lands.

GROWING SEASONS LOCATION WORLD AND LOCATION INDIA

Jatropha curcas plant has been distributed anthropogenic ally to different locations which are neither similar to each other, nor are the current cultivation areas. Presently *Jatropha* is growing in several states as well as in many districts in India which are presented here (Table 9.1) *Jatropha curcas* is growing in many regions in India as an experimental trial crop for prospecting biofuel.

Table 9.1: Distribution of *Jatropha curcas* in different areas of India

Sl. No.	States	Name of Districts
1	2	3
1.	Andhra Pradesh	Adilabad, Anantapur, Chittoor, Cuddapah, Kurnool, Karim Nagar, Mehboob Nagar, Nellore, Nalgonda, Prakasam, Visakhapatnam, Warrangal.
2.	Bihar	Araria, Aurangabad, Banka, Betiah (West Champaran), Bhagalpur, Gaya, Jahanabad, Jamui, Kaimur, Latehar, Muzzaffarpur, Munger, Nawada.
3.	Chhattisgarh	Bastar, Bilaspur, Dantewada, Dhamtri, Durg, Jagdalpur, Janjgir-champa, Kanker, Kawardha, korba, Mahasaund, Rajnandgaon, Raipur, Raigarh, Surguj.
4.	Jharkhand	Bokaro, Chatra, Daltenganj, Devgarh, Dhanbad, Dumka, Garhwa, Godda, Giridih, Gumla, Hazaribag, Jamshedpur, Koderma, Pakur, Palamu, Ranchi, Sahibganj, Singbhum (East), Singbhum (West).
5.	Gujarat	Ahmedabad, Amerli, Banaskantha, Bhavnagar, Junagarh, Jamnagar, Kutch, Rajkot, Surendranagar, Surat.
6.	Goa	Panaji, Padi, Ponda, Sanguelim.
7.	Himachal Pradesh	Bilaspur, Nahan, Parvanu, Solan, Unna.
8.	Haryana	Ambala, Bhiwani, Faridabad, Gurgaon, Hisar, Jind, Jhajjar, Mohindergarh, Punchkula, Rewari, Rohtak.

(Contd...)

1	2	3
9.	Karnataka	Bijapur, Bellary, Bangalore, Belgaum, Chikmagalur, Chitradurga, Daksina Kannada, Dharwad, Gulbarga, Hassan, Kolar, Mysore, Raichur, Tumkur, Udupi.
10.	Kerala	Kottayam, Quilon, Trichur, Thiruvananthapuram.
11.	Madhya Pradesh	Betul, Chhindwara, Guna, Hoshingabad, Jabalpur, Khandwa , Mand Saur, Mandla, Nimar (Khargaon), Ratlam, Raisena, Rewa, Shahdol, Shajapur, Shivpuri, Sagar, Satna, Shahdol, Tikamgarh, Ujjain, Vidisha.
12.	Orissa	Ahmednagar, Aurangabad, Amrawati, Akola, Beed, Buldana, Dhule, Nasik, Osmanabad, Parbhani, Pune, Ratnagiri, Raigad, Thana, Yavatmal.
13.	Punjab	Ferozpur, Gurdaspur, Hoshiarpur, Patiala, Sangrur.
14.	Rajasthan	Ajmer, Alwar, Barmar, Bilwara, Bikaner, Churu, Chittorgarh, Jaisalmer, Jodhpur, Kota, Sikar, Sawai Madhopur, Udaipur.
15.	Tamilnadu	Coimbatore, Chennai, Dharmapuri, Erode, Madurai, Periyar, Salem, Tirunelvelli, Vellore.
16.	Uttar Pradesh	Allahabad, Agra, Balia, Bulandshahar, Bhadohi, Baharaich, Chhitrakut, Deoria, Firozabad, Faizabad, Ghazipur, Hardoi, Jaunpur, Jhansi, Kaushambi, Lalitpur, Mainpuri, Partapgarh, Raibareli, Sultanpur, Shahjahanpur.
17.	Uttranchal	Chamoli, Dehradun, Pithoragarh, Rishikesh, Udhamsingh Nagar, Uttrakashi.
18.	West Bengal	Balurghat, Barasat, Burdwan, Cochbehar, Darjeeling, Hoogly, Howrah.

Source: GFU.

MATERIALS AND METHODS

The experiment was carried out at National Botanical Research Institute, Lucknow, situated at 26.50N latitude 80.50E longitude and altitude of 120 meter mean sea level in the sub tropical plains of North India, during 2006-2009 using 24 selected accessions. The soil of the experimental site is sodic land. The weather data on temperature, rainfall and relative humidity during this period were obtained from the Amausi meteorology department, Lucknow. An average maximum and minimum temperature varied from 32.1° C and 19.2° C. The experiment was laid Randomized Block Design (RBD) was used with 24 accessions of *Jatropha curcas* and 4 replication in 45 cm^3 refilled pits with the same soil at a spacing 2.5 m × 2.5 m. Corresponding to a density of 1600 plants/hac. Field performance of these accessions was evaluated periodically for four consecutive years (2006-09) in respect to growth and fruiting traits when plants initiated inflorescence. In case of plant mortalities, replacement of plant was done for initial two years. Data for various growth parameters and yield related traits were subjected to statistical analysis and presented as mean and standard deviation. Analysis of variance (F test) was applied to examine the significance of differences among the accessions. Values of critical difference were computed for each parameter. All calculations were done using window 2007 (MS Office-Excel programme). The details of chemical properties of soil have been presented in Table 9.2.

Table 9.2: Different Value of Chemical Parameters of Soil Under *Jatropha curcas L*

Sl.No.	Parameters	Value	Methods
1.	pH (1:2)	8.6	Glass Electrod/Elico/pH meter (Jackson, 1973)
2.	EC (µS/m)	422	EC meter
3.	Organic Carbon (%)	0.26	Walkley and Black method (Black, 1965)
4.	Available N (kg/hac)	147.46	Alkaline permanganate method (Subbaih and Asija, 1973)
5.	Available P (kg/hac)	46.25	Olsen method (Olsen et al, 1954)

TREATMENT COMBINATIONS:

Design	:	Randomized Block Design (RBD)
Replication	:	4
Treatment	:	24
No. of plant per bed	:	4
Plot size	:	2.5 m × 10m
Spacing	:	2.5m × 2.5m
Irrigation channel	:	1m
Bund	:	50cm
Road	:	1m

BOTANICAL FEATURES AND CULTURAL PRACTICES

It is a small tree or shrub with smooth gray bark, which exudes whitish colored, watery, latex when cut. Normally, it grows between three and five meters in height, but can attain a height of up to eight or ten meters under favorable conditions.

PROPAGATION: Cutting of about 20cm length with two diameters (2 and 3 cm) of each accession were examined for determining the efficient vegetative propagation protocol. These were planted in poly bags with a potting mixture of sodic soils, sand and FYM in 1:1:1 proportion. The experiment was carried out in 2009 in poly house as well as in open field condition to assess the root development. Preparation of nursery and cutting on *Jatropha curcas* L given below in Figure 9.1.

Fig 9.1: Preparation of Nursery and Cutting on *Jatropha curcas L*

LEAVES: It has large green to Pale green leaves, alternate to sub opposite, three to five lobed with a spiral phyllotaxis.

FLOWERS: The petiole length range between 6 to 23 mm. The inflorescence is formed in the leaf axil. Flowers are formed terminally, individually with female flowers usually slightly larger and occur in the hot seasons. In conditions where continuous growth occurs, an unbalance of pistillate or staminate flower production result in a higher number of female flowers.

FRUIT: Fruits are produced in winter when the shrub is leafless, or it may produce several crops during the year if soil moisture is good and temperatures are sufficiently high. Each inflorescence yields a bunch of approximately ten or more ovoid fruits. Three, bi-valved cocci is formed after the seeds mature and the fleshy exocarp dries.

SEED: The seeds become mature when the capsule changes from green to yellow, after two to four months from fertilization. The blackish, thin shelled seeds are oblong and resemble small Jatropha seeds.

IRRIGATION: It handles dryness very well and it is possible to live almost entirely of humidity in the air. Differences are expressed in what is optimum rainfall as some reading say 600 mm and some say 800 mm whilst some areas in India report good crops with rainfall of 1380 mm. Under irrigation 1500 mm is given.

WEEDING: Standard cultural practices are timely weeding, proper fertilization, surface ploughing and pruning with their management practices a yield around 10 to 15 kg fruit/tree can be obtained even if the plants did not reach full maturity.

ALTERNATIVE TO DIESEL: It is significant to point out that the non-edible vegetable oil of *Jatropha curcas* has the requisite potential of providing a promising and commercially viable alternative to diesel oil since it has desirable physicochemical and performance characteristics comparable to diesel for mitigating climate change by reducing emission of green house gases, meeting rural energy needs, protecting the environment and generating gainful employment, *Jatropha curcas* has multiple role to play. All attempts to increase its production and productivity, Oil extraction by application of appropriate technology, product development and diversification and policies that will protect and promote national interest would be welcome. Processer of Oil extraction on *Jatropha curcas L* given below in figure 9.2.

Fig. 9.2: Processer of Oil extraction on *Jatropha curcas* L

RESULTS AND DISCUSSION

Effect of growth and yield parameters of selected accessions of *Jatropha curcas* L. are presented in this chapter. The data recorded during course of investigation on all parameters are presented in tables and supported by the work done by other scientist in recent past.

A total of 24 accessions were introduced in field trials on sodic soil at Banthra. Most of them were planted during 2005-2006 except two accessions delayed in 2007-08 due to non-availability of planting stock. Four plants were raised in each replicate in a randomized block design with four replications. Three month old sprouted stem cuttings, received from different partner organisations were planted at a spacing of 2.5 m × 2.5 m (within a row among plants and between rows), corresponding to a density of 1600 plants ha^{-1}. Field performance of these elite accessions was evaluated periodically for four consecutive years (2006 to 2009) in respect to growth and fruiting traits when plants initiated inflorescence. In case of plant mortalities, replacement of plants was done for initial two years. Data for various growth parameters and yield related traits were subjected to statistical analysis and presented as mean and standard deviations. Analysis of variance (F test) was applied to examine the significance of differences among the accessions. Values of critical difference were computed for each parameter. All calculations were done using Window 2003-07 (MS Office - Excel programme).

Properties of the *Jatropha Curcas L* oil: Properties of the *Jatropha curcas* L oil given below in Table 9.3.

Table 9.3: Properties of the *Jatropha curcas* L Oil

Sl. No.	Property	Value
1.	Density	0.92 g/cm³
2.	Solidification Point	5 kin
3.	Ignition Point	340º C
4.	Viscosity	75 to 710-6m²/s
5.	Iodine value	13
6.	Saponification value	198
7.	Cetan Number	23/51
8.	Heating value	39,628 mj/kg
9.	Flash Point	240/110º C
10.	Carbon residue	0.64
11.	Distillation Point	295º C
12.	Kinematics Viscosity	50.73 cs
13.	Sulphur	0.13%
14.	Calorific value	9.470 Kcal/kg
15.	Pour Point	8º C
16.	Color	4.0
17.	Acid value	1.0-38.2
18.	Specific gravity	0.917/0.923
19.	Solidifying Point	2.0
20.	Refractive Index	1.47
21.	Palmitic acid	4.2
22.	Stearic acid	6.9
23.	Oleic acid	43.1
24.	Linoleic acid	34.3
25.	Other acids	1.4

Plant establishment after gap filling for two years ranged from 25 to 100 per cent in different accessions. A few accessions such as FRI E4 (25%), NBPGR Hissar Local and CSMCRI C5 (37.5%) showed poor plant survival in spite of repeated mortality replacement of plants indicating their inability to tolerate high sodicity and harsh soil conditions. Growth data recorded in different years revealed significant differences ($P<0.05$) in plant height, branches per plant and canopy spread among various accessions during different years from second year onward till fourth year (Table 9.4). The plant growth in terms of increase in height was relatively fast during second and third year in different accessions after that it has gone during the fourth year. Five accessions (NBPGR Chhatrapati, NBPGR Urlikanchan, NBPGR SKN J2, NBRI J05, and CSMCRI-C2) grew fast (266.31 to 309.31 cm) since beginning of their growth as compared to all other accessions (86.82 to 104.00 cm) (Table 9.3 & Fig. 9.3). The short height of some accessions like NBPGR Hissar local and CRIDA –JR -06 may be attributed to their late field plantation. As a consequence these accessions attained only 86.82 cm (CRIDA–JR-06) and 104.00 cm (NBPGR Hissar local) height after one and two years of growth, respectively. Number of branches per plant increased gradually in different years from first year onward. There were marked differences in number of branches (6.70 to 35.37 branches per plant) among different accessions at the age of four years (Table 9.3). Branching was profuse in accessions like NBPGR Chhatrapati, (35.37 branches per plant), NBPGR Urlikanchan (30.62 branches per plant) and NBPGR SKN J2 (29.87 branches per plant) while it was poor in FRI Dehradun E-5, CRIDA –JR -06 (6.75 branches per plant) and CRIDA-JR-06 (6.70 branches per plant) probably due to their lesser age. Accordingly, there was progressive increase in canopy spread with increasing number of branches in various accessions at different ages (Table 9.4). It varied greatly from 55.73 to 260.18 cm in different accessions with minimum in FRI-Dehradun-E-5 and maximum in NBPGR Urlikanchan depending on branching pattern. These differences among various accessions were statistically significant ($P<0.05$) in different years. The data of elite accessions screening trial, revealed superiority of few accessions viz. NBPGR Chhatrapati, NBPGR Urlikanchan, NBPGR SKN J2, NBRI J05, and CSMCRI-C2 in respect to their growth rate, adaptability to stress soil conditions and branching trait suggesting their suitability for plantations on sodic soil sites. However, some of the other accessions which are presently in second line need to be looked during subsequent growth. A few accessions viz. NBRI J05 and NBPGR-Hansraj showed greater variations in growth traits among plants within the accessions. This indicated need for further selection and confirmation.

Table 9.4: Growth Performance of Various Accessions of *Jatropha curcas* on Sodic Soil

Sl. No.	Accessions	Survival (%)	Height (cm)	No. of Branches per Plant (No)	Canopy Diameter (cm)
1.	NBRI J-05	100	276.06 ± 112.18	27.12 ± 13.95	224.12 ± 111.52
2.	NBRI J-18	75	213.00 ± 68.69	17.67 ± 8.49	154.25 ± 83.53
3.	CSMCRI, GJ-KGR-C1	100	234.00 ± 59.59	23.31 ± 6.41	206.94 ± 73.99
4.	CSMCRI, GJ-RAN-C2	100	266.31 ± 74.38	25.12 ± 9.83	194.12 ± 70.15
5.	CSMCRI, GJ-PCM-C3	100	220.81 ± 94.70	21.25 ± 10.42	168.25 ± 78.94
6.	CSMCRI, OR-KMP-C4	81.25	222.13 ± 71.22	20.46 ± 7.87	189.84 ± 73.84
7.	CSMCRI, OR-GPR-C5	37.5	265.83 ± 25.58	23.83 ± 6.14	202.67 ± 52.59
8.	NBPGR, SKN J2	100	287.81 ± 69.85	29.87 ± 15.49	202.37 ± 79.61
9.	NBPGR, SKN Big	100	233.50 ± 94.69	18.09 ± 10.71	169.81 ± 74.08
10.	NBPGR, Urlikanchan	100	307.00 ± 53.41	30.62 ± 7.34	260.18 ± 44.65
11.	NBPGR, Chattrapati	100	309.31 ± 42.69	35.37 ± 13.42	252.56 ± 59.66
12.	NBPGR, Hansraj	100	228.25 ± 111.15	23.62 ± 14.54	181.31 ± 97.22
13.	NBPGR, Hissar Local	37.5	104.00 ± 51.73	7.67 ± 1.97	68.00 ± 40.09
14.	CRIDA, JJ-05	93.75	228.60 ± 44.46	24.00 ± 6.76	195.73 ± 61.00
15.	CRIDA, LJ-05	100	220.56 ± 96.74	19.56 ± 11.40	169.44 ± 100.83
16.	FRI-UA-DD-0312-5 (E1)	87.5	214.14 ± 69.17	13.50 ± 5.15	141.78 ± 54.01
17.	FRI-UA-TG-0212-6 (E2)	100	107.62 ± 77.08	12.31 ± 7.54	105.12 ± 68.07
18.	FRI-UA-TG-0217-7 (E3)	87.5	170.07 ± 81.86	13.00 ± 6.54	126.28 ± 76.65
19.	FRI Dehradun FRI-UA-D-0312-9 E4	25	124.50 ± 72.89	10.00 ± 6.78	87.25 ± 73.19
20.	FRI-UA-DD-0312-9 (E5)	75	88.75 ± 36.24	6.75 ± 2.09	59.50 ± 21.85
21.	PAPL, Bangalore JPH 009	75	222.75 ± 42.55	18.00 ± 6.07	172.50 ± 52.31
22.	PAPL, Bangalore JPH108	75	208.58 ± 77.59	15.58 ± 5.21	142.42 ± 65.44
23.	EXCEL, Mumbai BHAVO 405 C1	81.25	245.69 ± 71.77	21.31 ± 10.03	185.82 ± 84.38
24.	CRIDA-JR-06	68.75	86.82 ± 28.38	6.70 ± 1.42	55.73 ± 9.74
	SEm		94.5	10.51	86.23
	Sediment		47.27	5.26	43.13
	CV (%)		33.42	3.72	30.5
	CD (if Fe>Ft)		33.22	40.69	40.1

Table 9.5: Seeding Characteristics of Various Accessions of *Jatropha curcas* on Sodic Soil

Sl. No.	Accessions	Fruit yield (ODW) (g)/Plant	Seed yield (ODW) (g)/Plant	Kernel yield (ODW) (g)/Plant	Oil Content (%)
1.	NBRI J-05	73.92 ± 35.26	35.08 ± 16.73	31.18 ± 14.87	24.31
2.	NBRI J-18	141.36 ± 83.02	81.67 ± 47.97	52.77 ± 30.99	30.1
3.	CSMCRI, GJ-KGR-C1	189.90 ± 92.20	126.30 ± 61.67	85.47 ± 41.71	24.13
4.	CSMCRI, GJ-RAN-C2	100.96 ± 90.94	63.76 ± 57.44	47.82 ± 43.08	28.87
5.	CSMCRI, GJ-PCM-C3	89.96 ± 89.68	53.69 ± 53.53	39.05 ± 38.93	24.11
6.	CSMCRI, OR-KMP-C4	52.38 ± 29.37	36.29 ± 20.34	27.22 ± 15.26	33.28
7.	CSMCRI, OR-GPR-C5	138.37 ± 114.85	138.40 ± 116.74	63.02 ± 65.97	28.96
8.	NBPGR, SKN J2	59.30 ± 53.58	33.31 ± 30.10	28.74 ± 25.96	26.95
9.	NBPGR, SKN Big	170.93 ± 112.82	101.59 ± 60.06	77.07 ± 50.87	29.85
10	NBPGR, Urlikanchan	271.52 ± 99.55	184.63 ± 67.69	124.9 ± 45.79	33.85
11.	NBPGR, Chattrapati	163.62 ± 117.22	112.45 ± 80.56	64.26 ± 46.03	29.95
12.	NBPGR, Hansraj	163.21 ± 93.05	116.30 ± 66.31	76.99 ± 43.89	26.59
13.	NBPGR, Hissar Local	52.80 ± 60.65	44.48 ± 51.09	26.25 ± 30.15	23.14
14.	CRIDA, JJ-05	31.60 ± 25.95	22.80 ± 18.72	6.60 ± 5.42	27.16
15.	CRIDA, LJ-05	113.48 ± 110.84	79.18 ± 77.34	46.28 ± 45.20	20.33
16.	FRI-UA-DD-0312-5 (E1)	89.03 ± 94.95	61.52 ± 65.61	41.01 ± 43.74	25.31
17.	FRI-UA-TG-0212-6 (E2)	59.24 ± 51.88	28.99 ± 25.39	20.82 ± 17.54	30.28
18.	FRI-UA-TG-0217-7 (E3)	151.47 ± 148.88	97.61 ± 95.94	57.68 ± 56.69	24.21
19.	FRI Dehradun FRI-UA-D-0312-9 E4	36.92 ± 61.63	17.01 ± 28.49	12.47 ± 20.89	25.59
20.	FRI-UA-DD-0312-9 (E5)	21.20 ± 14.40	11.88 ± 8.07	7.70 ± 5.22	11.34
21.	PAPL, Bangalore JPH 009	62.05 ± 66.68	41.56 ± 44.68	30.66 ± 32.95	28.05
22.	PAPL, Bangalore JPH108	29.68 ± 25.26	19.37 ± 16.38	13.84 ± 11.70	30.05
23.	EXCEL, Mumbai BHAVO 405 C1	100.94 ± 72.40	62.53 ± 44.85	39.87 ± 28.60	32.02
24.	CRIDA-JR-06	41.02 ± 37.59	25.54 ± 23.21	16.24 ± 14.83	11.03
	SEm	25.29	23.8	14.06	
	Sediment	35.77	33.65	19.89	
	CV (%)	53.45	74.6	64.39	
	CD (if Fe>Ft)	71.58	67.355	39.8	

ODW- Oven Dry Weight.

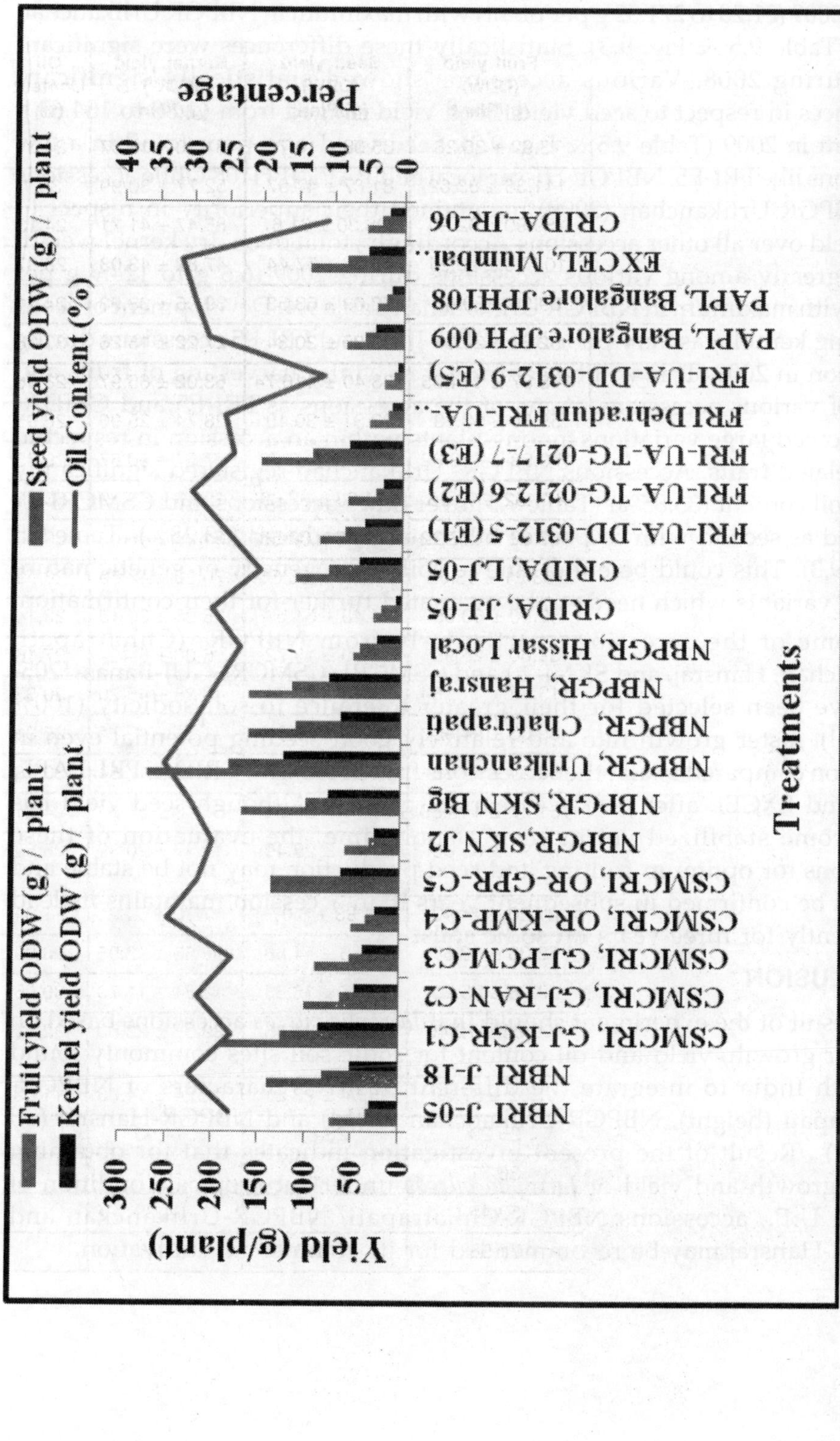

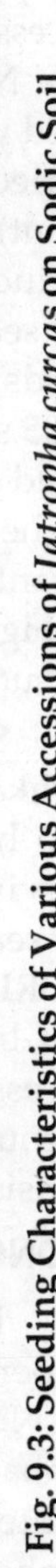

Fig. 9.3: Seeding Characteristics of Various Accessions of *Jatropha curcas* on Sodic Soil.

Oven dry fruit weight (ODW) differed markedly in different accessions during 2009 (21.20 to 271.52 g per plant) with maximum in NBPGR Urlikanchan (2009) (Table 9.5 & Fig. 9.3). Statistically these differences were significant only during 2008. Various accessions showed statistically significant differences in respect to seed yield. Seed yield ranged from 11.88 to 184.63 g per plant in 2009 (Table 9.5 & Fig. 9.3). Seed yield was poor to nil in a few accessions like FRI-E5, NBPGR Hissar local and PAPL JPH108 while accessions like NBPGR Urlikanchan (2009) maintained their superiority in respect to seed yield over all other accessions Accordingly, total oven dry kernel weight varied greatly among various accessions during 2009 (6.6 g to 124.9 g per plant) with maximum in NBPGR Urlikanchan Table 9.4. Development of seeds including kernel was very poor in CRIDA JJ-05 and FRI-E5 accessions during off season in 2009. This will be confirmed in winter harvesting of fruits and seeds of various accessions. Some of the accessions as FRI-E5 and CRIDA-LJ05 showed large variations among plants within an accession in respect to yield related traits. Accessions NBPGR- Urlikanchan registered significantly higher oil content (33.85%) (Table 9.5) over other accessions and CSMCRI-C-4 ranked as second with respect of oil content produced (33.28%) (Table 9.5 & Fig. 9.3). This could be either due to soil heterogeneity or genetic nature of such variants which needs to be evaluated further for their confirmation.

Some of the accessions particularly from NBPGR- (Chhatrapati, Urlikanchan, Hansraj, and SKNJ-2) and CSMCRI (CSMCRI-GUJ-Banas-1205-C1) have been selected for their greater tolerance to soil sodicity (100% survival), faster growth rate and relatively good seeding potential even in off season compared to all other accessions from CSMCRI, CRIDA, FRI, PAPL, NBRI and EXCEL after nearly 4 years of growth. Although seed yield has not become stabilized yet in such a short time, the evaluation of these accessions for optimum fruiting and seed production may not be stable and it could be confirmed in subsequent years if an accession maintains its lead consistently for three years on sodic soils.

CONCLUSION

Result of the experiment should that *Jatropha curcas* accessions based on superior growth, yield and oil content for sodic soil sites commonly found in North India to integrate the different positive characters of NBPGR-Chhatrapati (height), NBPGR-Urlikanchan (yield) and NBPGR-Hansraj (oil content) . Result of the present investigation indicates that for obtaining higher growth and yield of *Jatropha curcas* under sub-tropical condition of Central U.P., accessions NBPGR-Chhatrapati, NBPGR-Urlikanckan and NBPGR-Hansraj may be recommended for its commercial cultivation.

REFERENCES

Achten, W.M.L., Verchot, L., Franken, Y.J., Mathiji, E., Singh, V.P., Aerts, R. and B. Muys (2008). *Jatropha* Bio-desel Production and Use. Biomass & Bioenergy 32: 1063-1084.

Abhilash, P.C., Srivastava, P., Jamil, S. and N Singh (2010). Revisited *Jatropha curcas* as an Oil Plant of Multiple Benefits: Critical Research Needs and Prospects for the Future. Environmental Science Pollution Research 18: 127-31.

Achten, W.M.J., Maes, W.H., Aerts, R., Verchot, L., Trabucco, A., Mathijs, E., et al. (2010). *Jatropha*: from Global Hype to Local Opportunity. J Arid Environ. 74: 164-5.

Achten, W.M.J., Maes, W.H., Reubesns, B., Mathijs, E., Singh, V.P., Verchot, L. and B. Muys (2010). Biomass Production and Allocation in *Jatropha curcas* L. Seedlings Under Different Levels of Drought Stress. Biomass & Bioenergy 34: 667-676.

Adeoye O.K., Adeyemo A., Awoleye M.O., Owoloja A., Olunloyo A., Ajibade Y.A., Ayeni O.D. (2011). Effect of Different Tree Canopies on the Early Growth of *Jatropha curcas* Seedlings. *Continental J. Agronomy 5(1): 18-24.*

Behera, S.K., Srivastava, P., Tripathi, R., Singh, J.P. and N Singh (2010). Evaluation of Plant Performance of *Jatropha curcas* L. Under Different Agro-practices for Optimizing Biomass- A Case Study. Biomass & Bioenergy 34: 30-41.

Canakci M, Gerpen J.V. (2001). Biodiesel Production from Oils and Fats with High Free Fatty Acids. *Trans ASAE ; 44:1429-36.*

Frin, (2008): Forestry Research Institute of Nigeria an Annual Meteorological Report.

Ginwal, H.S., Phartyal S.S., Rawat, P.S., Srivastava, R.L.,(2005). Seed Source Variation in Morphology, Germination and Seedling Growth of *Jatropha curcas* L. in Central India. Silvae Genet. 54: 76-80.

Jackson, M.L.,(1958). Soil Chemical Analysis. Englewood Cliffs, New Jersey: Prantice Hall Inc.

Jones, N. and Miller J.H, (1992): *Jatropha curcas* a Multipurpose Species for Problematic Sites Land Resources Series *11:40.*

Jones, N. and J.H. Miller (1992). Jatropha Curcas: A Multipurpose Species for Problematic Sites. Washington DC: The world Bank.

Kaushik, N., Kumar, K., Kumar, S., Kaushik, N. and S. Roy (2007). Genetic Variability and Divergence Studies in Seed Traits and Oil Content of *Jatropha* (*Jatropha curcas* L.) Accessions. Biomass & Bioenergy 31: 497-502.

Lang, X., Dalai, AK., Bakhshi, N.N., Reaney, M.J., Hertz, P.B., (2001). Preparation and Characterization of Bio-diesels from Various Bio-oils. Bioresour Technol 80: 53-62.

Openshaw K.A. (2000). Rewiew of *Jatropha curcas*: An Oil Plants of Unfulfilled Promise. *Biomass Bioenergy; 19:1-15.*

Ogunwole, J.O., Patolia, J.S., Chaudhary, D.R., Ghosh, A. ad J. Chikara (2007). Improvement of the Quality of a Degraded Entisol with *Jatropha curcas* L. under Indian Semi-arid Conditions. Expert Seminar on *Jatropha curcas* L. Agronomy and Genetics 26-28.

Pramanik K. (2003). Properties and Use of *Jatropha curcas* Oil and Diesel Fuel Blends in Compression Ignition Engine. *Renewable Energy; 28:239-48.*

Ranade, S.A., Srivastava, A.P., Rana, T.S., Srivastava, J., Tuli, R., Easy. (2008). Easy Assessment of Diversity in *Jatropha curcas* L. Plants Using Two Single-prime Amplification Reaction (SPAR) Methods. Biomass Bioenergy. 32: 533-40.

Srivastava P. (2010). Evaluation of Soil Carbon Sequestration Polential of *Jatropha curcas* L. Plantation Growing in Varing Soil Conditions. *Ph.D., Synopsis Submitted to University of Lucknow.*

Srivastava P., Behra S.K., Gupta J., Jamil S., Singh N. and Sharma Y.K. (2011). Growth Performance, Variability in Yield Traits and Oil Content of Selected Accessions of *Jatropha curcas* L. Growing in a Large Scale Plantation Site. *Biomass and Bioenergy 1-7.*

Severino, L.S., Rosiane, L.S.L., Amanda, M.A.L., Maria, A.O.F., Ligia, R.S., Recardo, P.V., Katty, A.A.L.M., Valdinei, S. and H.C. Nair (2011). Propagation by Stem Cuttings and Root System Structure of *Jatropha curcas*. Biomass & Bioenergy 35: 3160-3166.

Shukla, S.K., Singh, K., Singh, B. and N.N. Gautam (2011). Biomass Productivity and Nutrient Availability of Cynodon Dactylon (L.) Pers. Growing on Soils of Different Sodicity Stress. Biomass & Bioenergy 35: 3440-3447.

Srivastava, P., Behera, S.K., Gupta, J., Jamil, S., Singh, N. and Y.K. Sharma (2011). Growth Performance, Variability in Yield Traits and Oil Content of Selected Accessions of *Jatropha curcas* L. Growing in a Large Scale Plantation Site. Biomass & Bioenergy 35: 3936-3942.

Tabatabai, M.A. (1994). Soil Enzyme, in: Weaver, R.W., Angle, S., Bottomley, P., Bezdicek, D., Smith, S., Tabatabai, A., Wollum, A. (Eds.), Methods of Soil Analysis Part 2 Microbiological and Biochemical Properties. SSSA Book Series, pp. 755-833.

CHAPTER

Flow-distance Dependent Biophysiochemical Impact of Coal Effluent on Nyaba River, Enugu South, Nigeria

M.C.Menkiti[1]; E.N.Adinna[2]; C.F Okey-Onyesolu[1]
N.U.Menkiti[3]; O.D.Onukwuli[1]

ABSTRACT

The environmental state of urban streams provides much information on activities and their impacts within the catchments area. This work therefore focuses on the biophysiochemical impacts of coal effluent on measured distances (20,40,60,80,100,120 m) down stream from the point of entrance into Nyaba River. The parameters tested for the samples include pH, turbidity, hardness, alkalinity, COD, E-Coli etc. The standard methods employed were APHA and AWWA. The results show that the pH varies from 1.98-5.85 while that of COD varies 7060-363mg/l. The results of E-Coli, TPC and total coliform are positive, indicating the presence of pathogens. With the exception of turbidity, total hardness, nitrate, calcium ion and COD, there is no other parameter that has consistent trend downstream from point of entrance. It is concluded

1. Chemical Engineering Department, Nnamdi Azikiwe University, Awka, Nigeria.
2. Geography and Metrology Department, Enugu State University of Science and Technology, Enugu, Nigeria.
3. Centre for Environmental Management and control, University of Nigeria, Enugu Campus, Nigeria.

that the impacts have both economic and social implications and that the water samples were not fit for human consumption since WHO standard was not satisfied.

Keywords: *Coal, Effluent, River, Biochemical, Physiochemical, Coal effluent*

INTRODUCTION

Coal is a solid, combustible carboniferous substance formed by the decomposition of vegetable matter without free access to air. The plant debris from which coal had its origin accumulated in peat swamps and in the presence of stagnant water and buried under rapidly increasing deposit of vegetable matter, which decomposed in almost complete absence of air. Assisted by micro-organism, a chemical transformation took place resulting in the formation of peat. These conversion processes, extending over many millions of years, were progressively leading to the highest rank coals, such as anthracite (Onwu, 1999).

Coal is presently one of the world's most plentiful energy resources, and is likely to quadruple by the year 2020 (Rose,2003;Essenhigh, 2004; Hegarty,2006). This is an indication that the continued importance of this raw material which Nigeria has its fair share of world's reserve is very obvious (Onwu,1999).

The important needs for coal utilization in a competitive market often requires rightly refined coal materials with its tendency to generate pollutant, of which coal washery effluent is a major component.

Granted that the coal production in the country is almost non-existence, nevertheless, the negative impact of the accumulated ponds of coal washery effluent discharges into our local water bodies should be a source of health concerns (EPA, 2010; FEPA, 1991; WQM, 1999).

With this in view, it calls in mind our locality where environmental protection is near absent and the discharge of such washery effluent is a common experience along Akwuke Coal Mine axis of Nyaba River. It is against this background that the study becomes imperative for river that provides a variety of uses for a large number of populations (WHO, 2003, ELC, 2002, Wright, 1996; Cairns, 1974).

As a contribution in this direction, this work attempts among others to assess the biophysiochemical impact (down stream from the effluent entrance point into the river) arising from the discharge of the washery effluent into the Nyaba River. The work is designed to provide an experimental data base evaluating water quality by comparing with established standards. Thus, the need for integrating the effects of these influences as a guide for proffering solution becomes imperative.

Armed with experimental data, health and environmental authorities will be in good standing to take a definite policy position to safeguard the health of the citizens and the aquatic environment of the study area.

STUDY AREA, SITE CHARACTERIZATION AND METHODOLOGY

Study Area

The study area lies in Akwuke, located within Enugu South L.G.A of Enugu Urban. For the purpose of easy identification, the study area is described based on the context of Enugu Urban.

Enugu Urban, the capital of Enugu state is located at the foot of Udi escarpment (Agukoronye and Adinna, 2003). Apart from Enugu South L.G.A., it contains other two councils namely, Enugu North L.G.A. and Enugu East L.G.A.

Relative Position: Enugu Urban is bordered by the following L.G.Areas: Udi, Igbo Etiti, Isi Uzo, Nkanu East and Nkanu West.

Absolute Position: Enugu Urban lies in lat 6°27′N and long 7°29′E (Agukoronye and Adinna, 2003).

Drainage Basin: Enugu Urban is within Nyaba drainage basin. Nyaba river traverse Enugu Urban and marks the boundary between Enugu Urban and Nkanu West along Enugu-Port Harcourt express road axis of the river course. Other streams passing through the metropolis include Ekulu River, Uwani River, Asata River, Ogbete River, etc.

Study Site

The study site is located along Nyaba River navigating through Akwuke coal mine complex. This section of the river lies just at the base of Udi hills.

Site Characterization

Nyaba River at Akwuke Coal Mine

- This is a sixth order river axis that marks the border between Enugu Urban and Nkanu West L.G.A.
- The stream is muddy in colour due to sand mining along its course

(i) *Sources of Pollution*
- Action of mass wasting due to the mining
- Faecal waste from humans and animals
- Discharges of coal effluent

(ii) *Uses of the river*
- Source of domestic water
- Source of sand for construction purposes
- Animal grazing ground
- Source of stones and gravels for construction purposes

(iii) *Flora and fauna prevalence*

Flora: The stream is surrounded by shrubs, herbs, trees, climbers and cassava plants. It has a good population of guinea grasses. The banks of the river have population of hydrophytes, spirogyra and saprophytic plants.

Fauna: The river environment is mainly dominated by birds, insects and rodents. There is also presence of cattle herds belonging to Fulanis camped near the river banks. No fishes were sited. However, the movements of monkeys are common uphill from the river.

Picture Showing Coal Effluent Pond Resulting from now Murribond Coal Mining Operation at Akwuke Coal Mine Enugu. This is a Typical Source of Coal Effluent into Nyaba River

Methodology

Sample Collection and Preparation (Armitage, 2005)

Nine 1-litre bottles were procured and corked on sterilization. The bottles were used to collect sample water after initial rinsing with the water sourced from the study site. The bottles were filled to the brim to expel any entrapped air within the bottles. The bottles were corked and not opened again until the commencement of the analysis (Wright, 1999).

The samples collected in August, 2004 were labelled showing the temperature, the date of collection, time and purpose of the samples (Mitchel and Stapp 2000).

Sample Characterization

The bio-physiochemical analysis on the water and effluent samples from the study site were done based standard methods of APHA, 1999 and AWWA, 1985. The sample characteristics determined were pH, TSS,TDS,TS, electrical conductivity, nitrate, iron, sulphate, total hardness, calcium, magnesium hardness, chloride. Alkalinity.plate count, total coliform.

RESULTS AND DISCUSSION

In over all, characteristics results of nine samples were determined. The characterization results considered a total of nineteen parameters for each sample at various distances down stream from the reference point.. Sample C is the reference point where the coal effluent from pond (Sample B) empties into the river. Sample A, 20m upstream from sample C, is the control. Sample D,E,F,G,H and I were 20,40,60,80,100 and 120m, respectively downstream from sample C. The characteristics results are graphically presented in figures 10.1 - 10.8.

Figure 10.1 presents the pH variation as a function of distance. Sample A has pH 6, indicating a more alkaline medium when compared to sample B that recorded pH 2. Sample B pH indicates clearly high acidic value normally associated with coal effluent (Menkiti, 2007a; Menkiti, 2007b; Menkiti, 2010; Menkiti and Onukwuli, 2012; Menkiti *et al*, 2011; Adamson, 1974). The high level of protonation prevalent in coal effluent, in addition to the presence of organic acids account for the low pH in most coal effluents. Samples C-D show upward movement in the value of pH; reaching a value of 5.85 at sample D. This can clearly be attributed to dilution effect due to sinking of pH as the distances from point C increase. However, none of the samples could meet with WHO standard since the pH< 6.5 (WHO, 2003).

Figure 10.2 presents the turbidity variation with distance. Sample A has value of 102 NTU, a value due to minimal interference before turbulence and cloudiness were introduced at point B. From samples B down to I, there is continuous reduction in the value of NTU from 38936 to 148. This is due to sinking effects as the particles and color settle to the river bed.

Presented in figure 10.3 is the hardness variation among the samples with distance down stream. Total, calcium and magnesium hardnesses are considered in figure 10.3. It is observed that magnesium hardness is the lowest of the three followed by the calcium hardness. The high value of calcium hardness is understood if it is noted that Enugu is a limestone belt, of which calcium is a major component. The high margin between values recorded for samples A and B is expected since sample B was a product of underground aquifer, a sure source for high level hardness. However, the sinking effects and other ancillary chemicals take away a large quantum of hardness recorded at point B.

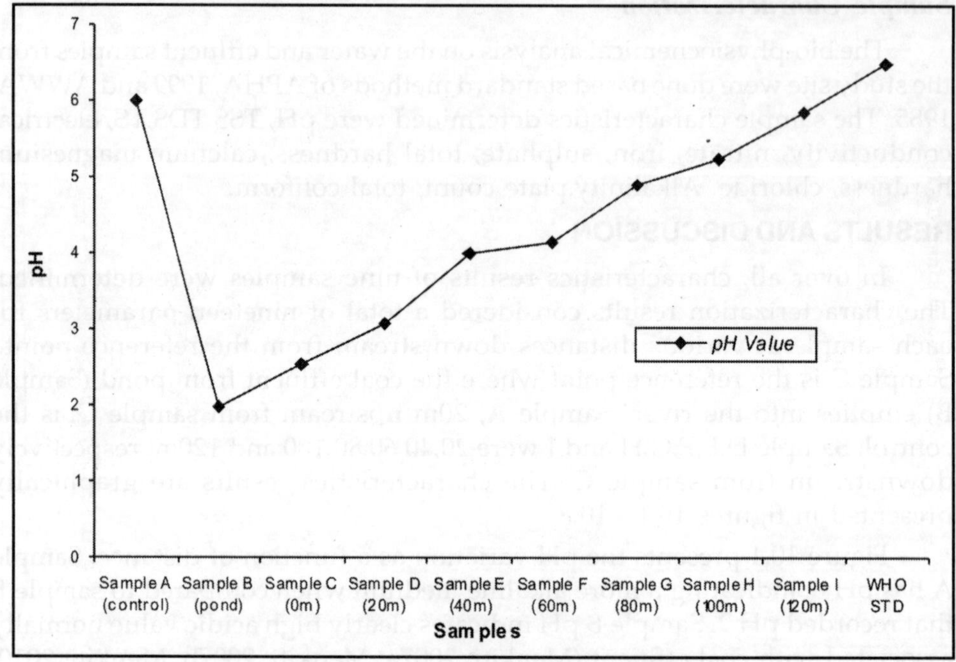

Fig. 10.1: Line Graph of pH Variation with Distance

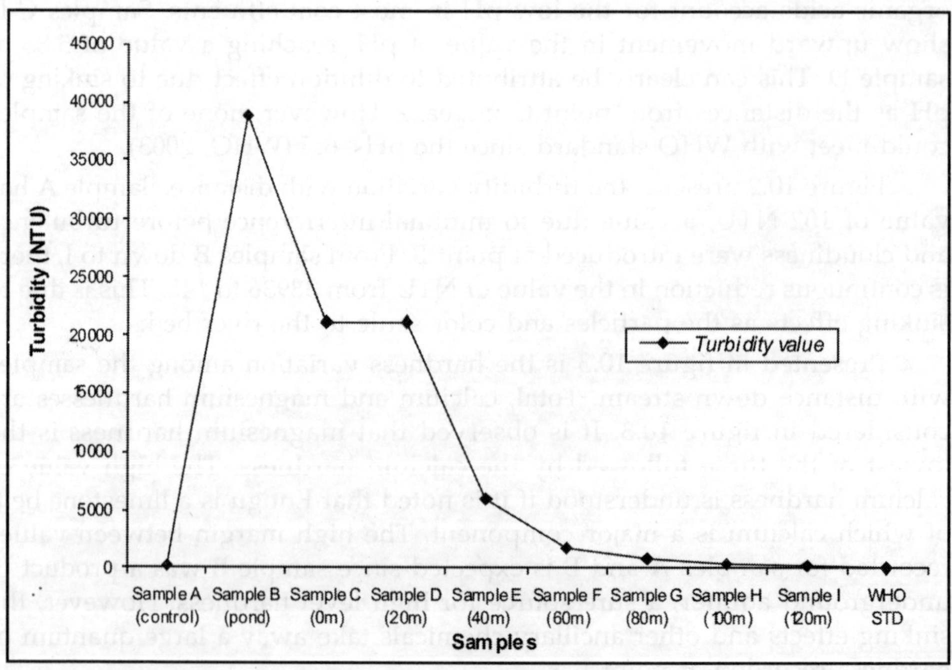

Fig. 10.2: Line Graph of Turbidity Variation with Distance

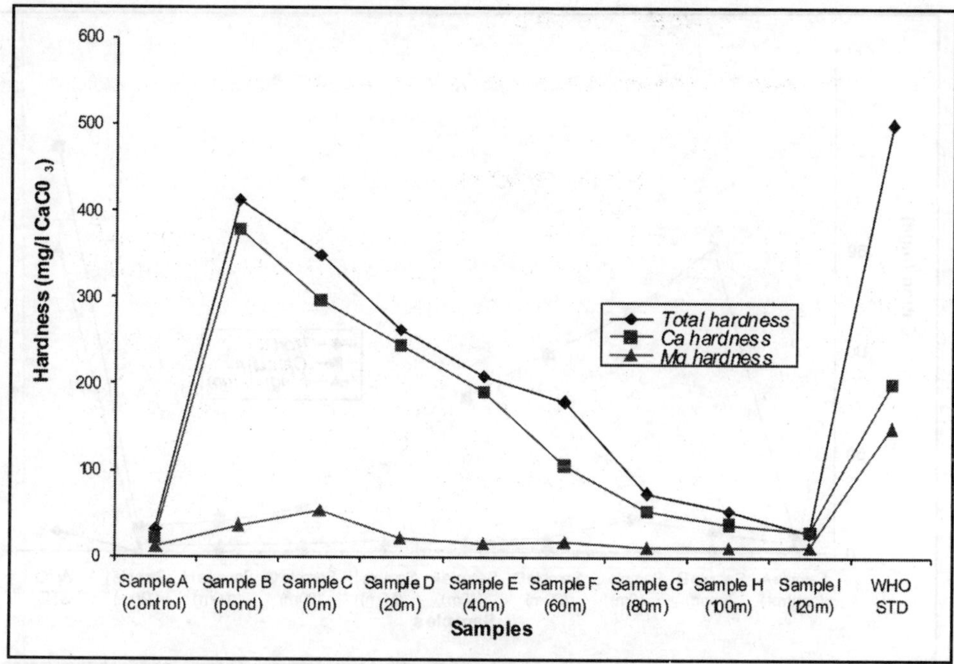

Fig. 10.3: Line Graph of Hardness Variation with Distance

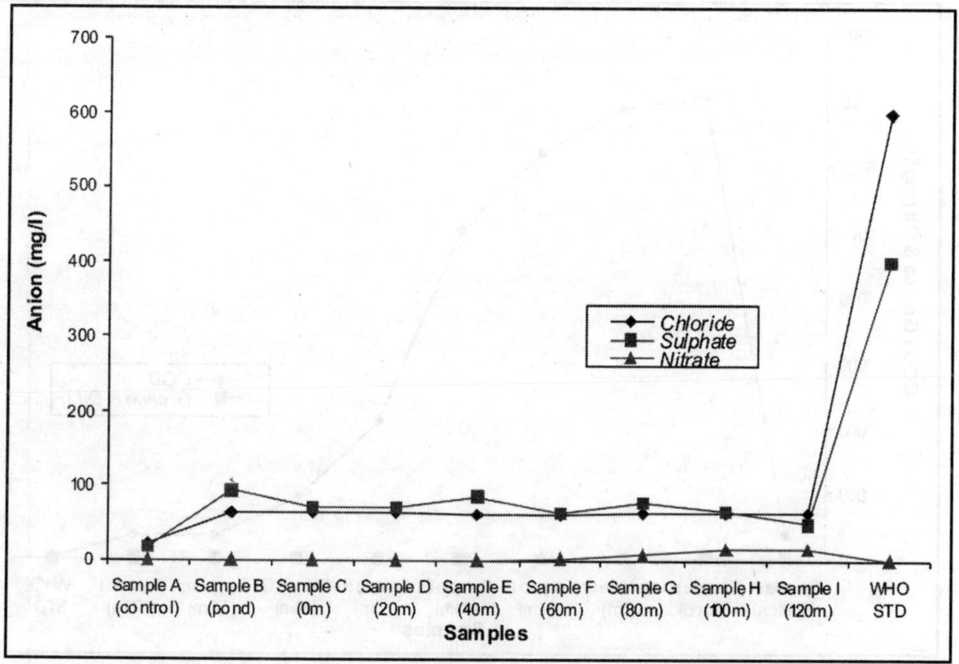

Fig. 10.4: Line Graph of Anion Variation with Distance

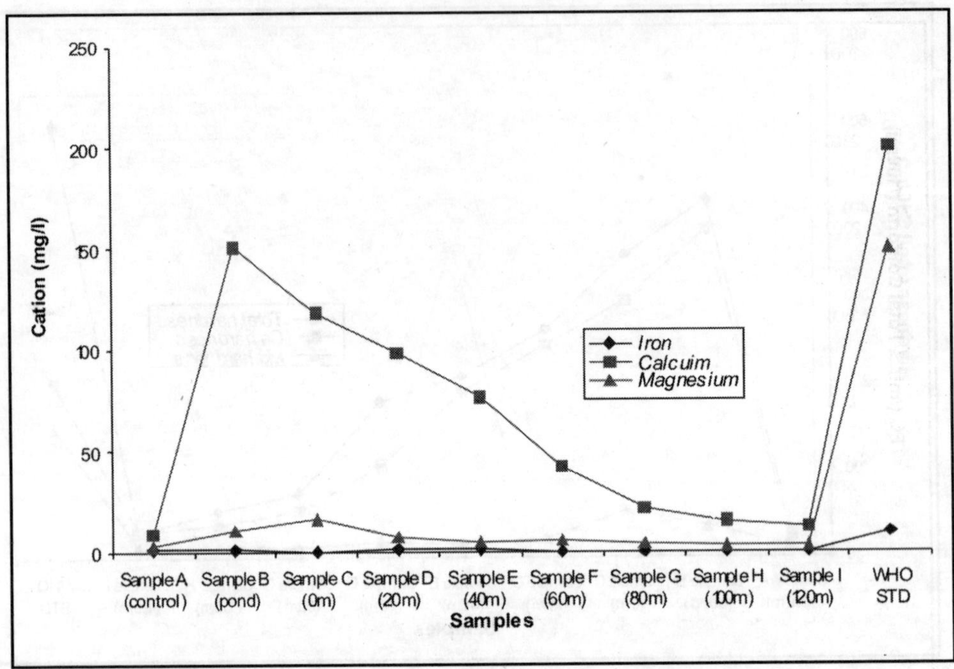

Fig. 10.5: Line Graph of Cation Variation with Distance

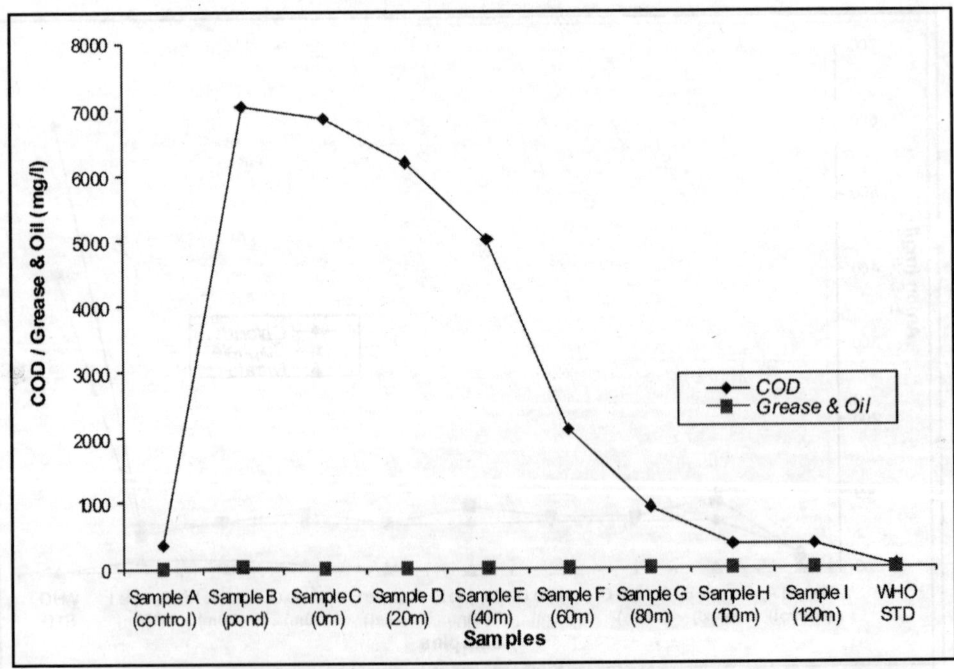

Fig. 10.6: Line Graph of COD/Grease and Oil Variation with Distance

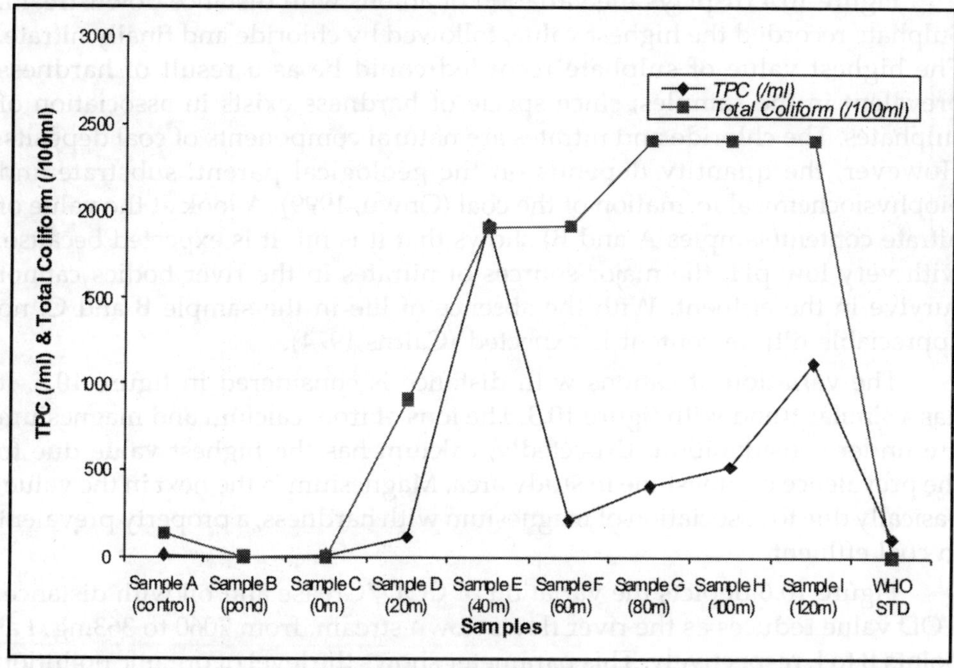

Fig. 10.7: Line Graph of TPC and Total Coliform Variation with Distance

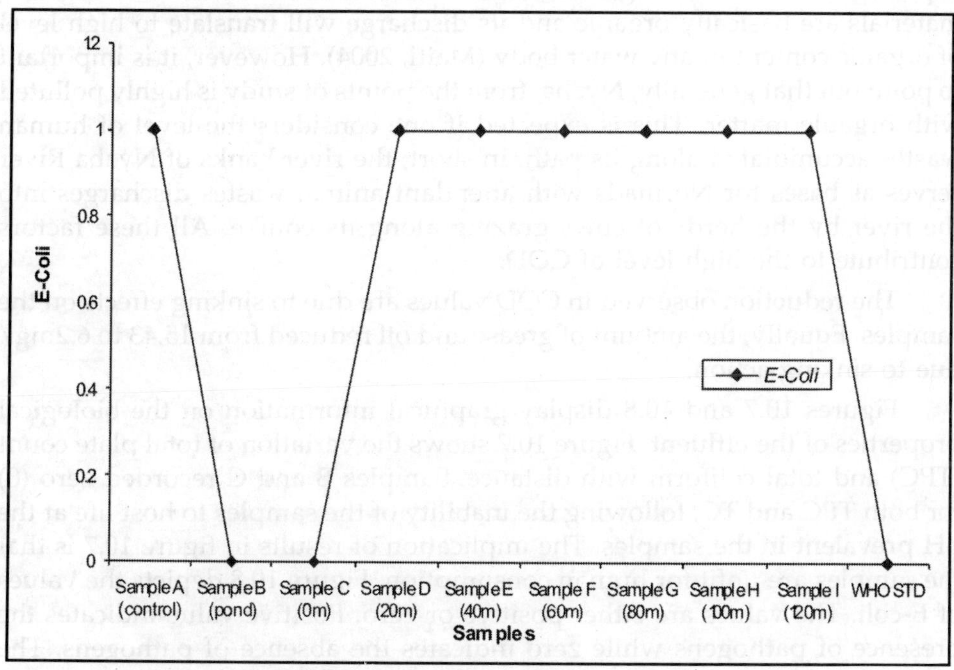

Fig. 10.8: Line Graph of E.coli Variation with Distance

Figure 10.4 displays the variation of anions with distance downstream. Sulphate recorded the highest value, followed by chloride and finally nitrate. The highest value of sulphate recorded could be as a result of hardness prevalent in the samples; since specie of hardness exists in association of sulphates. The chloride and nitrates are natural components of coal deposits. However, the quantity depends on the geological parent, substrate and biophysiochemical formation of the coal (Onwu, 1999). A look at the value of nitrate content(samples A and B) shows that it is nil. It is expected because, with very low pH, the major sources of nitrates in the river bodies cannot survive in the effluent. With the absence of life in the sample B and C, no appreciable nitrate content is expected (Cairns,1974).

The variation of cations with distance is considered in figure 10.5. It has a similar trend with figure 10.3. The ions of iron, calcium and magnesium are under consideration. Expectedly, calcium has the highest value due to the prevalence of limestone in study area. Magnesium is the next in the value, basically due to association of magnesium with hardness, a property prevalent in coal effluent.

Figure 10.6 depicts the variation of COD/Grease and oil with distance. COD value reduces as the river flows down stream, from 7060 to 363mg/l at points B to I, respectively. This parameter shows the level of organic pollution prevalent in this water body. The control COD values are very far from the stipulated standard of 3mg/l.This can be accounted for by the fact that coal materials are basically organic and its discharge will translate to high level of organic content in any water body (Maiti, 2004). However, it is important to point out that generally, Nyaba, from the points of study is highly polluted with organic matter. This is expected if one considers the level of human wastes accumulated along its path. In short, the river banks of Nyaba River serves as bases for Normads with attendant animal wastes discharges into the river by the herds of cows grazing along its course. All these factors contribute to the high level of COD.

The reduction observed in COD values are due to sinking effects on the samples. Equally, the amount of grease and oil reduced from 15.43 to 6.2mg/ due to sinking action.

Figures 10.7 and 10.8 display graphical information on the biological properties of the effluent. Figure 10.7 shows the variation of total plate count (TPC) and total coliform with distance. Samples B and C recorded zero (0) for both TPC and TC, following the inability of the samples to host life at the pH prevalent in the samples. The implication of results in figure 10.7 is that the samples are unfit for human consumption. Figure 10.8 depicts the values of E-coli. The values are either positive or zero. Positive value indicates the presence of pathogens while zero indicates the absence of pathogens. The zero value recorded for samples B and C (Fig. 10.8) is due to low pH that cannot sustain life. Clearly, figures 10.7 and 10.8 show that the samples are unwholesome and not fit for human consumption.

There exists some observed general trends among the parameters and samples. One of such trend is the acidic nature of the samples tested. Basically, this is expected in a coal mine region. Coal deposits and effluent are known to inject acidity into water bodies when allowed to be washed into streams (Adamson, 1974). Indeed, the high level of acidity is apparent when one observes that all the pH values, determined are lower than the control pH taken 20 meters upstream from the point where the effluent discharges into the Nyaba river.

Comparison of the results with the WHO standard shows that sulphate, chloride, Mg hardness, iron content and total hardness all lie within the stipulated limit. The low level of these parameters could be attributed to the sinking ability of the river. This is plausible considering the fact that the samples were collected in August, just at the thick of the rainy season. Hence, accumulation of the chemicals must have been highly reduced. On the other hand, pH value, turbidity, electrical conductivity, TDS and COD lie out side the stipulated standard.

Of the parameters tested in the samples, only Fe, Total hardness, turbidity and pH has a definite trend. The values of the parameters decrease down stream. Generally, this is as a result of sinking of the parameters down the stream. However, a major explanation for the sustenance of this trend may be due to absence of human activities that can easily upset the trend. Basically, the one that can easily be upset by human action is the turbidity due to sand mining. However, what was prevalence in the study site was stone mining near the river course.

The absence of trend in other parameters tested is reflection of human and animal interference. Basically, the riverbank is a host to nomads and community settlements. The variation can occur due to discharge of different kinds of wastes at various points in the river by the nomads and community members. The flushing of farm chemicals at various points could also contribute to this variation. Indeed, water run off also contributed its quota in the variation experienced in the water samples.

In order to give the work more scientific support, correlation of values of parameters and distance down the stream was calculated. Only pH, Nitrate, TC, Grease and Oil have positive correlation coefficient. The rest of the parameters have negative correlation. Of course, the pH correlation value is expected following the trend exhibited which shows that there is relationship between the distance down the stream and level of acidity of the river . The positive correlation coefficient remarks there is a relationship while the negative values indicate that there is no relationship. Tables 10.1 and 10.2 present the overall correlation coefficient and samples deviation from the control sample, respectively. The higher the deviation, the higher the disparity

Table 10.1: Correlation Coefficient

Sl. No.	Parameter	Value
1.	Ph Value	0.98784787
2.	Turbidity	-0.80198851
3.	Total Hardness	-0.87978282
4.	Calcium Hardness	-0.95071379
5.	Magnesium Hardness	-0.91743041
6.	Chloride	-0.22659601
7.	Sulphate	-0.65870166
8.	Nitrate	0.95294241
9.	Iron	-0.94813635
10.	Electrical conductivity	-0.84720907
11.	TDS	-0.84721925
12.	Total Alkalinity	-0.84721925
13.	Calcium	-0.95071379
14.	Magnesium ion	-0.91770226
15.	TPC	0.07913754
16.	Total Coliform	0.69463307
17.	E-Coil	–
18.	COD	-0.94000309
19.	Grease & Oil	0.12551848

Table 10.2: Deviation Between the Control Sample (A) and Samples C, D, E, F, G, H, I

Sl. No.	Parameter	Mean Value	MD	SD
1.	pH-Value	4.46	1.05	1.18
2.	Turbidity	6419.15	7390.2	27568.10
3.	T. hardness	125.25	89.63	109.11
4.	Ca hardness	122.33	91.25	97.59
5.	Mg hardness	18.42	9.27	13.32
6.	Chloride	57.86	15.05	23.06
7.	Sulphate	63.44	12.83	18.35
8.	Nitrate	5.18	5.49	6.11
9.	Iron	2.04	1.46	1.67
10.	Elec. Conductivity	787.40	216.2	268.30
11.	TDS	441.18	120.90	150.16
12.	T. Alkalinity	4.07	1.01	1.78
13.	Ca^{2+}	48.99	36.50	39.11
14.	Mg^{2+}	5.52	2.78	3.99
15.	T.P.C.	539.37	489.56	623.76
16.	T. Coliforn	1206.63	944.18	996.48
17.	E-Coli			
18.	COD	2769.87	2282.88	2538.55
19.	Grease & Oil	9.42	2.73	3.64

CONCLUSION AND RECOMMENDATION

There was apparent impact on the biophysiochemical properties of the river at the conditions of the study. The samples considered were unfit for human consumption. Among the parameters tested in the samples, only Fe, total hardness, turbidity and pH has a definite trend, decreasing down stream. Generally, this is as a result of sinking of the parameters down the stream. The impacts could be attributed to both anthropogenic and abiotic factors, apart from the effluent effects. On economic aspect, appreciable amount of resources would be required in treatment of the water to conform with WHO standard. This will enhance the tourism potential of the study area known for recreational beach. Since this work was carried out during the rainy season, it is recommended that the work should be conducted during the thick of dry season.

REFERENCES

Adamson, G.F.S (1974): Some Modern Aspects of Coal Cleaning and Their Influence on Avoidance of River Pollution, Effluent Water Treat. J, Vol. 5 No. 143, P. 1081.

Agukoronye and Adinna, E.N. (2003): "Indoor Pollution in Enugu Urban" in Adinna E.N., Attah, V.I., Ekpo A.B. (eds) Environmental Pollution and Management in Tropics.

APHA (1999): American Public Health Association; Standard Methods for the Examination of Water-diary Products, 15th Ed., New York.

Armitage, P.D. (2005): The Environmental Quality of Small Urban Water Course, the Bourine Stream (Dorset), Assessed with Macro Invertebrate Date, Institute of Fresh Water Ecology, River Laboratory, East Stoke, Wareham, Dorset, USA.

AWWA (1985): American Water Works Association; Standard Methods for the Examination of Water Effluent, New York, USA.

Cairns, J. (1974); Coal Mining Effluent; Industrial Waste Water Treatment, Academic Press, New York, USA.

ELC (2002): Environmental Literacy Council; Water Quality, USA.

EPA (2010): Central Pollution Control Board; Environmental Standard: Coal Washeries; USA.

Essenhigh, R.H. (2004): Coal Processing and Conversion; Journal Institute of Fuel, Vol. 4, No. 7, pp. 239-244, Newcastle, UK.

FEPA (1991): Guideline and Standard for Environmental Pollution Control in Nigeria, Abuja.

Hegarty and Moody B.E.: (2006) Coal Processing Technology; Chemical Engineering Progress, Technical Manual Society, New Jersey, USA.

Maiti, S.K. (2004): Study on Settling Behaviour of Coal Washery Effluent – A Case Study; Proceedings of NSEEMA, India.

Menkiti M.C.(2007a): Biophysical Impact of Coal Effluent on Measured Distances of Nyaba River, Akwuke Coal Mine, Enugu, Enugu State, M.Sc (Envt. Mgt.) Thesis, Department of Geography and Meeteorology, ESUT Enugu, Nigeria.

Menkiti, M, C (2010): Sequential Treatment Coal and Brewery Effluents by Biocoag-flocculation and Activated Carbon Adsorption, Ph.D Thesis, Chemical Engineering Department, Nnamdi Azikiwe University, Awka, Nigeria.

Menkiti, M.C (2007b): Studies on the Coagulation and Flocculation Coal Washery Effluent: Turbidimetric Approach, M.Eng. Thesis, Department of Chemical Engineering, Nnamdi Azikiwe University, Awka, Nigeria.

Menkiti, M.C. and Onukwuli, O.D. (2012); Impact of pH Variation on Coag-flocculation Behaviour of Chitin Derived Coag-flocculant in Coal Washery Effluent Medium. *Journal of Mineral and materials characterization and engineering* . Vol. 10, No. 15, pp. 1391-1407. U.S.A.

Menkiti M.C., Chime, T.O. and Onukwuli (2011): Bioadsorption of Suspended and Dissolved Particles from Washery Effluemt onto Fluted Pumkin Sed Shell Biomass, World Journal of Engineering 8(2) 179-190.

Mitchel and Stapp, W (2000): Field Manual for Water Quality Monitory: An Environmental Education Programme for Schools, 12th ed. Kendall / Hunt Publishing Co. Debugue Iowa, USA.

Onwu, D.O. (1999): Coal Fundamentals and Conversion Technology, Immaculate Publication Ltd, Enugu.

Rose, H.J (2003): Chemistry of Coal Utilization; John Wiley & Sons Ltd., UK.

WHO (2003): Guideline for Drinking Water Standard, 2nd Ed., Geneva, Switzerland.

WQM (1999): Water Quality Monitory; Technical Guide Book, The Oregun Plan for Salmon and Watersheds, Version 20, Oregun Dept of Environmental Quality, Salem Oregun, USA.

Wright, E.D. (1996): RIVPACS – A Technique for Evaluating the Biological Quality of Rivers in US, European Water Pollution Control, pp. 15-25, UK.

CHAPTER

Relationship of Rotifers with Environmental Factors in Derelict Water Bodies of Western Region U.P.

Habeeba A. Kabeer*; Saltanat Parveen

INTRODUCTION

Water is the essence of life on earth and totally dominates the chemical composition of all organisms (Wetzel, 1983). The ubiquity of water in biota as the fulcrum of biochemical metabolism rests on its physical and chemical properties. The present domain of life existing on earth has evolved in water (Hosetti, 2002). It is the most abundant part of the living and as such performs important role in metabolism. It is chiefly a limiting factor among land animals in which the amount is subjected to great fluctuations. About 70 per cent of the earth surface is covered with water (Wetzel, 1983). Most of the freshwater is frozen as polar ice in polar region (Antarctica and Greenland) and is out of reach to humanity (Prakash, 2001). The amount of freshwater available on the earth today is not more than that was available two thousand years ago when the earth's population was less than 3 per cent of its current size (Prakash, 2001). According to Odum (1983), freshwater habitats occupy relatively a small portion of earth's surface but its importance is far greater than their actual area. It has provided both food and drink and has been

Limnology Research Lab, A.M.U., Aligarh (UP), India.

used for recreation, transport, energy, cooling, disposal and much more. Hence, the freshwater ecosystem is highly useful in human civilization in their day to day life.

Climatology of Western Region and Description of Derelict Water Body

Climatic factors like wind, rainfall, temperature, pressure and humidity play very important role in the ecology of aquatic as well as terrestrial environments (Barclay, 1966). Panday and Tripathi (1988) have also reported the role of climatic factors in the ecology of aquatic environment. These factors control organic production in all the waterbodies by affecting circulation and exchange of essential nutrients (Rawson, 1951).

Aligarh, a district of Uttar-Pradesh in Northern India, is located in the central Ganga Yamuna Doab at latitude 27° 54′N and longitude 78° 4′E. It experiences the tropical monsoon type of climate with marked North-East and South-West monsoons. The year can be broadly divided in to the following five seasons:

1. Winter season (December to January).
2. Post –Winter (February to March).
3. Summer season (April to June).
4. Monsoon season i.e. season of general rains (July to September).
5. Post-monsoon season, i.e. season of retreating monsoon (October to November).

The winter season is marked with a gradual fall in temperature. Days are moderately warm but nights are cool. The region experiences a relatively good humidity and is mostly rainless. The winds during this season blow very slow.

The Post-winter season is marked with gradual rise in temperature, bright sunshine absence of cloudy days, a gradual lengthening of the photoperiod and a lower relative humidity.

The summer season is marked with a gradual rise in temperature with bright sunshine. The temperature shows a gradual increase in April, May, June and July. It is with lengthening photoperiod and a lower relative humidity. Hot dry winds of great velocity are a regular phenomenon during the season. Wind blows with a force of gale during day, falls off very rapidly in the evenings and nearly calm down during nights. These fast winds are locally called as *loo*. The occurrence of dust and thunderstorms caused by convection currents is a peculiar phenomenon of the hot weather season. There are no rains during the summer months except for the small amount accompanied by the thunderstorms. The wind velocity causes wave actions and strong currents and, as a result, fragmentation of filamentous algae and fragile organisms take place. *Microcystis sp.*, a colonial form, produce smaller irregular and loosely constructed colonies due to wave actions.

Summer season is followed by the monsoon season. During this season, rains start pouring. The rains generally begin in the month of July and last till the end of September to early October. This season is characterized by a gradual fall in temperature, more numerous cloudy days, relative low light intensity, and gradual shortening of the photoperiod, high relative humidity and cyclonic weather. The months of July and August have steady rains. Rains also affect the morphometry of wetlands. The density of plankton gets affected by flooding of the wetlands during monsoon as the number of plankton per liter of water decreases considerably, showing an inverse relationship with the intensity of rainfall. The monsoon season is followed by a period of transition from rainy to dry and cool weather. This is the season of retreating monsoon and is termed as post-monsoon season. This season is characterized by a further fall in diurnal and nocturnal temperatures and a gradual decrease in photoperiods and relative humidity. The average rainfall in October is 0.790 mm and the relative humidity in this month come down to 56.90 per cent. As the sky clear and the sun shines, the day temperature rises while due to the dryness of the air there is a tremendous decrease in the night temperature.

Variations in air temperature are affected by the cold, dry and hot wind action during different seasons of the year. The winter is usually very cold whereas the summer is quite hot. The months of November, March and April are found to be moderate. The temperature changes in winter are influenced by the rainfall and cold winds, while the summer is influenced by the dry and hot winds.

Description of Water Body

Wetlands directly or indirectly have an enormous ecological, commercial and socio-economic importance and values, which are rich in components of bio-diversity, life, flora and fauna of important local, natural and regional significance (Gopal, 1995).

Aligarh and its adjoining areas are richly well off with wetlands which support an extensive and regular fisheries of various kinds. They are surrounded by two river systems Ganga and Jamuna with their many tributaries.

Derelict water body: This water body, locally termed as Dhobighat is a perennial fresh water sewage fed wetland, situated at a distance of about 2 kms from University campus. It has achieved golden jubilee in its age and is almost rectangular in shape. It is a shallow eutrophic wetland covering an area of about 0.57 hectare with its depths varying from 1.50 m during monsoon to 0.60 m during summer. Its source of replenishment is mainly rainwater which enters as a surface run-off during rainy season and through a drain coming from the adjacent locality and overhead tank.

This wetland is used as a drainage basin into which drainage water sweeps from the surrounding locality and also for bathing and washing purpose. Organic nutrients are added in the pond through a drain which brings sewage from adjacent locality. Many washermen use this wetland for washing the clothes, thus adding certain chemicals and colours to its water almost everyday that bring certain physico-chemical and biological changes in its flora and fauna regularly. The water of this wetland is turbid due to luxuriant growth of microscopic algae and the colour or stains of the washing chemicals used by washerman. Its main fish inhabitants are air breathing fishes, like *Esomus danricus, Heteropneustes fossilis, Clarias batrachus, Channa punctatus* and *Colisa fasciatus* along with other aquatic organisms, like frogs, water snakes, worms and certain tortoises etc. which were encountered during the course of study.

ROTIFERA

Introduction

Rotifera, one of the oldest groups and a minor phylum of invertebrates, include animals commonly termed as "Wheel Animalcules" because of their characteristic "wheel organ" or "corona" (Sharma, 2001). Rotifers are the most important soft bodied invertebrates in the fresh water plankton and benthos and characteristically inhabitants of inland waters (Hutchinson, 1967). Further, the members of this group are known to exhibit worldwide occurrence from the Arctic and Antarctic regions to the tropics. The rotifers occur in an endless variety of aquatic and semi aquatic habitats, including limnetic and deepest regions of the largest lakes and smallest puddles. They are found in damp soil and vegetable debris, in mosses that may be netted or dampened only occasionally (Pennak, 1978). About 95 per cent of the known rotifer species, belonging to superclass Eurotatoria, inhabit freshwaters (Sharma, 2001) except two genera and few species which are marine (Wetzel, 1983).

They were originally treated as Infusoria due to their conspicuous ciliation and microscopic size and, hence, were not distinguished from unicellular organisms. The terms "Rotifera" or "Rotatoria" had long been invariably used for this primitive group; their nomenclature status was first questioned and reviewed (Ricci, 1983) at international symposium held at Uppsala, Sweden in 1982 and the former term was accepted to be valid by the rotiferologists for all future applications. Rotifers exhibit high population turnover rate in nature and therefore, respond more quickly to environmental changes than any other group of aquatic organisms. About three-quarters of the rotifers are sessile and associated with littoral substrates. They also act as valuable indicators of trophic conditions of water (Sladecek, 1983). Locomotion through water is mostly dependent on the peripheral cilia. Many plankton and limnetic species remain in permanent suspension without ever coming in contact with a substrate. Such locomotion is often a combination of twisting on the longitudinal axis and spiral movements of the whole animal. A few plankton genera, such as *Filinia, Hexarthra* and *Polyarthra* move by sudden jerks and leaps, owing to sudden beating movements of their long appendages (Pennak, 1978). Various investigators have designated certain species as monocyclic, dicyclic or acyclic and perennial, according to whether their annual population curves have one, two, several or no pronounced peaks. *Brachionus angularis* and *Keratalla cochlearis* are often considered dicyclic with spring and autumn maxima, but are sometimes perennial (Pennak, 1978). *Polyarthra* is dicyclic, polycyclic or perennial (Pennak, 1978). *Keratella quadrata* may be most abundant in spring or autumn, or it may be perennial (Pennak, 1978). *Asplanchna priodonta* is variously considered monocyclic, dicyclic or perennial (Pennak, 1978). Some of the common genera, like *Asplanchna, Pleosoma, Synchaeta* and *Trichocerca* feed on other rotifers and all kinds of small metazoan, either in the plankton or on a substrate. The great majority of species are omnivorous and ingests all organic particles of the appropriate size. Common examples are *Cephalodella, Filinia, Keratella, Lecane, Euchlanis, Epiphanes and Brachionus.*

Important publications related to rotifers are those of Donner (1965), Ruttner-Kolisko (1974), Pontin (1978), Pennak (1978), Sladecek (1983), Wallace and Snell (1991), Sharma (1991, 1995, 1996, 1998, 2000, 2001), De Smet (1995, 1996), De Smet and Purriot (1996) and Melone *et al.* (1998), Deneke (2000) Weithoff (2004, 2005), Obertegger, *et al.* (2008), Wacker and Weithoff (2009), Hartwich *et al.* (2010).

RESULT AND DISCUSSION

Rotifera formed the most abundant group. This group was represented by six genera viz *Brachionus, Keratella, Notholca, Filinia, Hexarthra, and Asplanchna.* The monthly variations in density of various genera of Rotifers (No/m^2) in the selected water bodies are given in Table 11.2. The population density of Rotifers ranged from a minimum of 723 No/m^2 during July, 2009 to a maximum of 1282 No/m^2 in January, 2010. Total per cent contribution of Rotifers ranged from 23.47 per cent during December, 2009 to 35.12 per cent during September.

Statistically Rotifera recorded a significant negative correlation with water temperature ($r = -0.769$, Fig-1), whereas with D.O., it showed significant positive correlation ($r = 0.599$) (Table 11.1) (Fig. 11.1). It showed negative correlation with TDS ($r = -0.171$) (Table 11.1).

Among the common and widely distributed species of *Brachionus, B. calyciflorus, B. bidentatus* and *B. angularis* are common species in Indian waters. Species of *Keratella, Notholca,* and *Brachionus,* are semi-planktonic in nature.

Table 11.1: Showing Correlation Between Rotifers and Different Environmental Factors

Rotifera	NO_3-N	-0.654
Rotifera	PO_4-P	-0.542
Rotifera	D.O.	0.611
Rotifera	W.T.	-0.769
Rotifera	TDS	-0.171

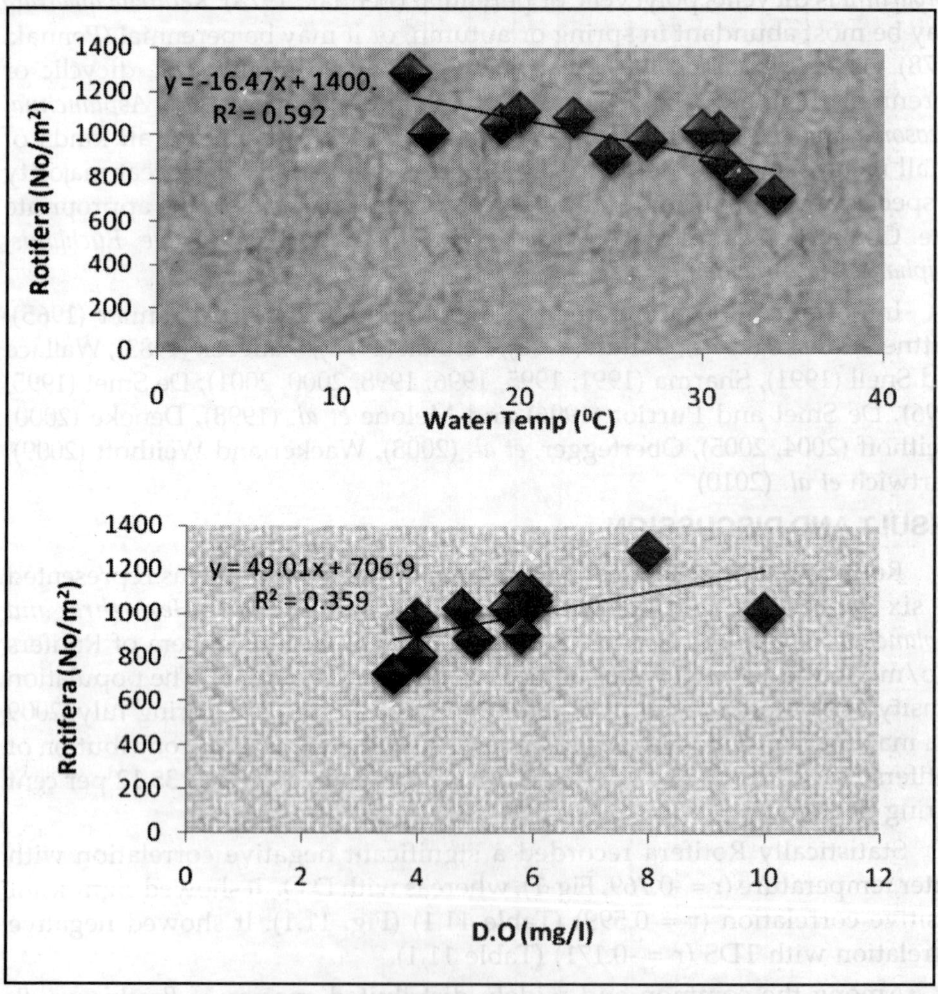

Fig. 11.1 Regression Lines Showing Relationship Between Dissolved Oxygen (mg/l) and Water Temperature (°C) with Rotifers

Table 11.2: Monthly Distribution and Abundance of Rotifers (No/m^2)

Rotifers	February' 09	March	April	May	June	July	August	September	October	November	December	January' 10
Brachionus calyciflors	72	212	72	58	112	55	45	195	202	151	97	105
B. bidentata	169	84	156	138	151	142	151	201	92	145	226	218
B. angularis	198	92	312	115	201	92	272	84	218	312	156	226
Keratella tropica	175	95	58	86	38	42	27	149	172	175	69	96
K. quadrata	68	73	78	29	115	35	24	47	56	56	85	32
Asplanchna priodonta	72	145	68	92	171	29	129	136	21	99	95	72
Filinia longiseta	173	92	39	91	78	125	58	59	115	63	45	98
Notholca sp.	39	59	67	125	98	91	79	82	75	28	42	139
Hexarthra sp.	83	52	125	68	56	112	98	68	129	72	191	296
Total	1049	904	975	802	1020	723	883	1021	1080	1101	1006	1282

Whereas *Polyarthra, Hexarthra, Conochilus, Filinia* and *Asplanchna* are planktonic or semi-planktonic in nature (Sharma, 2001). They depict cyclomorphosis and exhibit different ecotypes (Khan and Alam, 1999). They have been designated as indicator of organic pollution in eutrophic water bodies (Sharma, 2001).

Brachionus calyciflorus: Anterior occipital margin with four broad based spines, median occipital spines distinctly longer than laterals, (Sharma, 1998 a). It was low in density. Density varied from minimum 45 No/m^2 during August, 2009 to maximum 212 No/m^2 during March, 2009 (Table 11.2).

Brachionus bidentata: Anterior margin with occipital spines, lateral and medians longer than intermediate occipital spines (Sharma, 1998 a). Its population density varied from a minimum of 84 No/m^2 in March, 2009 to a maximum of 226 No/m^2 in December, 2009 (Table 11.2).

Brachionus angularis: Anterior margin is with two median occipital spines. Posterior spines lacking (Sharma, 1998 a) . Its density varied from a minimum of 84 No/m^2 in September, 2009 to a maximum of 312 No/m^2 in April, 2009 (Table 11.2).

Keratella tropica: Six anterior occipital spines are present, median occipital spines are longest, pointed and out curved; Posterior spines unequal and variable in length, the right spine generally longer than the left, the left posterior spine much reduced in some specimen (Sharma, 1998 a). Its density was found to vary between 27 No/m^2 during month of August, 2009 and 175 No/m^2 2009 during November, 2009 (Table 11.2).

Keratella quadrata: Six anterior occipital spines are present, median spines longest and curved (Sharma, 1998 a). It showed variations between 24 No/m^2 in August, 2009 and 115 No/m^2 in June, 2009 (Table 11.2).

Asplanchna priodonta: Body is illoricate, transparent, polymorphic and with thin cuticle, body shape sacciform, bell shaped or with humps or projections; Foot absent; Corona comprised of a broken single ring of cilia (Sharma, 1998 a). It showed minimum density (21 No/m^2) in October, 2009 and maximum density (171 No/m^2) during June, 2009 (Table 11.2).

Filinia sp.: Body is thin, barrel shaped and with two long movable antero lateral setae and one long immovable posterior seta usually folded ventrally (Sharma, 1998 a). It showed minimum density (39 No/m^2) in April, 2009 and maximum density (173 No/m^2) during February, 2010 (Table 11.2).

Notholca sp.: Its lorica is oval to elongate and spindle shaped, with six occipital spines. Dorsal plate is with longitudinal striations; Foot absent. It showed minimum density (28 No/m^2) in November, 2009 and maximum density (139 No/m^2) during January, 2010 (Table 11.2).

Hexarthra sp.: Body is conical with six arms like appendages and pinnate bristles at their tips. Corona wavy, with double band of cilia and with or without ventral lip (Sharma, 1998 a). It showed minimum density (52 No/m^2) during March, 2009 and maximum density (296 No/m^2) during January, 2010 (Table 11.2).

REFERENCES

De Smet, W.H. (1995) - Rotifera. 3- The Notommatidae and Scaridiidae. In: *Guide to the Identification of Micro-invertebrates of Continental Waters of the World*. Vol. 8 (Eds. H.J. Dumont and T. Nogrady). SPB Academic Publishers, Amsterdam, The Netherlands.

De Smet, W.H. (1996) - Rotifera. 4- The Proalidae (Monogononta). In: *Guide to the Identification of Micro-invertebrates of Continental Waters of the World*. Vol. 9 (Eds. H.J. Dumont and T. Nogrady). SPB Academic Publishers, Amsterdam, The Netherlands.

Deneke, R. (2000) - Review of Rotifers and Crustaceans in Highly Acidic Environments of pH Values _3. *Hydrobiologia*, 433: 167-172.

Donner, J. (1965) - Ordnung Bdelloidea (Rotatoria Radertiere). Best Bucher Z. Bodenfauna Europas, *Berlin*, 6: 1-297.

Gopalkrishnan, T.C. and Nair, K.K. (1995) - Subtidal Benthic Macrofauna of the Mangalore Coast, West Coast of India. *Indian J. Mar. Sci.*, 27: 351-355.

Hartwich, M., Wacker, A and Weithoff, G. (2010) - Changes in the Competitive Abilities of Two Rotifers Feeding on Mixotrophic Flagellates. *J. of Plankton Res.*, 32 (12): 1727-1731.

Hutchinson, G.E. (1967) - *A Treatise on Limnology*: An Introduction to Lake Biology and the Limnoplankton. Vol. 2. John Wiley & Sons Inc., New York, 115 pp.

Khan, A.A., Alam, A. and Gaur, R.K. (1999) - A Comprehensive Study of Water Quality Parameters in the River Ganga Between Narora and Kannauj: Primary Production. In: *Freshwater Ecosystem of India* (ed. K. Vijaykumar) Daya Publishing House, N. Delhi, 287-294.

Melone, G., Ricci, C., and Segers, H. (1998) - The Trophy of Bdelloidea (Rotifera): a Comparative Study Across the Class. *Can J. Zool*, 76: 1755-1765.

Obertegger, U., Flaim, G. and Sommaruga, R. (2008) - Multifactorial Nature of Rotifer Water Layer Preferences in an Oligotrophic Lake. *J. Plankton Res.*, 30: 633-643.

Odum, E.P. (1983) - *Basic Ecology*. Saunders College Publishing, Holt Saunders, Japan, 613 pp.

Parrish, C.C. (1998) - Lipid Biogeochemistry of Plankton, Settling Matter and Sediments in Trinity Bay, Newfoundland. I. Lipid classes. *Org. Geochem.*, 29: 1531-1545.

Pennak, R.W. (1978) - *Freshwater Invertebrates of United States*. 2nd Ed. Johan Wiley and Sons Inc., New York, 803 pp.

Pontin, R.M. (1978) - A Key to Freshwater Planktonic and Semi-planktonic Rotifera of British Isles. *Freshwat. Biol*. Assoc. Sci. Publ., 38: 1-178.

Prakash, S., Ansari, K.K. and Sinha, M. (2001) – Seasonal Dynamics of Zooplankton in a Freshwater Pond Developed from the Wasteland of Brick - Kiln. *Poll Res.*, 21: 81-83.

Rawson, D.S. (1951) - The Total Mineral Content of Lake Water. *Ecol.*, 32: 669-672.

Ricci, C. (1983) - Rotifera or Rotatoria? *Hydrobiologia*, 104: 1-2.

Ruttner-Kolisco, A. (1974) - Plankton Rotifers: Biology and Taxonomy. *Die Binnengewasser, Suppl.*, 26: 1-146.

Sharma, A. (1999) - *Limnological Studies of Ban- Ganga and Distributional Pattern of Stream Bottom Fauna*. Ph.D. Thesis, University of Jammu.

Sharma, B. K. (1998 a) – *State Fauna Series 3: Fauna of West Bengal*, ZSI. Part 11: 341-361.

Sharma, B.K. (1991) - Rotifera. In: *Animal Resources of India: Protozoa to Mammalia*. State of Art. *Zool. Surv*. India, 69-88.

Sharma, B.K. (1995) - Freshwater Rotifers (*Rotifera: Eurotatoria*): Fauna of West Bengal: State Faunal Series, *Zool. Surv*. India, 3 (13): 1-121.

Sharma, B.K. (1996) - Biodiversity of Freshwater Rotifers in India: A Status Report. Proc. *Zool. Soc*. India, 49: 73-85.

Sharma, B.K. (1998) - Faunal Diversity in India: Rotifera. In: *Faunal Diversity of India*. (Eds. J.R.B. Alferd, A.K. Das and A.K. Sanyal). *Zool. Surv. India*, Envis Centre; 57-70.

Sharma, B.K. (2000) - Synecology of Rotifers in a Tropical Flood Plain Lake of Upper Assam. *Indian J. Anim. Sci*., 70: 880-885.

Sharma, B.K. (2001 a) - Zooplankton Diversity: Freshwater Planktonic and Semi-Planktonic Rotifera. In: *Water Quality Assessment, Biomonitoring and Zooplankton Diversity* (Ed. Prof. B.K. Sharma). Department of Zoology, North Eastern Hill University, Shillong, Meghalaya, 190-210 pp.

Sharma, B.K. (2001) - Biological Monitoring of Freshwaters with Reference to Role of Freshwater Rotifera as Biomonitors. In: *Water Quality Assessment, Biomonitoring and Zooplankton Diversity* (Ed. B.K. Sharma). Ministry of Environment and Forests, Government of India, New Delhi, 83-97.

Sharma, B.K. and Lyngskor, C. (2003) - Planktonic Communities of a Sub-tropical Reservoir of Meghalaya (N.E. India). *Indian J. Animal Science*, 73 (2): 88-95.

Sharma, B.K. and Michael, R.G. (1987) - Review of Taxonomic Studies on Freshwater Cladocera from India with Remark on Biogeography. *Hydrobiologia*, 145: 29 33.

Sharma, B.K. and Sharma, S. (1999) - Freshwater Rotifera (Rotifera: Eurotatoria). In: Fauna of Meghalaya. *State Fauna Series*. Zool. Surv. India; 4 (9): 11-161.

Sharma, B.K. and Sharma, S. (1990) - On the Taxonomic Status of Some Chadoceran Taxa (Custacea: Cladocera) from Central India. Rev. *Hydrobiol. Trop*., 23: 105-133.

Sharma, B.K. and Sharma, S. (1997) - Lecanid rotifers (Rotifera: Monogononta: Lecanidae) of North-Eastern India. *Hydrobiologia*, 356: 159-163.

Sharma, K.P., Goel, P.K. and Gopal, B. (1978) - Limnological Studies of Pollued Freshwater I. Physico-chemical Characteristics. *Int. J. Ecol. Environ. Sci*., 4: 89-105.

Sharma, M. (2002) - *Studies on the Impact of Anthropogenic Influences on the Ecology of Gharana Wetland, Jammu*. Ph.D. Thesis, University of Jammu.

Sharma, O.P. (2003) - Zooplankton Production Using *Eichhornia cressipes* as Biofertilizer. *Fishing Chimes*, 23 (7): 42-45.

Sladecek, V. (1983) - Rotifers as Indicator of Water Quality. *Hydrobiologia*, 100: 169-201.

Wacker, A. and Weithoff, G. (2009) - Carbon Assimilation Mode in Mixotrophs and the Fatty acid Composition of Their Rotifer Consumers. *Freshwater Biol*., 54: 2189-2199.

Wallace, R.L. and Snell, T.W. (1991) - Rotifera. In: *Ecology and Classification of North American Freshwater Invertebrates* (Eds. S.H. Thorpe and A.P. Covch). American Press, New York, 187-248.

Weithoff, G. (2005) - On the Ecology of the Rotifer *Cephalodella hoodi* from an Extremely Acidic Lake. *Freshwater Biol*., 50: 1464-1473.

Wetzel, R.G. (1975) - *Limnology*. W.B. Saunders Co. Philadelphia, 743pp.

Wetzel, R.G. (1983) - *Limnology*. 2nd Ed. Saunders College Publishing Co., New York, 767 pp.

CHAPTER

The Relationship of Zoobenthic Community with Different Water Parameters

Habeeba A. Kabeer*; Saltanat Parveen

INTRODUCTION

The organisms associated with solid liquid interface are ordinarily termed as Benthos (Haeckel, 1891). The term Benthos is derived from two Greek words *"Ben"* meaning 'the collection of organisms living in or on the sea or lakes' and *"Thos"* 'the bottom of sea or lakes'. Hutchinson (1967) defined benthos as an association of species of plants and animals that live in or on the bottom of a body of water. Benthic fauna are especially of great significance for the fisheries that they themselves act as a food of bottom feeding fishes (Walker *et al.*, 1991; Vijaykumar *et al.*, 1991) forming an important part of the food chain. Benthos plays a critical role in the natural flow of energy and nutrients. As benthic invertebrates die, they decay leaving behind nutrients that are reused by aquatic plants and other animals. These animals are widespread in their distribution and can live on all bottom types, even on manmade objects. They can be found in hot springs, small ponds and large lakes. Some are even found in the soil beneath puddles. Many species of benthos are able to move around and expand their distribution by drifting with currents to a new location during the aquatic phase of their life or by

Limnology Research Lab, A.M.U., Aligarh (UP), India.

flying to a new stream during their terrestrial phase. Most benthic species can be found throughout the year, but the largest numbers occur in the spring just before the reproductive period. In colder months, many species burrow deep within the mud or remain inactive on rock surfaces. Many aquatic insects undergo a complete metamorphosis - the transition from egg to larva to pupa and finally to adult. They remain in the water for most of their lives (typically one month to four years). After becoming adults, the majority of insects live for only a brief time, usually a few hours to a few days, while they locate mates and reproduces.

Study degree of relationship between benthos density and physicochemical factors and given the result on a single sheet with the help of CCA analysis.

This would be helpful in knowing the status of benthic diversity in a waterbody and their conservation from biodiversity point of view.

Temperature constrains the various processes in aquatic ecosystems differently and therefore, a general warming of the water column will change trophic interactions and ecosystem functioning (Beaugrand and Reid, 2003; Alheit *et al.*, 2005). Increasing temperatures could also change the balance between pelagic and benthic secondary production. Sedimentation rate of organic matter during the spring bloom has been shown to decrease due to higher zooplankton grazing effect and bacterial respiration in the water column if the temperature increases (Keller *et al.*, 1993 and Müren *et al.*, 2005). Thus, the total sedimentary input to sustain the benthos may decrease if more material is channeled through the pelagic grazing food chain (ErikssonWiklund *et al.*, 2009). Higher bottom water temperatures will also increase pelagic microbial remineralisation of the settling particulate organic matter and this effect will be more pronounced in the deeper water column and the longer the sinking material is exposed to pelagic respiration (Hansen and Bendtsen, 2006). Changes in the temperature could probably also change the species composition of the benthos according to their feeding ecology (Coyle *et al.*, 2007).

According to Wetzel (1983) transparency of water allows light penetration, which has far reaching effects on all aquatic organism including their development, distribution and behaviour etc. Therefore, light is often an important limiting factor in the development and distribution of flora and fauna in aquatic habitat. The transparency of water body depends upon the turbidity (Chandler, 1944; Hutchinson, 1975; Haque, 1991) which is caused by dissolved substances and suspended matter, both living and non-living. Light availability at depth is affected directly by the presence of TSS and plankton in water column and by macrophytes and sediment accumulation on the surface (Carter and Rybicki, 1985). According to Hutchinson (1975) transparency, the depth to which light penetrates in water body can be used as a reliable indicator of productivity. Transparency acts as an index of water quality and plays a key role in reflecting the pond productivity (Mohanty, 1999).

Conductivity is the measure of capacity of a substance or a solution to conduct electric current. Conductivity is an important factor which gives an indication of total salt concentration. Fresh water bodies in their natural state have very low conductivity values whereas polluted water shows higher values of conductivity (Trivedy *et al.*, 1985).

The pH is very important chemical characteristic of natural water and is closely related to many biological phenomena, mineralization, oxidation and reduction in water bodies. pH indicates the concentration of hydrogen ions in water. It expresses the intensity of acidity or alkalinity depends upon the amount of absorbed CO_2, on H^+ ion arising from the dissociation of carbonic acid (H_2CO_3) and OH^- ions arising from the hydrolysis of bicarbonates buffering the water. According to Welch (1952) it is an important means of understanding the chemical conditions prevailing in the natural waters. pH of water is considered to be one of most important chemical factor affecting the productivity of the water body. In general pH is influenced directly by the carbon dioxide concentration in the water, which in turn regulates photosynthetic and respiratory activities (Talling, 1976).

Carbon dioxide is an extremely important constituent of an aquatic environment (Welch, 1952). This gas is very much necessary for bacterial growth and green plants. The primary source of inorganic carbon for photosynthesis and the generation of organic substance in an aquatic ecosystem are largely dissolved carbon dioxide and bicarbonates (Wetzel, 2001). The presence of carbon dioxide in the environment, gives the opportunity to plants and phytoplankton to synthesize their food and produce oxygen, which is the basic need for all life forms. Variation in CO_2 concentration may have an adverse effect on physiological functions of the biotic lives present in aquatic ecosystem. Inorganic carbon utilization in natural water is balanced by respiratory generation of carbon dioxide by aquatic organisms and by influxes of carbon dioxide and bicarbonates with incoming surface run off and from atmosphere.

Dissolved oxygen is essential for the respiratory metabolism of organisms. The amount of DO in a water is only one fortieth to the twentieth of that present in equal volume of air when the two are in equilibrium although their partial pressure are the same. The distribution of O_2 in the aquatic medium is governed by diffusion from air, photosynthesis of micro and macrophytes and loss due to respiration and chemical and biotic oxidation. Generally the water masses show high fluctuation in the oxygen content during day and night. Thus the O_2 regime exhibits both diurnal and seasonal variations and that many environmental parameters influence the concentration of the O_2 content in an aquatic environment. Most of the organisms except anaerobic bacteria need oxygen. Dissolved oxygen is one of the most important parameter in water quality assessment and reflects the physical and biological process prevailing in the waters. Its presence is essential to maintain higher forms of biological life in water. The effects of waste discharge in the water body are largely determined by the oxygen balance of the system (Trivedy and Goel, 1984).

Depth of a pond has an important bearing on the physical and chemical qualities of water. It determines the temperature, circulation pattern of water and the extent of photosynthetic activity. The seasonal and spatial differentiation in the meteoric rains are the factors responsible for balancing the depth (Augustyn, 1979) and it varies from year to year (Kant and Anand, 1979) depending upon the monsoon rains, evaporation, siltation and water abstraction. The water depth thus, fluctuates seasonally causing seasonal irregularities.

METHODOLOGY

Collection of Water Samples

The subsurface water (about 30 cm depth) from littoral region of selected ponds was collected monthly with the help of Ruttner water sampler bottle with the capacity of two litters during the period, from February, 2009 to January, 2010. Parameters like Air and Water temperature, Depth, Transparency, Conductivity, pH, D.O., free CO_2, Alkalinity were analysed between 8:00 AM and 9:00 AM at the site. For remaining physicochemical analysis, water samples were filled in cleaned plastic bottles and brought to the laboratory.

Collection of Sediment Samples

Sediment samples were collected monthly between 9:00 AM and 10:30 AM with the help of Ekman-dredge of size 15 cm × 15 cm. After collection, sediment samples were kept in plastic bags, labeled and were brought to the laboratory. A part of the sediment sample was put in oven at 105° C for drying and grinded in a Gate-Mortar for sediment analysis.

Separation of Bottom Fauna and Identification

For benthos analysis, samples were mixed and diluted with tap water to prepare slurry in a bucket and sticks, leaves, debris were removed. Then slurry was divided into ten subsamples. Each subsample was passed through sieves, B.S. No. 30 (mesh # 500 μm) and B.S. No. 72 (mesh # 200 μm) arranged former above the latter so that smaller organisms (meio) were retained on the smaller sieve. Sieving yielded residue including mixture of animals and sediment. The sample retained on first sieve was emptied in shallow dish and organisms were sorted by using brush, forceps and pipette against a white background. To facilitate the sorting few drops of 10 per cent aqueous solution of Rose Bangal was added. Organisms retained on second sieve were washed into a tray and then samples were taken in vials and labeled. Organisms were preserved in 70 per cent ethyl alcohol solution for qualitative and quantitative analysis. For larger animals, insect larvae and oligochaetes about 2 ml of preserved sample was taken in a calibrated petri-dish and studied under dissecting microscope.

For smaller organisms, about 1 ml of preserved sample was taken on Sedgewick Rafter cell and studied under an inverted microscope (Metzer). Individuals were identified up to genus or species level as could be possible and number of each taxon was noted. Density was determined per meter square area and result was expressed as ind/m^2. Identification was done with the help of keys given in Edmondson (1959), Needham and Needham (1962), Pennak (1978) and Tonapi (1980).

Water Analysis

Physico-chemical parameters were analyzed on monthly basis from February, 2009 to January 2010. Each chemical parameter was repeated at least three times and the average of the three readings was taken to minimize the error. Physico-chemical analysis was done with the help of method given in Trivedy and Goel (1984).

Canonical correspondence analysis (CCA): The data of benthic community and water and sediment quality variables were drawn up in the form of one matrix and were analysed by canonical correspondence analysis (CCA) using PAST programme, version (2.10) by Hammer and Harper (2001), separately in Pond. CCA diagram was performed to determine relationships between 20 environmental variables and 10 groups of benthos. It is a non-linear technique used to relate variations in the environmental factors. Benthic data were log transformed to approach the assumed condition of normality and homoscedasticity of the data to standardize the data sets. The constrained ordination axis corresponds to the direction of the greatest variability of the data set that can be explained by the variables (Leps and Smilauer, 1999). In graph, environmental factors are indicated by the length of arrow, length of line represents the degree of relationship between benthic groups and environmental factors, the angle between arrow shaft and ordination axis indicates the degree of correlation between environmental factors. In addition the analysis make vertical lines connecting a particular group with the line of environmental factors, closer the connecting point on the line of environmental factors to arrow shows stronger positive correlation. Distribution pattern of groups in benthic community are represented by points, points of group and environmental factors indicates the distribution of groups and characteristics of benthic community variance along the gradient direction of each environmental factor.

RESULT AND DISCUSSION

The eigen value, value of p and Cumulative percentage variance of groups-environment relation of axes 1-4 are given the table below respective figures 12.1.

Table 12.4

Axis	Eigenval	p	%
1.	0.01699	0.3069	40.35
2.	0.007541	0.1584	17.91
3.	0.006264	0.08911	14.88
4.	0.005375	0.3861	12.77

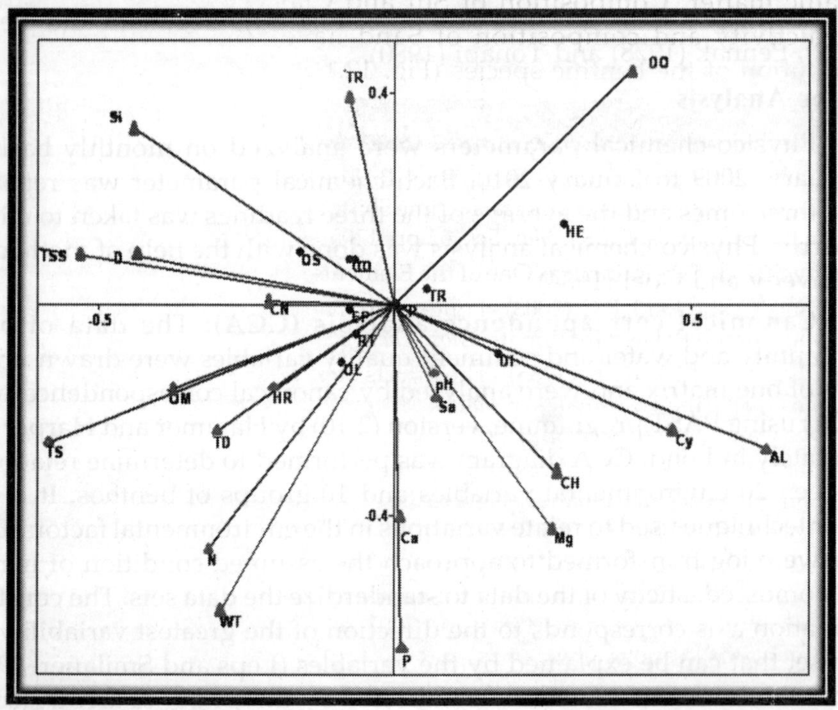

Fig. 12.1: Canonical Correspondence Analysis (CCA) Diagram of 20 Environmental Parameters (Water Temperature-WR, pH-pH, Dissolved-oxygen- DO, Nitrate-N, Phosphate-P, Alkalinity-AL, Hardness-HR, Calcium-Ca, Magnesium-Mg, Transparency-TR, Chloride-CH, Conductivity-CN, Depth-D, Total Dissolved Solids-TD, Total Suspended Solids-TSS, Total Solids-TS, % Organic Matter-OM, Composition of Sand-Sa, Silt-Si, Clay-Cy) and 10 Benthic Groups (Cladocera-CL, Copepoda-CP, Ostracoda-OS, Rotifera-RT, Oligochaeta-OL, Diptera-DI, Coleoptera-CO, Hemiptera-HE, Trichoptera- TR and Ephemeroptera-EP) in Pond

In this Pond total Trichoptera and Hemiptera showed positive correlation with Dissolved oxygen whereas Diptera showed high positive correlation with Clay composition and Alkalinity. Copepoda showed high positive correlation with Clay, Sand, Chloride, pH and Mg. Other groups like Rotifera, Oligochaeta and Ephemeroptera showed high negative correlation with Water temperature, Nitrate, Hardness, TDS, per cent Organic matter, TS and Conductivity and Cladocera, Coleoptera and Ostracoda showed high positive correlation with Transparency, TSS, depth and Composition of Silt. CCA analysis indicates that, in Pond important factors affecting benthos distribution are Water temperature, Dissolved oxygen, Nitrate, Phosphate, Alkalinity, Calcium, Magnesium, Transparency, Chloride, Depth, Total dissolved solids, Total suspended solids, Total solids, per cent Organic matter, Composition of Silt and Clay. However, pH, Hardness, Conductivity and composition of Sand have a lesser influences on the distribution of the benthic species (Fig. 12.1).

REFERENCES

Alheit, C. Mollmann, J., Dutz, G., Kornilovs, P., Loewe, V., Mohrholz and Wasmund, N. (2005) - Synchronous Ecological Regime Shifts in the Central Baltic and the North Sea in the Late 1980s. *ICES J. Mar. Sci.*, 62 pp. 1205-1215.

Augustyn, N. (1979) - Rainfall as One of the Elements of Pond Water Balances.

Beaugrand, G. and Reid, P.C. (2003) - Long-term Changes in Phytoplankton, Zooplankton and Salmon Related to Climate. *Glob. Change Biol*, 9: (2003), pp. 801-817.

Carter, V. and Rybicki, N.B. (1985) - The Effects of Grazers and Light Penetration on the Survival of the Transplants of *Vallisneria americana nichx.* in the Tidal Potomac River, Maryland. *Aquatic Botany*, 23: 197-213.

Chandler, D.C. (1944) - Limnological Studies of Western Lake Erie. IV- Relation of Limnological and Climatic Factors to the Phytoplankton of Western Lake Erie. *Trans. Amer. Microsc. Soc.*, 63: 203-236.

Coyle, K.O., Bluhm, B., Konar, B., Blanchard, A. and Highsmith, R. C. (2007) - Amphipod Prey of Gray Whales in the Northern Bering Sea: Comparison of Biomass and Distribution Between the 1980s and 2002-2003, *Deep Sea Research Part II*: Tropical Studies in Oceanography.

Edmondson, W.T. (1959) - *Ward and Whipple's Freshwater Biology*, 2nd Ed. John Wiley & Sons Inc., New York, 1248 pp.

Eriksson Wiklund, A.K., Dahlgren, K., Sundelin, B. and Andersson, A. (2009) - Effects of Warming and Shifts of Pelagic Food web Structure on Benthic Productivity in a Coastal Marine System. *Mar. Ecol. Prog. Ser.*, 396: (2009), pp. 13-25.

Haeckel, E. (1891) - Plankton studies. Jenaische Zeitschr. *F. Naturw.*, 25: 232-336.

Hansen and Bendtsen, J. (2006) - Klimabetingede Effekter på Marine økosystemer. Faglig rapport fra DMU No. 598, *the Ministry of Environments*, 50: pp.

Haque, N. (1991) - Studies on Hydrobiology of Some Polluted Ponds of Aligarh Region. *Ph.D. Thesis*. Aligarh Muslim University, Aligarh, India.

Hutchinson, G.E. (1957) - *A Treatise on Limnology*: Geography, Physics and Chemistry, Vol. I, John Wiley & Sons Inc., New York, USA, 1016 pp.

Hutchinson, G.E. (1967) - *A Treatise on Limnology*: An Introduction to Lake Biology and the Limnoplankton. Vol. 2. John Wiley & Sons Inc., New York, 115 pp.

Hutchinson, G.E. (1975) - A Treatise on Limnology: Chemistry of Lakes, Vol. 1, Part II, *John Wiley & Sons Inc.*, New York, 660 pp.

Kant, S. and Anand, V. K. (1979) – Interelation of Phytoplankton and Physical Factors in Mansar Lake, Jammu (J & K). *Indian J. Ecol.*, 5 (2): 134-140.

Keller, W., Yan, N.D., Howel, T., Molat, L.A. and Taylor, W.D. (1993) - Changes in Zooplankton during the Experimental Nutrilization and Early Reacidification of Bowland Lake, Near Sudbury, Ontario. *Canadian J. Fish. Aquat. Sci.*, 49: 52-62.

Mohanty, R.K. (1999) – Effects of Water Turbidity and its Management in Aquaculture. *Fish World*, 3: 24-25.

Müren, U., Berglund, J., Samuelsson, K. and Andersson, A. (2005) - Potential Effects of Elevated Sea-water Temperature on Pelagic Food Webs. *Hydrobiology*, 545: 153-166 pp.

Needham, J.G. and Needham, P.R. (1962) - *A Guide to the Study of the Freshwater Biology*. Holden-Dey Inc., Francisco, 108 pp.

Pennak, R.W. (1978) - *Freshwater Invertebrates of United States*. 2nd Ed. Johan Wiley and Sons Inc., New York, 803 pp.

Talling, J.F. (1976) - The Depletion of Carbon Dioxide from Lake Water by Phytoplankton. *J. Ecol.*, 64: 79-121.

Tonapi, G.T. (1980) - *Fresh Water Animals of India*. Oxford and IBH Publishing Co., New Delhi, 341 pp.

Trivedy, R.K. and Goel, P.K. (1984) - *Chemical and Biological Methods for Water Pollution Studies*. Karad, India; 215 pp.

Trivedy, R.K., Garud, J.N. and Goel, P.K. (1985) - Studies on Chemistry and Phytoplankton of a Few Fresh Environmental Publications Water Bodies in Kohlapur with special reference to Human Activity. *Poll. Res.*, 4(1): 25-44.

Vijaykumar, R., Ansari Z.A. and Palekar, A.H. (1991) - Benthic Fauna of Kakinada Bay and Back Waters, East Coast of India. *Indian J. of Mar. Sci.*, 20: 195-199.

Walker, I., Henderson, P.A. and Sterry, P. (1991) - On the Pattern of Biomass Transfer in the Benthic Fauna of an Amazonian Black Water as Evidenced by 32 P Level Experiment. *Hydrobiol.*, 215: 153-162.

Welch, P.S. (1952) - *Limnology*. McGraw Hill Book Co. Inc., New York. 538 pp.

Wetzel, R.G. (1983) - *Limnology*. 2nd Ed. Saunders College Publishing Co., New York, 767 pp.

Wetzel, R.G. (2001) - *Limnology—Lake and River Ecosystems*. Academic Press, San Diego, pp. 1006.

Index

N

O